INDUSTRIAL MARKETING

An Analytical Approach to Planning and Execution

INDUSTRIAL MARKETING

An Analytical Approach to Planning and Execution

LAWRENCE FISHER, M.Sc.(Econ.), A.I.S.

Sponsored by the Industrial Marketing Council

BRANDON/SYSTEMS PRESS • PRINCETON • NEW YORK

To K. L. F.

FOREWORD

The development of industrial marketing and the education and
training of marketing management are determined in part by
the availability of published material dealing with both the
theory and scientific operation of marketing. Despite an increasing demand both in industry and in business education,
there has been a serious lack of such material for many years.
It was for this reason that the IMC sponsored *Industrial Marketing,* and the Council is now pleased to be associated with a
textbook written by an author who is not only well known in
the world of business education, but is also a leading member
of the Industrial Marketing Research Association, which is a
constituent body of the Council.

Lawrence Fisher was one of the early pioneers in the professional organization of industrial marketing and a founder
member of one of the regional industrial marketing research
groups which helped to found the Industrial Marketing Research Association in 1963; since then he has played an active role
in the Association's affairs. He is a professional economist and
statistician, having been an executive in companies concerned
with the marketing of industrial products for thirteen years
before entering business education, and his experience in this
area in the last six years has enabled him to organize highly
successful seminars on industrial marketing at the Polytechnic
School of Management Studies in London, where he is senior
lecturer in marketing.

The Industrial Marketing Council is indebted to Lawrence
Fisher and to Michael Hewlings, the Chairman of IMC's Pub-

lications Committee, for this textbook, which, thanks to the author's widespread experience, will become a standard work of great value to everyone engaged in industrial marketing and business education.

D. W. NEWILL

Founding Chairman, IMC

ACKNOWLEDGMENTS

This is to record my debt to the many people who have contributed ideas and suggestions in connection with this book, including the following: Balint Badroghy (Peter Ward [Interplan] Ltd.), Gordon England (Economist Intelligence Unit Ltd.), Bernard Hippsley (Associated Industrial Consultants Ltd.), Professor Kenneth Lawyer (Case Western Reserve University), Percy Reynolds (Market Communication), the staff of Roles & Parker Ltd., W. Robert Staton (McAlley Associates Ltd.), Eric Ward (The Polytechnic School of Management Studies), Dr. W. Westgate, and R. Williams (Metal Box Ltd.), and for continual help and encouragement from Mike Hewlings (Chairman, IMC Publications Committee). None of these people is, of course, in any way responsible for any deficiencies which may remain.

L.V.F.

INDUSTRIAL MARKETING COUNCIL
Founded in 1964 by associations concerned with industrial marketing, the Council aims to provide a forum for discussion and coordination of activity among member associations in their common endeavor to improve techniques and standards in industrial marketing.

Members: British Industrial Marketing Association.
Industrial Marketing Research Association.
Scottish Industrial Marketing Association.
EVAF–UK

CONTENTS

The role of industrial marketing. How to use a business book.

1
Marketing in Perspective   1
Marketing as customer orientation. Marketing as problem solving.
Marketing as service. Marketing as a synthesis with the environment. Marketing as an anticipation of change. Marketing and
business planning.

2
Understanding Industrial Markets   11
Customers and users. Market characteristics. The concept of market segmentation. Making the buying decision. Informal influences.

3
Marketing and Corporate Strategy   27
The rise of corporate strategy. The objectives of a company. Strategy development. Reviewing company resources. Tests of strategy.

4
Preparing a Marketing Plan   41
What is a plan? Period of the plan. Developing the marketing

plan. The development of strategies. The elements of the plan. Setting out the plan.

Direct mail. Setting the advertising budget. Assessing the effectiveness of advertising. The role of the advertising agency. Making the most of advertising.

14
Print, Promotion, and Public Relations   191
The forms of print. Aspects of promotion. P.R. in marketing.

15
Price Determination   201
The arithmetic of short-term pricing. Price and the buyer. Price elasticity. Competition. The meanings of cost. The full-cost model. The "marginal cost = marginal revenue" model. The break-even model. Improved break-even analysis. Contribution/volume ratio.

16
Special Aspects of Pricing   223
Pricing and the product life-cycle. Market segmentation pricing. Product-line pricing. Marginal-cost pricing. Tendering.

17
Channels of Distribution   233
The role of the intermediary. Supplier/distributor relationships.

18
Organizing the Marketing Function   241
The marketing manager. The basis of organization. Departmental organization. Establishing a marketing department.

19
The Skills of the Manager   251
The function of management objectives. Dealing with people. The language of business. Tests of performance. Budgeting. The capital investment decision. The age of the computer. Towards quantified marketing. On being a manager.

Notes and References   265

Index   269

LIST OF ILLUSTRATIONS

PREFACE

THE ROLE OF INDUSTRIAL MARKETING

Industrial marketing has an important part to play in the nation's economic growth. It is one of the agents of change and advance, bringing progress through innovation to its customers in industry. In Britain there has been no shortage of demand in the past quarter of a century; indeed, successive governments have often considered there was an excess. The deficiency has been in the ability to satisfy demand and to generate a sufficient volume of exports to pay for the needed imports. Industrial marketing has a truly creative role in the economy, not only because it provides the major part of exports but because it also brings more effective production to its customers. It adds to the nation's wealth by providing customers with the means whereby demand can be more effectively satisfied and, at the same time, provides real income with which this wealth may be purchased for their employees, shareholders, and the government.

Compared with the amount which has been written on consumer marketing, the literature on industrial marketing is still sparse, although the practical problems do differ from those in the consumer field. Industrial marketing is noteworthy for the variety and range of challenges which it provides, and for this reason demands a more fundamental approach than consumer marketing.

It is hoped that the present text will go some way toward providing a perspective of its subject. It does not set out to provide a set of model solutions to industrial marketing problems; even if such an encyclopedic approach were possible, it would have become out of date before it went to press. At the other extreme, the object has been to avoid such generality as to be of no operational significance. The aim is to show the steps by which industrial marketing practice evolves and adapts dynamically, and how it fits in with the other parts of the business enterprise, in the hope that the individual reader can use this as a springboard for the development of ideas to fit his own firm, his own customers, and his own products. Each firm is different from every other, and next year it will be different again from what it is today.

HOW TO USE A BUSINESS BOOK

A business book is a tool for its user. It is a tiny item of capital investment from which the reader aims to achieve a payoff in the years ahead.

But a tool has to be used, and using a book effectively requires some thought. For this book the reader might like to consider the following plan:

1 Read through quickly, skipping those parts which appear to require rather deeper thought.
2 Then read through more slowly, adapting the book to your own particular needs, by underlining or otherwise indicating points that interest you, and making your own marginal or other notes.
3 Now set out to penetrate more deeply, spending time on the complex sections and following up the references, especially on those aspects of most interest.
4 Finally integrate the book into your own plans for continual personal development and updating of your knowledge. These plans should include the regular reading of selected periodicals and new literature, selective attendance at seminars, and association with others seeking to advance in this field.

1

Marketing in Perspective

In the well-known verse by John Godfrey Saxe, six blind men went to see an elephant and each of them came back with a different idea of what the beast was like. One fell against the animal's side and compared it with a wall, the second thought its leg was like the trunk of a tree. So it went on: its tusk was a spear, its tail a rope, its trunk a snake, its ear a fan. Not one of them was able to visualize the beast as a whole.

This story has its analogy with marketing today. There are many ways of approaching this subject and each of them emphasizes a different aspect. Marketing effectiveness means seeing all these aspects, not separately but as part of a unified whole.

This book is not concerned with the niceties of definition. It is concerned with understanding what marketing is about and how it can be used to generate turnover and profits. The first step is to appreciate the meaning of the term and to develop the "marketing" attitude of mind. This is what lies behind the persistent appeals for market orientation in business.

Businessmen concerned with industrial products have sometimes tended to identify marketing with some of its more striking manifestations: mass advertising, television commercials, supermarket goods with 2 cents off. If this view of marketing were correct, then there would be no place for a book concerned with industrial marketing. In fact, these manifestations reflect only one part of the very wide area comprised in the word "marketing."

Studying the marketing "elephant" closely reveals six major aspects, which taken collectively give a broad insight into the subject and suggest how business problems may profitably be approached from the marketing point of view.

MARKETING AS CUSTOMER ORIENTATION

A business exists in order to sell something. This is true whether that business be privately owned or nationalized. In general, whoever controls the business seeks to achieve a higher and increasing level of profit and can do this only by achieving sales on satisfactory terms. The act of sale is the consummation of the purpose of business.

But consummation involves two parties. It must offer satisfaction both to the businessman and to the customer. Products are not made to satisfy the technicians who have lavished so much loving care on them, nor to satisfy research workers who have written learned papers about them, nor to satisfy directors who have masterminded them. They are made to satisfy the customer. The whole enterprise is set up to serve that purpose.

"Satisfying the customer" is an elusive idea. It is partly a matter of producing the right piece of hardware—the tangible physical product which has been thought out down to the last detail in terms of what will meet the customer's needs and desires. The customer also has associated requirements. He wants more than the product: he requires many intangible extras, and he is not always clear in his own mind what these intangibles are. He may want reassurance: "Am I wise in choosing this product from this maker?" He may want advice on using it, or after-sales service, or a host of other things. Much of the skill in marketing is concerned with designing a total blend of tangibles and intangibles which strikes the right balance between cost to the manufacturer and benefits to the customer.

The hallmark of a marketing man is that he thinks *first* about the customer and his present and potential needs. He envisages how the product is to be used, by whom, when, and where. He strives to understand the mental and emotional struggles and the departmental politics preceding the decision to buy a product. He realizes that a "better" product is not necessarily the one which is machined to the finest tolerance, but is the product which offers the potential customer what he wants on terms which can be shown to be acceptable. The idea for the product and its accompanying services is conceived from study of the customer, and the resources of the firm are directed to turning the idea into a product and the product into sales.

Nevertheless, customers can be awkward. You produce this "better" product. Do buyers form a line outside the sales manager's door and keep the representatives' telephones busy? Alas, no—or at least, very rarely. Marketing must provide a further impetus to action through the techniques of communication, salesmanship, and promotion.

The marketing man studies in detail the whole buying process to make sure that he applies the impetus to buy his product in the manner and at the point which gives it maximum leverage.

It is equally important to ensure that no minor impediments exist to deter a prospect from buying or using a product. There is sometimes a temptation to say or think: "That's only a small inconvenience. Let's leave the customer to deal with it; it won't cause him much bother." The marketing approach is to say: "It's only a small point. Let's correct it; it won't cause *us* much bother." When products are similar and price differences small, the final choice of source of supply may turn on the smallest detail.

MARKETING AS PROBLEM SOLVING

The problems of concern in the marketing process are those of the prospective customer. He has not just one problem which a supplier must aim to help him to solve, but a whole constellation of problems in relation to the product.

This is true in consumer marketing, and it is most strikingly true in industrial marketing. The housewife buying the most obvious of household products, whether it be a packet of detergent or a tin of soup, is facing a much wider set of problems than simply "How shall I wash the clothes?" or "What shall I serve with lunch?" She is concerned with such questions as "How can I make the family happy?" "How can I save time?" and a whole range of others.

The buyer of industrial products is similarly placed. He must be satisfied that the product is suited for his purpose, that delivery, service, and price are within acceptable limits. He may also require assistance with such issues as "What will the boss say?" "Is it safe?" "Is the supplier reliable?" "How do I store it, finance it?" It is important to realize that a favorable decision to buy may involve the buying company in a number of associated problems to be solved, and that the seller should identify at least the most crucial of these and consider what he can do to help solve them. Part of the basic analysis of a marketing situation is to identify the customer's constellation of problems.

An ability to see marketing in terms of the issues which executives in the prospect companies must resolve is of immense value in developing the best marketing approach. The supplier who sets out to answer all the prospective customer's problems is far more likely to get the business.

MARKETING AS SERVICE

Nobody wants your product.

This is a useful cautionary note for everyone in marketing. People never want a product—they want the service which the product renders them. Although a company is selling hardware, the need for the hardware is based on the service which is required from it.

Awareness of this point helps in marketing analysis in two ways. Firstly, it is closely related to the problem-solving approach. If there is clarity about the service which the buyer seeks from the product, it is easier to envisage the other problems which he has to solve in obtaining that service. The marketing strategy can then be designed to solve these. This approach is based on the idea that the supplier tries to offer the most effective way of providing the customer not with a product, but with the service which is his ultimate aim. In consumer marketing, the emphasis is on customer satisfaction; the service approach is recommended as a convenient interpretation for industrial customers.

In industrial marketing, the prime satisfaction which is the customer's ultimate aim is in general the attainment of profit. This is achieved by the combined interaction of a vast range of specific individual services throughout the company. Thus for a paint brush the specific service might at first be described as "to apply paint." Even this may not be subtle enough. Major mass-production runs may be dealt with by spraying or dipping. Perhaps the prime service a paint brush offers is the application of a protective or decorative coating to a relatively small nonstandardized surface.

This illustration shows that defining the service which the enterprise seeks to provide is by no means easy. Yet it is important, particularly in the long run. Unless a company knows what service it aims to provide, it does not know who its competitors are, even though it is well aware of all the other companies which provide the same product. The service of packaging, for example, can be provided through the physical media of paper, tin, glass, and plastic.

Over time, the ways in which a particular problem is

solved or a particular service rendered are always changing. If a company considers itself in the business of providing a specific product, then it may find itself without a market when the market for its product is invaded by something else which does the job better.

When a company's executives define the nature of the service which the company seeks to render, they tell the world —and all their subordinate staff—what business they are in. They define who their competitors are. Above all, they are able to perceive the changes which need to be made within the company to mesh in with the changing needs of customers, and they are far more likely to anticipate these changes in sufficient time to make the necessary adjustments in their capital equipment, staff, skills, and other resources.

This principle is difficult to apply to its fullest extent in relation to basic products such as iron and steel and perhaps also to some nonferrous metals, timber, and some plastics. These serve the customer and compete with each other on the basis of their differential advantages in multifarious applications. The marketing executive is faced with the problem of seeking new applications in which the relative considerations of weight, strength, durability, ease of processing or fabricating, price, and everything else which can be summed up in the phrase "fitness for purpose" can be so blended in his product that it gains sales. Nevertheless, in view of the increasing ingenuity of the chemical industry, it would be a bold man who would take it for granted that iron and steel are always going to remain at their present level of importance in the economy.

MARKETING AS A SYNTHESIS WITH THE ENVIRONMENT

Customer orientation is an excellent thing, but it must be related to the enterprise's search for profit. Serving the customer does not mean following the whim of every fickle jade in the market without measuring the gain and counting the cost. That way lies financial disaster.

A businessman looking out from his office chair at the competitive environment which surrounds him sees a host of products he might consider making, a host of problems he can help to solve, a host of services he could render. But his resources are limited, and he must therefore select some limited area on which to concentrate. He cannot tackle every problem in the world.

How does he decide? Essentially this is a marketing decision, for he must say to himself: "Where in this total environment are the best opportunities for my firm?" This is the key long-term decision which conditions others. Success depends in part on choosing the opportunity. How big is it? What is present and prospective competition from other firms? Or from other products providing the same service? Is it a growing market which offers a widening future horizon for a range of products?

On the other hand, some apparent opportunities are unlikely to be successfully exploited by a particular firm because it lacks certain skills or assets. These are areas of relative weakness. True, weaknesses may be corrected over time, but in making an approach to the market it is necessary to recognize the weaknesses which exist, to evaluate their implications and to consider realistically the possibilities of correcting them.

This question has two sides, the firm and the environment, and successful marketing involves a synthesis between the two. Study of the company shows that it has certain skills and resources which permit it to exploit some opportunities in the marketplace better than others. One company has knowledge of rubber technology, another has a sales force calling on 95 percent of the architects in the country, yet another is sited near an important center of the steel industry, and so on. Each of these skills and assets makes certain classes of opportunity more likely to be successful.

The first step in marketing is to choose the emerging opportunity which is most attractive over time to *your* company. It must be most attractive both from the point of view of the magnitude of the opportunity and the strength of the competition and from that of its meshing with the pattern of your firm's strengths and weaknesses.

Planned modifications are made to the company to improve its ability to succeed in its chosen area. It is adjusted in anticipation of change, so that the most rewarding relationship between the firm and its environment is maintained.

In a sense, this interpretation of marketing is the most fundamental. It is perhaps the most difficult to absorb, but it influences the entire approach to marketing of the present book. It is the basic justification for the inclusion of Chapter 3 on corporate strategy. Once it is accepted that marketing is a *total* blending or synthesis of the firm and its environment to achieve profit for the firm and satisfaction for the possible customers, then the earlier views can be regarded as the development of different aspects of this definition in greater detail. It indicates that the idea of marketing runs throughout the company, with each individual considering his own contribution in the light of the ultimate marketing objectives.

Fig. 1 illustrates what this means in practice.

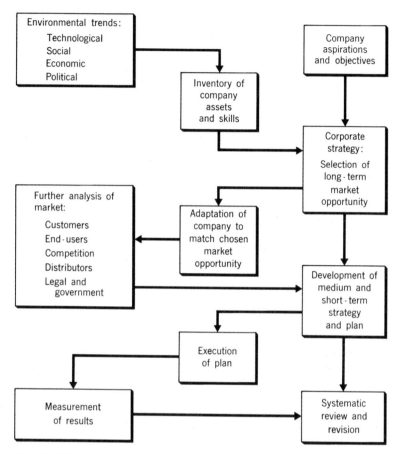

Fig. 1. The company and the environment

     The company builds up information about the market, its present state, and its possible future state. This is essentially information about its prospective customers and the pressures upon them, about competitors, or possible government or political action. It compares its own abilities with the opportunities revealed by this analysis. This leads to the long-term policy decision: "What business should our company be in?"

     This overall decision conditions the other marketing decisions which have to be made. These decisions can be classed under six major headings:

    1 Identifying market targets by industry or customer.
    2 Determining the products to be offered.
    3 Determining the services to be provided.
    4 Deciding the price and terms of sale.

5 Deciding on communications policy.
6 Deciding the channels of distribution.

These decisions are closely related and interdependent; they are not separate but are interwoven into a close, harmonious market strategy. Any change in policy under one heading reacts on all the others, and the two skills of a marketing man lie firstly in developing this policy and secondly in implementing it.

MARKETING AS AN ANTICIPATION OF CHANGE

Having developed a synthesis with the environment, it soon becomes apparent that this is not a static relationship. The environment changes, and never has change been so rapid and pervasive as it is today. Technological advance develops at an unprecedented rate; new methods, new materials, new machines become available more quickly than ever before. They also become obsolescent more quickly than ever before. The marketing strategy is thus in constant need of review and development. Not only the marketing strategy—the basic question "What business should the company be in?" must be reexamined too.

This is exemplified by the recent history of John Brown & Co. Traditionally the name of this company has been virtually synonymous with shipbuilding. Yet by 1968 its interest in this field had shrunk to a trade investment (representing one-third of the equity of an associated company) included in the balance sheet at less than $5 million out of a figure for total assets in excess of $103 million. The company's profits and turnover came from machine tools and cutting tools, chemical engineering and pipelines, containers, commercial vehicle bodies, and general engineering.

Industrial products can also lose markets because of changes in the pattern of consumer behavior, as is illustrated by the following extract from *The Statist*, March 25, 1966:

> From a 50 per cent rate in the early 1960s, Crown Cork, a subsidiary of Crown Cork and Seal of Philadelphia, first cut its dividend to 25 per cent in 1962 and thereafter took the controversial decision to drop out of the dividend lists altogether. . . .
>   Since the end of last century Crown Cork had been producing bottle closures for its two main customers—the brewers and the soft drink manufacturers . . . when keg and draught beer gained ground in the early 1960s at the

expense of bottled brews (and soft drink sales simultane-
ously declined under pressure from a new tax and bad
summer weather), the company was in no state to cope
with reduced demand for its product.

Crown Cork eventually diversified into aerosol cans and began
manufacture of aerosols in 1964. The parent company in the
United States had pioneered aerosols in 1946, eighteen years
earlier. (*The Statist* too has had its problems, and has since
ceased publication.)

Change must be accepted as an inevitable part of the
environment. So far as is humanly possible, the direction of
probable change must be anticipated, and policy altered in
good time.

The marketing reaction to change is positive. Here is
something new, a new opportunity which no one else is satisfying. If a firm can anticipate this change, then it can consider
whether there is an opportunity to enter this emerging market
and can choose a time and circumstances which give it an edge
on possible competitors.

Indeed, a company may set out to create demand for its
products by accelerating change. It may be the first in the field
with a new product, although not every company is able to exploit this type of situation. Or it may follow innovation by a
market leader by providing variations which are particularly
suited to some small segment of the total market.

MARKETING AND BUSINESS PLANNING

In the last decade there has been a great deal of talk
about marketing, and industrials have been exhorted to adopt
the marketing concept rather in the way that nineteenth-century
evangelists called on sinners to repent.

Now it is very easy to say, "I repent and will hereafter
lead a better life," but when it comes to actually living the good
life, the flesh and the devil can play havoc with good intentions.

The analogy with the present situation in marketing is
that it is very easy to say, "I will adopt the marketing concept,"
but it is much harder to put those bold words into practice.
They can only be put into practice by planning and organization throughout the company.

The attitudes outlined above should permit the development of an overall sense of purpose for the entire company,
which can lead to the identification of the objectives for each
sector of the company and ultimately for each individual in it.

So far as is possible, these should be quantified, starting with figures for the expected market performance and working from this to the related production, personnel, purchasing, and other objectives. This is to be backed with an adequate control system which facilitates the comparison of progress against expectation and thus makes possible the review of performance and of targets.

"Marketing" is not a take-over bid for the company by the marketing department. It is an approach to the entire operation of the company which associates management at all levels with the ultimate objective of the business and requires from them systematic and efficient management procedures to get the best results from the resources available to the company. Without this management approach, whatever grand phrases are spoken about "the marketing concept" are a snare and a delusion, for the behavior of the individuals who make up the enterprise will be little different from what it was before.

2

Understanding Industrial Markets

What is different about industrial markets?

In industrial marketing, the manufacturer is concerned with goods or services which are to be marketed to buyers who will use them in connection with the goods and services which they in turn produce.[1] It is thus contrasted with consumer marketing where goods and services are sold (either directly or through middlemen) to buyers who will use them for the personal satisfaction of themselves and their families. The interpretation of industrial marketing includes the supply of institutional buyers (for example, the armed forces, hospitals, and local authorities).

The distinction is thus not determined by the nature of the goods but by the nature of the market for which the product is destined; some goods such as typewriters, tape recorders, and gasoline may be sold to both consumer and industrial markets. There is in fact no firm line separating the industrial from the consumer market, and the differences of approach are often differences of degree, with ideas being *adapted* from one sector to another. Nevertheless, the difference of degree may be quite considerable, and the approach to the typical industrial market shows marked dissimilarity from the approach to the typical consumer market.

It is customary to analyze the goods and services offered to industrial customers into a number of different classes. The list below is a typical analysis, but it is by no means the only or even necessarily the most important factor in developing the marketing strategy of a company. The *total* marketing situation has to be analyzed and strategy fitted into it. Nevertheless, this analysis does suggest some preliminary ideas:

1 CAPITAL GOODS

These are goods which will be used over a period of time by the customer. They will commonly be capitalized in the accounts and written off over a number of years. Often they will involve significant expenditure and be a major decision for the buying company.

2 RAW MATERIALS, PROCESSED MATERIALS, COMPONENTS, SUBASSEMBLIES

These items share the common feature that they enter directly into the customer's product, become physically part of it, and in this way pass onward incorporated in the goods he sells. Accordingly, they are often part of the customer's direct variable cost and affect the salability of his product. Sometimes the customer's customer may be able to identify the qualities which they give in the product which he, in turn, buys. Raw materials commonly have a relatively wide range of applications, but as they are processed into more advanced products, so they tend to be more closely adapted to a specific class of application. (Products which are marketed to a wide cross-section of industry are often referred to as being in horizontal demand; those marketed to a narrow market are referred to as being in vertical demand.)

3 CONSUMABLES

These are items used up in a relatively short period without actually becoming part of the customer's product. They cover a considerable range, and include such items as lubricants, fuel and power, and stationery.

4 SERVICES

These cover a wide range from those services which provide a long-term benefit and are thus analogous to a capital item, although not treated as such in the accounts of the buying company (the services of a management consultant are an example of this), to other services such as those of banking, transport, and insurance, which are more analogous to a consumable product.

CUSTOMERS AND USERS

Certain standard terms have been adopted in this book to aid in describing market structure:

The *intermediate* manufacturer is a customer who buys products (such as those described in number 2 above) and incorporates them (with or without processing) as part of the product which he himself makes.

The *indirect* customer is the intermediate manufacturer's customer. Thus a synthetic-fiber manufacturer may sell his product to a processor (an intermediate manufacturer), who sells it, after processing, to a textile manufacturer (an indirect customer). In the chain from the first manufacturer to the final consumer there may be many links. The final consumer is an indirect customer as far as the industrial marketer is concerned.

The *end-user* is the buying organization or individual who physically retains possession of the goods which he buys. This would apply to consumables, capital equipment, and services. The individual consumer who buys for the benefit of himself or his family is, of course, also an end-user.

The term *customer* has been used freely and includes potential customers in the target market; it is not restricted to current customers.

Institutions are organizations such as hospitals, defense services, and charitable bodies whose prime motive is not commercial business but the serving of some other purpose. Buying decisions cannot be related to commercial results in terms of expected profit, but the institutions operate within budget constraints which may be severe.

The demand for all industrial goods is a *derived* demand: it originates from an actual or (more generally) an anticipated final demand from some consumer. The relationship between the demand for the industrial product and the demand in the consumer market varies from one class of product to another. If the demand for automobiles falls, the demand for original equipment (e.g., batteries) also falls, and the equipment supplier quickly feels the reaction.

In many markets, however, the reaction is not so quick, nor the relationship so clear-cut. The supplier of a synthetic fiber has a market which is affected by the change in demand for a wide range of final products. Moreover, between the fiber supplier and the consumer are a number of intermediaries holding stocks in one form or another; these stocks may be of fiber, yarn, fabric, or garments. If consumer demand changes, the reaction on the original fiber supplier, both in timing and in magnitude, depends partly on the change in consumer demand and also on policy decisions made by the stockists. A fall in final demand may lead stockists to reduce the size of their stocks. If this happens, the change in final market demand may be greatly magnified by the time it reaches the fiber supplier, reflecting both the change in final demand and the change in stocks. The reverse may happen when demand expands.

Changes in demand for industrial products may also occur independently of a change in final demand if intermediate manufacturers alter their methods. The replacement of glass bottles by plastic containers for, say, the packaging of lubricants reacts on the demand for both plastics and glass. Methods of production which economize on the use of a product, by putting a thinner layer of tin on a metal can or improving the efficiency of fuel utilization, also affect the demand for the materials concerned. Such changes may occur very quickly as a result of a policy decision by one very big buyer, or they may occur as a result of a series of changes, each of them relatively minor, made by a wide range of customers.

Capital goods have not in general a quick direct link with the final demand for a particular consumer product. Nevertheless, their demand is often very sensitive to change in the general state of the economy. When a government considers it necessary to cut back on the total demand of the economy, raises interest rates, and restricts the supply of credit, the demand for many types of capital goods in the home market falls proportionately more than the demand for consumer goods.

MARKET CHARACTERISTICS

Although certain types of industrial and consumer market show similarities of structure, it is possible to distinguish the *typical* industrial marketing situation from its consumer counterpart by a number of features.

The pattern of buyer demand usually differs. The majority of consumer products in Great Britain have customers numbering thousands and often millions. Each one of these buyers represents a small part of the total demand. (There are a few possible exceptions, such as a small tailor, or a company making yachts for well-to-do clients.) In the industrial markets, a small number of buyers is common. In the United Kingdom, the Central Electricity Generating Board is the dominating customer for switchgear, and the company making accessories for portable pumps will find only eight to ten customers. The National Coal Board purchases over 90 percent of certain types of mining ropes. It is a common phrase in many industries that

20 percent of the buyers represent 80 percent of the business, and this is a convenient generalization. Of course, there are exceptions: there are many thousands of farmers in the United Kingdom, and of builders and small offices.

The amount of money involved in an industrial sale is also generally far higher than it is in the consumer transaction. Its related financial implications may also be greater in other ways. The purchaser is himself in business, and if he includes a component of poor quality in *his* product, his own sales and reputation will be affected. If he installs an item of equipment which breaks down, his entire production line will be thrown out of gear. If goods fail to arrive on time or, worse still, do not arrive at all, then the outcome will be most serious.

Thus the buying decision is given much greater thought and there are almost always some logical, objective criteria to be satisfied by the product. These criteria include, explicitly or implicitly, the specifications which the product must meet, its price, and other terms relating to the sale, and also the cost and other implications of using and maintaining, the product. The importance of confidence in continuity of supply on fair terms also ranks high. Often companies will go out of their way to buy components and raw materials from two or more suppliers so that this continuity is assured. Equally, executives may be reluctant to buy from a relatively unknown supplier because they lack confidence in his ability to meet his commitments. Price and specification are not the only rational factors in a buying decision.

In consumer buying, irrational as well as rational considerations frequently operate. It is difficult to decide how far the same can be said of industrial buying. There are certainly some factors which are frequently relevant other than objective and explicit criteria. Confidence is very important, and confidence in a supplier may depend upon the image of the company as well as on the facts of the situation. The purchase of computers in their early days was more an act of faith than a conclusion based on the careful analysis of cost and return. Indeed, one heard stories of computers bought as company status symbols, and it is difficult to discount these entirely. ("If you quote me," said one informant, "I shall deny it.")

Organization theory[2] suggests that there will in fact be three classes of interest at work in the minds of individuals making the decision:

   1 The interests of the company—for example, its need for profit, for increased turnover, and for the avoidance of unreasonable risk.

2 The interests of the department to which the individual belongs—for example, its efficient operation and its success within the company.
3 The interests of the individual—for example, his desire to stand well with his superiors, to develop his career and his own self-interest, and to satisfy his own normal social and ego needs by winning the respect of his colleagues and meeting the standards which he sets for himself.

Often these three motives will be consistent with each other. Sometimes the interests of the company may not be very obviously involved (for example, in the last resort, the make of calculating machine bought will scarcely have an identifiable effect on the company's profits), and then departmental and personal interest may be more important. There may also be times when neither company nor departmental interests are apparently involved, perhaps because competitive offerings are very similar in price and specification. The customer's decision may then turn on such factors as what is a fair and reasonable apportionment of business between different suppliers, or on other minor factors of a personal character, such as good relations with the representative of the supplier.

Salesmen are, of course, extremely conscious of the nonobjective criteria in industrial buying. Certainly every buying decision except, perhaps, routine repeat buying involves some degree of fear or at least doubt. It is necessary that the marketing man recognizes that this factor is at work, and devises his marketing action accordingly. Finally, however much the industrial buyer may laugh at the ordinary consumer who buys toothpaste with a stripe in it, nevertheless one British company thought it worth while marketing a water-suction hose with a stripe on it. Sometimes such devices succeed in focusing the customer's attention on a product, and help him remember it more vividly when the time comes to buy.

In addition to the product actually purchased, industrial customers generally require a great deal of other service before or after the sale. Sometimes it is presales advice: a survey may be carried out to recommend the type of office forms to be purchased or the particular grades of lubricant to be used. Often it is after-sales service, the maintenance of the equipment or perhaps the temporary provision of replacement equipment while the customer's equipment is out of order. It may be the training of staff who use or maintain the equipment. It may be design or marketing service: packaging companies may design an efficient and attractive selling pack for a client and advise on the marketing program for the client's product.

One other factor must be mentioned in this preliminary review of considerations affecting the industrial decision to buy. This is the widespread implications of "reciprocal buying." This is the practice by which Company A, who is purchasing goods from Company B, applies pressure to Company B to reciprocate by making purchases from Company A. This practice is widespread and is a normal ingredient in the commercial life of today.

Frequency of purchase may also be a factor affecting market demand problems. For some products the same customers buy regularly; this applies to packaging and raw materials. For others, individual customers buy rarely and a key marketing function is customer identification; an example of this is conveyors.

Industrial markets are also frequently distinguished by greater geographical concentration, which in certain industries is most striking. The glass industry is heavily concentrated at St. Helens; the woolen and worsted industry is still primarily in the West Riding of Yorkshire; and automobile manufacture is still restricted to a small number of centers. In some types of business this fact may be relevant to the organization and operation of the sales force, to the location of warehouses, and to other aspects of marketing. For small companies, the problem "What business should I be in?" may well be solved by looking first at the question "What possible customers do I have within easy distance?"

The final point to be made about the special characteristics of a typical industrial market is the importance of technological change. The market can be tremendously affected in the short term by new ways of doing things, and the industrial marketing man must be continually watching for innovation—new opportunities for improved products, new competing products, new methods adopted by customers, and new applications—which may react on his market. This watch will be accomplished in many ways: through the salesmen who will report new developments, through technicians who hear a whisper of a new technological advance at a scientific conference, through the press, and through formal market research. This, indeed, is one reason, among others, why *everyone* in a company should be market-conscious. The salesman may only hear about a new development by the time a rival has marketed a product. The technologist, on the other hand, has a good chance of hearing about a development long before the stage of application and can thus give his company a chance to take action to exploit the opportunities which it creates.

THE CONCEPT OF MARKET SEGMENTATION

No analysis of an industrial market would be complete without consideration of the way in which it could be segmented or broken down into "submarkets." Market segmentation, which has been much discussed in the literature of consumer marketing in recent years, has long been an established feature of much industrial marketing. A clear understanding of the concept will, however, permit it to be used more systematically as a basis for a profitable and effective policy.

It is common to speak of the market for nuts and bolts or for oscilloscopes. In fact, different groups of buyers may have different market characteristics. Some may seek product features which are of no interest to others; some may be sensitive to price variation, whereas others may be relatively insensitive; some may be keen to take up new ideas, while others are more conservative; and some may require a great deal of technical service, while others have their own staff specialists to undertake this function.

Thus the total market may be classified into segments, with the buyers in one segment differing in general from the buyers in another. It may be possible to devise different marketing strategies for different segments satisfying the special requirements of each. This can gain the supplier a competitive advantage, although usually with some consequent increase in cost.

Market segmentation can be exploited to advantage in a large number of different ways. In launching a new product which in its early marketing phase is likely to be expensive, the initial launch may be slanted toward a certain segment of the market comprising industries to which its offered advantages are particularly valuable. If the product resists corrosion, it may first be marketed to those industries where this problem is most serious. A marketing department may be organized so that specialists develop knowledge of particular segments and devise appropriate products or models and market strategy.

There are many ways of segmenting industrial markets. The commoner ways are discussed below, but this list should not be regarded as exhaustive. The imaginative marketing man will look out for other natural divisions between parts of his total market.

Industry segmentation is probably the commonest form of segmentation in industrial markets. Products are designed or adapted to meet the requirements of particular industries, and the marketing methods are adapted to meet the requirements of those industries.

Size of customer is another way in which analysis can be carried out. It may be an advantage to segment the market between large and small buyers. Thus a small manufacturer with low overheads may set out to deal with the low-volume customers whom the bigger company ignores. At the other extreme, one really big customer may be sufficiently important to be treated as a market segment on its own. If, for example, it was desired to develop the use of a particular product in the automobile industry, the supplier could prepare formulations suited to the needs of a particular company and analyze its models one by one to show where his product could be used to advantage.

Applications for a product may also be a basis for segmentation. For example, equipment for R&D purposes may be made to finer tolerances, require more supplementary features, and command a higher price than the corresponding product for general plant use. The R&D market may justify attention as a separate segment. The electronic components market may be divided between computer applications, consumer durables applications, and so on.

Regional segmentation is sometimes found. A small supplier may concentrate on supplying one part of the country only and thus be able to give prompt and individual service together with low transport costs. As some industries are regional in character, it may be possible to associate regional and industrial segmentation and to concentrate on supplying, for example, the West Riding textile industry. In international marketing, segmentation on a country or area basis may be essential.

Market segmentation recognizes that different types of purchaser (and even the same purchasers on different occasions) have different needs. Identification of segments permits the marketing executive to focus his efforts more clearly and sharply on the needs of the segment and thus to match his offering to it with more precision. This reduces the size of the potential market to which this particular approach is appropriate, but it generally improves the possibility of marketing the product successfully. If a segment is identified which has not been satisfied by competitors' offerings, then a product adapted for that segment should command higher profit, and the attack on the segment should give better returns for a given marketing effort. On the other hand, the identified segment needs to be large enough to justify all the costs involved.

MAKING THE BUYING DECISION

This section deals with one of the basic essentials in the successful marketing of industrial products: the intensive study of the procedure by which the decision to buy a product is made in a customer company. Although the product may be sold to a limited company, which has neither a body nor a soul, the decision to buy is made by people. Even if the actual process of making the buying decision is done by a computer (as is beginning to happen today), some person programed the computer and decided the rules which were to be the basis of its decision. No marketing plan can be made without thoroughly considering who makes the decision to buy and how it is made. Who are these people? What is their role in the buying decision and what criteria do they apply?

A simple mnemonic is the "3 S" approach: specify (the product), select (the supplier), and sign (the authorization). Each "S" represents one stage toward the buying decision; each stage may involve a different person. This formula is perhaps too simple, but it is valuable when circumstances do not justify more subtlety. For example, it is of value to teach industrial salesmen this at an early stage so that they become aware of the need to make their presentation to the right man.

Specification and other matters relating to the setting of standards will commonly be the responsibility of some clearly authorized and appropriately qualified person, such as a research chemist, works engineer, transport manager, and so on. In some circumstances, the specification may be made more informally; specification of typewriter requirements is in some firms *in fact*, if not in theory, largely in the hands of the typing staff, who will have views on whether a wide carriage is needed, whether a key release is necessary, and so on.

When goods are being regularly ordered and reordered, specification will not be reexamined on every occasion. However, a seller who has to offer a product of a different and in some way superior specification must contact the appropriate person in the prospect company to effect a change in the policy on this matter.

The actual placing of the order will normally be through the buyer or purchasing officer. The authority of this executive differs from firm to firm and is sometimes not very clear. While a great deal depends upon the quality of the individual concerned, his authority is probably highest on regularly purchased materials where he has developed special knowledge in relation to the products or has developed a skill in anticipating price movements and negotiation of terms with suppliers. On some products of a technical nature, however, he may have only the right to recommend a list of suppliers, and if the specification is very restrictive there may in fact be only one supplier able to meet it.

Finally, approval of purchases of any size will commonly have to be made by a superior. This is not necessarily an approval of each individual order but may be the scrutinizing of a schedule or the determination of policy.

This is a greatly simplified approach. A deeper approach regards the buying decision as being made after a network of communication between individuals in the buying company. Each individual has a decision to make as his contribution toward the total buying decision. The marketing executive has to identify what decisions have to be made, who makes each decision, and what criteria he applies.

The following is a simple example illustrating the purchase of a calculating machine for use in a market research department. What happened was this: The statistician who was known to be anxious to speed production from his calculating section was approached by a machine operator, who complained that her present machine was slow and lacked certain features which, she said, were needed for the special work of that department. In particular, she said that there was no device for extracting a square root.

After investigation, the statistician approached the market research manager, who first checked with the accounts department that his departmental budget was sufficient, and then agreed to requisition a machine made by Company X. The requisition was signed by the general manager (commercial) and sent to the buying department.

The buyer responsible for office supplies referred to his records and phoned back to say that there were two other companies making models with "much the same" features. He suggested that it might be possible to satisfy the market research department's need on more favorable terms than by buying the model first suggested. He sent suppliers' literature from his files to the M.R. department for information and consideration. Following study of this literature by the statistician and consultation within the M.R. department, a representative from one of the companies was invited to call and demonstrate, and as a result a purchase was made.

This simple example of a buying procedure is worth examining to identify elements which are common in many industrial buying situations.[3]

First, the need was identified and a decision made to request a replacement. In this case, the need was identified by the operator of the machine in the course of daily use. It is common when the need is for a *replacement* of equipment that it is identified by people who are concerned with the equipment regularly, either as operators or through responsibility for its supervision or maintenance. Replacement recommendations for machinery may come, for example, from the works manager. Where, however, there is to be expansion, the proposals are often initiated by a higher authority; for capital equipment, for example, the proposal may arise at board level.

There are, however, many ways in which identification of need can occur: from regular review procedures, from complaints about poor quality or slow delivery, from value analysis and customer product improvement, from new construction or other innovation in the factory, and finally, from the marketing initiative of suppliers.

The need having been identified, there is a search process to develop a list of acceptable suppliers. The statistician in this example might well have been satisfied with the make that first came to his mind, but the buyer searched further and consulted his files. He identified three possible sources, decided these were sufficient and suitable for recommendation, and terminated his search. Of course, if he had been pressed he might easily have searched further, consulted trade directories and buyers' guides and widened his inquiries. However, in this example he felt satisfied after identifying three sources. Clearly, if the search for sources is limited it is important to a would-be supplier to be one of the companies short-listed as a suitable supplier; his name must come readily to mind and the name must be acceptable.

Finally, there is a process of selecting one supplier. The statistician's original request had been, in effect, a partial specification for the machine, but the subsequent discussion process developed this so that criteria were established sufficient to discriminate between the various possible models. Thus was the total decision reached to make a purchase of a particular item from a specific supplier.

If there are a number of departments in the company which use calculating machines, there may be more than one communication network. These may overlap. For this product they probably would, and the office supplies buyer would be a member of all the networks connected with calculating machines.

A further step in the analysis is to try to identify those who have most power in making this decision. They are the key characters in the communication network. If some individuals carry more weight, then the would-be supplier must take care that proper promotional communication is directed toward them. This promotion will then have more leverage: effort will produce greater response. The test is not solely formal authority.

A senior director is apparently more powerful than the technician, but if in buying a specific product he relies on the advice of the technician, then the latter is the key man.

In general, the role of the buyer is greater where commercial considerations are important—where prices fluctuate and there is, therefore, a need to keep in touch with the market and judge price trends, or where delivery dates really matter or past supplier performance is in question.

The technician has more importance where the product is complex or where the buying company is developing an unfamiliar use. In these circumstances, there may be differences between the products offered by different suppliers, which may be hard to evaluate. Technical influence will then be heavy in the buying decision.

Top management will, of course, figure more strongly in the decision process in the small company. Apart from this, there will be active high-level interest in a purchase which will have widespread influence in the company or have substantial implications for its future profitability. Where the product represents commercial and technical innovation in the company of such a scale as to involve widespread reorganization and retraining of staff and operatives, where the cost is so great that it represents a significant strain on the company's resources, where the company is moving into the unknown so that the risk involved in the purchase has an importance to the company as a whole, all these are circumstances in which the top brass of the company will come actively into the decision-making process. Reciprocal buying arrangements are also generally the subject of high-level consideration.

Each market situation requires analysis. One can cite cases where the marketing staff of the buying company will be the key, because the purchase will have a direct and noticeable effect on the sales of the product. In turn, this may mean that the indirect customers will perceive a change in what they receive, so the original suppliers may see an argument for "back-selling" campaigns.

Ideally, a marketing man would like to motivate all decision-makers and buying influences affecting the purchase decision. Sometimes this is possible, but at other times it is impracticable or uneconomical. The general policy is to apply most promotional pressure at key points where leverage is greatest, with supplementary action at other points.

In summarizing this section, one may suggest that the buying procedure—and therefore the marketing strategy to match it—is largely determined by two main variables: *product complexity*[4] and *commercial uncertainty*. Product complexity arises as a result of the impact of the technology of the product

Table 1 Factors in product complexity

Low ←——— PRODUCT COMPLEXITY ———→ HIGH	
Standardized product	Differentiated product
Technically simple	Technically complex
Established product	New product
Previously purchased	Initial purchase
Existing application	New application
Easy to install	Specialized installation
No after-sales service	Technical after-sales service

Table 2 Factors in commercial uncertainty

Low ←——— COMMERCIAL UNCERTAINTY ———→ HIGH	
Little investment	High investment
Small order	Large order
Short-term commitment	Long-term commitment
No consequential adjustments	Substantial consequential adjustments
Small potential effect on profitability	Large potential effect on profitability
Easy to forecast effect	Hard to forecast effect

on the existing knowledge of the customer. Commercial uncertainty arises when the purchasing decision involves business risk to the customer, because of its potential implications for his future profits. To some extent product complexity and commercial uncertainty are related. The main considerations affecting product complexity and commercial uncertainty are set out in Tables 1 and 2.

These factors interact to set the stage for the buying decision to be made. This interaction is illustrated in Fig. 2.

Where the buying situation is low in both product complexity and commercial risk, the buyer is the key man in the

Commercial uncertainty	Product complexity	
	Low	High
Low	Buyer emphasis	Technologist emphasis
High	Policy - maker emphasis	Total involvement

Fig. 2. The pattern of buying decisions

decision, but as product complexity increases, the technologist takes over and the buyer's influence declines. Increase in commercial risk without increase in complexity leads to the development of specialized buyers and the closer involvement of senior directors, accountants, economists, and others on the commercial side of the business. Where the product is complex and risk is also high, many decision-makers participate in the buying decision, and the situation is one of total involvement of many people at many levels.

Because of the frequent association of product complexity and commercial risk, most buying decision processes are close to the principal diagonal from top left to bottom right. Buyer emphasis is most clear in the purchase of a small quantity of a standardized product. Total involvement is exemplified by the initial purchase of electronic products of an advanced type to become standard components in widely used electronic equipment.

Technologist emphasis is illustrated by the purchase of a new item of moderate cost for the R&D department. Policy domination occurs where, for example, a large purchase is made of a standardized material on a basis which involves speculation about the future course of prices.

These differences are reflected in the approach to marketing strategy. In the buyer corner, the emphasis is on regular calling by the representative. In fact, where the unit of sale is very small and infrequent, the prime responsibility for the final sale may well be handed over to a distributor or agent. Moving to the opposite corner, there is total involvement with a number of people from the supplier meeting a number of people from the customer. Frequently this will be a relationship which can be very lasting; in fact, the customer company can become so dependent on the supplier for spares, service, and—perhaps above all—information on advances in technology affecting the product that there is a real cost to the customer if the relationship is severed. A supplier who can create this situation is well placed to maintain and expand business against competition.

INFORMAL INFLUENCES

So far the discussion has centered on the buying decision-makers, people whose roles are determined by their official authority in the buying company or their recognized roles as consultant, architect, designer, and so on. In general, if straightforward inquiries are made about who makes the buying decision, the replies will describe these people. But they in turn are subject to influence from a range of others with little or no authority in the formal sense.

Shop-floor workers are sometimes of consequence where, for example, an obvious change in the product is involved which directly affects them. On one dock it was proposed to replace chain by wire rope slings. This was resisted by the labor force on grounds of safety; they held that when chain began to wear, this was obvious and visible, but with wire rope this might not be so and the rope might break without warning, thus endangering their lives. Another, perhaps more surprising, case was reported by a participant in a seminar. A salesman had been supplying thread to a company of clothing manufacturers and had taken care to sell the machinists. When a rival's product of the same specification was purchased, there were immediate complaints that it broke more easily in use, and production was impaired.

Distributors, installers, and other intermediaries between buyer and seller may not always appear to be formally consulted, but they and their service and sales staff will sometimes be in a position of advising or commenting on what is to be bought.

If the buying customer is an intermediate manufacturer, his customers also can influence what is to be purchased, as perhaps their customers can also, and sometimes the chain can be followed right through to the final consumer. For a few products this has led to the development of what is known as back-selling. Here the supplier of industrial products may plan a campaign of promotion and persuasion to the final consumer so that he will ask for or accept the consumer product incorporating the industrial seller's components or material. This in turn reacts on the retailer and through him back along the chain of intermediate manufacturers. A well-known example in the fibers field is Bri-Nylon, which is very heavily promoted to the consumer; and this promotion is supported at intermediate points in the chain from fiber manufacturer through to the consumer. Perhaps Harris Tweed is an even older example.

For some products which go to government or local authorities, many influences both inside and outside the buying institution may come to bear, including the electorate itself.

Finally, when this analysis is complete, calculation and costing come in to express the facts in figures and forecasts, and the knowledge developed by market analysis must be supported by sound judgment, good management, and a sensitivity to the buying situation and so lead on to a strategy and plan.

3

Marketing and Corporate Strategy

At first sight a chapter on corporate strategy may seem out of place in a book on industrial marketing. There is, however, a good reason for its inclusion at the very beginning. Marketing begins when the corporate strategy of the firm is determined, and it cannot be expected to achieve its most effective contribution unless that strategy is clearly defined.

In Chapter 1 it was stressed that marketing implies that in the long term the firm must be adapted to the changing environment. Corporate strategy is the process by which that adaptation takes place in a controlled fashion.

THE RISE OF CORPORATE STRATEGY

Corporate strategy has come very much to the fore for two main reasons. First there is the high rate of obsolescence not only of individual products but of entire ranges of products, so much so that the whole basis on which a business is founded can be overthrown. The rapid and accelerating rate of technological advance which is largely responsible needs no elaboration here—it is the subject of the businessman's everyday observation. Its effect is accentuated by the more rapid changes in consumer tastes which react on the demand for industrial goods.

Technological advance has produced a secondary reaction through the advent of the age of rapid mass communication and fast travel. Whereas at one time ideas took decades and even centuries to spread and become accepted, now a worthwhile new idea is soon known universally and adopted in more advanced countries and communities.

Changes in the pattern of international trade have opened new markets and closed some old ones. Such groupings as EEC and EFTA have increased competitive advantages in some countries and reduced them in others. The reduction of international trade restrictions under GATT has often made it possible to think of a much wider area as the natural market for a product.

Finally, it would be wrong to underestimate the increasing impact of business education. This has whetted the edge of competition and has awakened a new generation of managers to a realization of what can be done, and has built up their determination to do it.

Developments such as these can damage and ultimately destroy the market opportunity on which a company has focused and on which its prosperity has been built. A company may then find itself with its traditional markets gone and an array of resources—using that word as a short description not only of its physical assets but also for the skills of its managerial staff, specialists, and operatives—which are ill suited to compete in any other market. The best operating decisions on product planning, salesmanship, and promotion may well be limited in what they can do to relieve the gloom.

It is not uncommon to find companies struggling with little success with the problems of marketing, under circumstances which suggest that the root of their problems is to be found in an earlier failure to adopt a suitable approach to the changing outside world.

The broad trends which bring about such a situation are often visible years in advance, not only to the statistician, market researcher, and economist, but to any perceptive businessman who reads, absorbs, and thinks about the contents of the leading daily and weekly press, and of the more serious television programs. If a company appreciates the broad significance of these trends in time, it can seek out other suitable areas of market opportunity to which it can adapt and from which it can profit. Yet despite this possibility, there have been companies making such products as, for example, small arms and steam locomotives which have waited until later than they should to adapt.

Corporate strategy is not to be thought of solely as negative, staving off threatened disaster, but as the positive approach to the achievement of growth and profits. Change closes some doors but also opens others, and a company which is in no way threatened will, if it is infused with an entrepreneurial spirit, wish to address itself to the question "Can we do better by identifying and setting out to exploit new market opportunities in the future?"

The second and related reason why corporate strategy is now so important is the time and cost involved in creating that complex of fixed assets and corporate skills which make up a modern business. Buildings, plant, and other expensive equipment must be matched to each other to create a cohesive unit fitted to the market purposes which they are to serve. They must be backed by qualified staff—executives, sales representatives, and R&D scientists—of the right background and training and workers with appropriate skills and experience. Once these skills and assets are established, they substantially determine which market opportunities the company is equipped to exploit and which it must leave alone.

Strategy seeks to lay down guidelines designed to achieve the maximum possible harmony of today's decision with the environment of the future. Each of the many decisions made every day in a firm affects some detail of its assets, competences, and philosophy. Their collective effect over a period of years is to reconstruct it. Unless constrained by some wider approach, it will be sheer chance if the company achieves a structural pattern which is suited to take advantage of the unfolding environment.

The dominating principle of corporate strategy is that company top management should study the trends apparent today in order to identify the emerging market opportunities of the future, select those in which it is likely to succeed, and begin the process of adaptation in good time. At this early stage it may not be possible, and it would probably be premature, to specify particular products. The first step is to establish a company staffed with people with the right knowledge and experience and ally to this an appropriate blend of major assets so that it is in a position to compete in its chosen market opportunity with whatever medium- and short-term approach is necessary. At the same time, while adaptation is taking place, the company must maintain current business, and there are delicate problems of management control during the adaptation stage.

Ansoff, perhaps the best-known writer in this field, says:

> Strategic decisions are primarily concerned with external, rather than internal, problems of the firm and specifically with the selection of the product-mix which the firm will produce and the markets to which it will sell. To use an engineering term, the strategic problem is concerned with establishing an "impedance match" between the firm and its environment or, in more usual terms, it is the problem of

deciding what business the firm is in and what kinds of businesses it will seek to enter.[5]

The periods for which business decisions are made can be classified into three:

1 The *strategic* period: this is the longest and is the period for which quantitative forecasting is of little value because the uncertainties involved create a wide margin of error.
2 The *long-term* period: the nearer period of time, such as is commonly covered by the long-term forecast, the expected limits of error not being so great as to destroy the value of forecasting.
3 The *operating* period: the short-term decision-making period which characterizes the regular cycle of operations throughout the company.

In the strategic period, the concepts of corporate strategy and of marketing tend to converge and to become substantially indistinguishable. The strategic decisions control the marketing policy which is followed in the long-term period, and this in turn is the framework for the marketing plan and the individual managerial operating decisions.

THE OBJECTIVES OF A COMPANY

Ask a businessman to state the objective of his company. The traditional answer is supposed to be "To make as much money as possible" or "To maximize profits." Such replies focus on the economic objectives of the business and offer these formulae as a first approximation to them.

Although a complete set of objectives of the company will include certain noneconomic purposes, it is useful to look at the economic objectives first. Most businessmen, if pressed, would probably seek to qualify this traditional view. A typical comment might be: "In the long term, of course—I don't mean you charge as much as you can today and end up with no customers next year," or perhaps a suggestion that the objective is "to maximize the long-term return on equity."

It is certainly convenient to assume that it is the intention of management to seek some such objective. Nevertheless, this view must often be subject to a very qualified interpretation.

Even if the interests of the equity shareholders are the prime concern all major management decisions are made with some degree of uncertainty as to their outcome. Because of this element of risk, some writers have emphasized that the first objective is survival. This may well lead a company to decisions which do not offer the maximum probable return. They may prefer a course of action which offers somewhat less but with greater certainty as to its achievement. The executive of a company which has been selling electronic equipment for defense purposes may have observed that a change of government policy could lead to the termination of major contracts and imperil company prospects. The company may, therefore, prefer a more flexible and low-risk strategy and seek to expand non-defense markets for its products, even though this may reduce probable profits at least for some years. Some balance has to be struck between expected profit and the risk involved in attaining this profit.

It is, however, by no means clear to what extent the policy of a company should be directed to seeking the maximum benefit for the shareholders. There are many voices which argue that this is only one responsibility, and the ordinary shareholder himself is not particularly active in seeking to defend his interest. "It is only *after* a disaster has happened that the shareholder's voice is normally heard," says one writer.[6]

A company is under pressure from many other groups seeking to protect some interest or other. The government and semigovernment agencies in Great Britain such as the Prices and Incomes Board and the Monopolies Commission have been established to safeguard some concept of the public interest, described with varying degrees of precision.

Trade unions press the interests of their members, and customers are frequently influenced by the concept of a fair price. The position of the shareholders, although not unheeded, is only one among a number of competing groups. The executive's policy reflects a balancing out of all these pressures.

This is not the place to explore this matter deeper. For many purposes of analysis, profit maximization is a convenient assumption, although it is in practice generally modified, explicitly or implicitly, by social, ethical, and personal considerations.

Every board of directors must define its own set of economic objectives. These will depend in part on its own philosophy, as discussed above. They will also depend on the individual circumstances of a company. One may be interested in short-term profits and short-term liquidity (for example, a family company which the proprietors wish to sell), but if short-term profits are secure, most look to the longer run. Entrepreneurial individuals initiating a small new company may often accept high risk as a necessary accompaniment of the objectives of high growth rate and high profit. They have much to gain and little to lose. A well-established company may seek more moderate levels of risk, growth, and return. Consideration of risk may induce a company to seek a more flexible pattern of resource allocation by broadening its markets or entering different industries.

Economic objectives will be amplified by other objectives which reflect the philosophy and attitudes of the owners or top executives of the company. Some of these will be ethical. There are well-known British companies which have clear ideas about the values of their executive. These imply responsibilities to the community, which are reflected in the company's plans. They will also have their own predilections: one group of executives has an inner drive to expand their business, another may prefer a quieter, safer existence and seek to avoid competition. Certainly, senior executives will have difficulty in running a business whose objectives conflict with their own personal dispositions.

The first step in developing a set of objectives is little more than the specifying by informed executives of their aspirations for the company. These aspirations will almost certainly have to be modified as analysis proceeds. Thus the start is a somewhat arbitrary set of objectives, such as:

> Return on capital employed to exceed 20 percent.
> Growth rate to exceed 5 percent per annum.
> R & D skills to be developed in new growth areas.
> Ethical and social objectives.

These objectives will have to be checked, revised, and supported by policies indicating broadly how they are to be met. As they stand, they do not guide executives toward those decisions which are in the long term most consistent with them.

It is therefore necessary to identify the strategic guidelines which, disseminated throughout the organization, will act as constraints on shorter-term policy decisions at all levels.

In practice, it does not seem to be easy to draw a clear line between the objectives and the strategy by which they are to be pursued, but the following headings indicate the general content of the statement of strategy.[7]

1 The market opportunity to be met: the need to be filled and the markets to be served (what business are we to be in?).
2 The policy by which (1) is to be attained, e.g., by takeover and divestment, or by building up from within.

3 The character of the competition to be offered.

4 The particular competences and assets which are to be developed or maintained to achieve that result.

STRATEGY DEVELOPMENT

Aspirations will be modified progressively in the search for a sound strategy. Sometimes this may mean that they become less ambitious, as study reveals that they are not capable of achievement. However, there should be no undue rush to cut back on initial hopes. Moreover, if it appears easy to achieve the aspirations first specified, then they may be too modest and might well be raised.

The initial resources are also capable of alteration and development, but this requires time and foresight, and there is some limit to what can be achieved. As the manager examines different possible lines of business in parallel, he considers the feasibility of developing a pattern of resources to match the requirements for effective competition in the business under review.

At the beginning, the executive is faced with aspirations (what it is desired to achieve), expectations (what is likely to be achieved with present policy), and resources (a heritage from past management decisions selected to suit current or past markets).

The chosen corporate strategy seeks to lay down guidelines for the reallocation of resources over time, so that the expected outcome will be to achieve objectives which represent the highest feasible aspiration of the company. Study of resources and refinement of objectives continue progressively throughout the process of strategy development.

The central problem is to assess in what line of business the company is most likely to achieve the desired level of results.

There are various ways in which the business may be defined. It can be answered in terms of the product, and many companies might well seek this definition. "We make flat glass" is a definition of the company's business in these terms, whereas "We are in the electronics business" defines a company in terms of its technology, and "iron and steel" in terms of the materials used. To the marketing man, the most valuable description is in relation to the class of customer needs which the company's products seek to satisfy and the classes of customer which it seeks to serve.

Basically, the search is for a "common thread"[8] which

unites the different activities of a company in a meaningful way, gives point and coherence to the whole of its activities, and directs those activities toward an optimum level of results.

Thus it will be desired to specify whether the product mission (the class of needs to be satisfied) is to be varied and whether the groups of customers to be served are to be varied. The natural starting point is to examine the probable results to be obtained from remaining in the company's present business, and to compare this with the aspirations (or tentative objectives) which have been specified. Perhaps the company's objectives may be satisfied by selling the same class of goods (including the natural development of other products consistent with the same overall purpose) to the same class of customers.

Suppose, however, that a review of trends indicates to the company's executive that this is unlikely to achieve its reasonable hopes for the future. Take, for example, the company manufacturing steam locomotives which sees that its natural market is likely to be lost to electric or diesel-electric traction, and that steam cannot challenge this competition successfully. The executive will therefore search more widely.

There are three possibilities. First, the executive might say: "We are in the business of providing traction for rail and similar types of transport. Let us therefore set to and develop into a new technology and manufacture electric and diesel-electric locomotives."

However, after taking a good hard look at the implications of this decision, the executive might have further thoughts. It might be argued: "To develop that totally different type of technology in a reasonable span of years so that we can compete effectively with existing manufacturers looks a pretty tough job. Let us therefore find a market opportunity in which we can offer a different class of product using our present technology." Both these are forms of related or concentric diversification and both involve an assessment of a suitable market opportunity which can be satisfied with goods and services (as yet undefined in detail) which can be produced by the company using its know-how, fixed assets, and funds which it has or which it can reasonably hope to develop in the available time.

If examination of the two foregoing possibilities fails to produce an acceptable opportunity, then the company may examine the third difficult possibility of conglomerate diversification, moving both to new markets and to new technologies. This step is one which usually requires a high order of management skill, and it could be argued that in the conglomerate it is this skill which is a link relating the new development to the original base from which the company is moving. The purpose still remains the search for an appropriate market opportunity, to which the company can be adapted.

Success in corporate strategy depends upon choosing a market matched to the company's feasible pattern of resources, a term which here includes not only its balance-sheet assets, but also the less tangible company skills, know-how, and experience. A necessary stage is therefore the preparation of an inventory of company resources: in particular, it is desired to identify those resources which the company has which are uncommon—differentiated or specialized resources. The company may be able to achieve a competitive advantage by turning them to account, and markets in which they can be utilized deserve careful scrutiny. Table 3 makes clear what is implied by such an inventory:[9]

Table 3 Inventory of company resources

Financial strength	Money available or obtainable for financing research and development, plant construction, inventory, receivables, working capital, and operating losses in the early stages of commercial operation.
Raw material reserves	Ownership of, or preferential access to, natural resources such as minerals and ores, brine deposits, natural gas, forests.
Physical plant	Manufacturing plant, research and testing facilities, warehouses, branch offices, trucks, tankers, etc.
Location	Situation of plant or other physical facilities with relation to markets, raw materials, or utilities.
Patents	Ownership or control of a technical monopoly through patents.
Public acceptance	Brand preference, market contracts, and other public support built up by successful performance in the past.
Specialized experience	Unique or uncommon knowledge of manufacturing, distribution, scientific fields, or managerial techniques.
Personnel	Payroll of skilled labor, salesmen, engineers, or other workers with definite specialized abilities.
Management	Professional skill, experience, ambition, and will for growth of the company's leadership.

The analysis thus covers the facilities and equipment which are possessed, the experience available, the suitability of the organization for various purposes, and the ability of management. This is obviously a lengthy process which requires impartial assessment. Success in a particular business depends in the long run on whether a company's pattern of resources can be made appropriate to its market—appropriate, that is to say, as compared with competitors, for the higher the qualities of competitors' assets and skills and the more closely they match to the market opportunities, the higher will be the standard by which the company should judge itself.

As each possible market is studied (as described above), the analyst will be attempting to answer the following questions:

1 What are the trends in the business being studied?
2 What are the requirements for success in it?
3 How far do competitors match these requirements?
4 Is it possible that my company's present pattern of skills and assets can be developed to match these requirements as well as, or better than, competitors?
5 Can we therefore expect to compete successfully, and what competitive policy would achieve success?
6 By what steps can we proceed from our present pattern of resources to the required pattern?

The outcome of this process of analysis is to determine a strategy such that the company can systematically move into its chosen business with a substantial expectation of achieving corporate objectives.

An interesting and related approach to the problem of choosing suitable diversification has been developed by an English writer, Ward.[10] He seeks to identify in the analysis of companies certain "differentiated" assets or skills, that is to say, resources which are in comparatively short supply and which therefore form a basis for advance. From a study of these, he seeks to draw out a "dynamic product area" which is a description of a particular product mission: a class of need which is likely to persist over time and within which a succession of product ideas may be generated for different classes of customer. Ward quotes as an example a manufacturer who defined himself as being in the "materials separation" business, and points out that although the need for a particular type of material may vanish, it seems likely that some form of materials separation will be required. This concept is closely related to that of corporate strategy. Ward provides the following list of criteria for a satisfactory dynamic area:

> A dynamic area may take many forms, but must achieve a satisfactory balance between the too general and the too specific. Ideally it should:

1 Be capable of continued application and usefulness, irrespective of changing social, industrial and market needs. (Will it last?)
2 Be likely to embrace a large number of individual products, including many selling in growth markets. (Does it afford enough scope for seeking products?)
3 Not be limited to a single market, market area or industry. (Does it offer a sufficient breadth of market?)
4 Be simple to identify and describe and sufficiently definite to focus a product search. (Can it be expressed in a few words and readily be understood?)
5 Be in the general stream of social and industrial change. (Is it likely to yield new developments?)
6 Not be strongly associated with another company or industry. (Is it unique?)
7 Be consistent with the company's experience and image. (Does it embrace any existing products or activities?)
8 Relate in some degree to markets in which the company is already well established. (Will it provide an opportunity to use the company's present sales facilities and outlets?)

These criteria should of course be treated with discretion. A good dynamic area may sometimes fail particular requirements.

Having identified a probable area, the company can compare the degree of success which it expects to achieve with its aspirations and, if it is satisfied that the best possible strategy has been formulated, obtain equilibrium by adjusting the aspirations so that they become its final objectives.

In determining this relationship, the company will have considered how far it can build on present resources, and by what competitive policies success in its chosen mission/market relationship is likely to be achieved. A company strong on R&D may seek to succeed by technical leadership. Another less strong in this aspect, perhaps smaller and with lower administrative costs, may prefer the role of a follower. It may leave major innovation to others and be content to come in later with minor variations built on the benefits of observing their experience. One company may take over an existing company in its planned area, while another may spread out from its present base.

The development of a corporate strategy is not an easy task, and this simple outline of basic principles should not disguise this fact. It is easy to sit down and list trends which are creating opportunities, such as the growing use of the computer, natural gas from the North Sea, the container revolution, and the building of the national highway system.

These in turn create demand for many subsidiary and related requirements. Few firms will have the enormous resources and know-how necessary to enter the direct manufacture of computers (although even here careful market segmentation has enabled some companies which are not giants to find a niche). But the supply of requisites, such as random access disks, may be possible. It is still necessary to study the current and potential competition to consider what are the factors which determine success or failure in this field and whether the company is likely to succeed. Where a company is extending into new fields, there is often an advantage if this leads to the further exploitation of those *distinctive* resources which are not widely available in other companies. This gives a competitive advantage, and there may be economies from fuller utilization of those resources and sometimes from a better balance between different skills or assets.

Conversely, there is always some degree of risk when a company leans too heavily on one resource, whether it be a market, a product, a skill, a person, or an idea. Individual markets, products, skills, people, and ideas are perishable and there is a need, therefore, to balance the advantages of exploiting the special qualities of a company to their fullest extent and the risk of building too heavily upon a narrow base.

TESTS OF STRATEGY

Developed fully, the strategy now sets out the company's intended business and the means by which it seeks success. Communicated to all managerial levels, it indicates what strengths are to be developed, what weaknesses are to be remedied, and in what manner. Thus plans and operating decisions are developed in a manner which gradually brings the company into the relationship with the emerging pattern of market opportunities which analysis has shown to offer the highest prospect of success.

The following tests of the appropriateness of a strategy have been recommended:[11]

1 Is the strategy identifiable and has it been made clear either in words or in practice?
2 Does it fully exploit domestic and international environmental opportunity?
3 Is the strategy consistent with corporate competence and resources, both present and projected?
4 Are the major provisions of strategy and the program of major policies of which it is comprised internally consistent?

5 Is the chosen level of risk feasible in economic and personal terms?
6 Is the strategy appropriate to the personal values and aspirations of the key managers?
7 Is the strategy appropriate to the desired level of contribution to society?
8 Does the strategy constitute a clear stimulus to organizational effort and commitment?
9 Are there early indications of the responsiveness of markets and market segments to the strategy?

4

Preparing a Marketing Plan

Planning is important in any field of business management and perhaps most important of all in marketing.

The marketing plan is fundamental to virtually every other plan prepared within the business; from it flows the timing and volume of revenue, the demands on production, the development of the technology required, the size and characteristics of the labor force, and so on. It serves to integrate and synthesize the business.

Yet it is still common for planning to be neglected in the marketing of industrial products. The marketing plan is apt to prove difficult to prepare, especially in companies undertaking this task for the first time. It aims to mesh the business with the uncontrollable environment in such a way as to achieve the best possible results for the company. The plan must therefore be based upon forecasts and assumptions about future changes in that environment, and must be capable of modification should these anticipations prove to be amiss.

The executive who embarks for the first time on preparing an industrial marketing plan will find it a very long-drawn-out process. It is by no means unusual for the preparation of an initial marketing plan to take nine to twelve months.

Yet the development of the plan can reasonably be expected to bring great benefits, not only by its direct effect on the efficiency of operations within the company, but also from the deeper insight into the operation of the company which is obtained during its preparation. It communicates throughout the company's organization an understanding of the character and purpose of the business and shows each department its role in relation to the ultimate creation of sales and profit. Decisions can then be made with a fuller understanding of their implications, and the quality and timeliness of the decision-making thus improved.

If there is a well-prepared plan, company executives will be more aware of the effect on the company of the many facets of environmental change and will become more flexible in the face of change.

The plan is based on the company's forecasts and assumptions about the way the world will probably behave. It can be very clear that there are some other important possible developments which cannot be ignored; for example, an overseas competitor which has been researching the market may decide to enter it. Reserve strategies may be devised and plans may be prepared against such major contingencies.

An obvious, extreme case of the devaluation of the pound in 1967: some companies had contingent plans for this eventuality which permitted an early attack on export markets. A company which has a long-term contract with a major customer that is due to expire must plan for the possibility that the contract may not be renewed even if it can reasonably expect renewal.

WHAT IS A PLAN?

A plan—almost any plan—consists of a number of components. These components are not always separately identified in the planning process, but it is an advantage to recognize what they are to ensure logical development of a comprehensive plan.

The following is a broad indication of the components of a complete plan:

1 OBJECTIVES

Objectives are a statement of what the plan aims to achieve. Frequently, the objectives are initially a broad, perhaps rather hopeful, statement of what the executive would like to achieve. In the course of the planning process they are refined to become a more precise quantitative or qualitative identification of what can reasonably be expected as the outcome of an efficiently prepared and executed plan. At this stage the term "goals" is sometimes used to describe the precisely defined objectives, and this practice will be followed here. It should be stressed that goals must be so specific that the subordinate executives can derive from them the general character of the action required and the yardsticks by which performance is to be judged. There is also much to be said for the view that the goals should be feasible but at such a level that the executives must "stretch" to achieve them.

2 STRATEGY

A broad statement describing the general principles to be applied in attaining the goals. It answers the question "How are these results to be attained?"

3 ELEMENTS

As the plan is worked out more fully, so the individual tasks to be carried out are scheduled in such detail as is necessary to show what is required from each department as its contribution to the complete strategy. These are, in fact, the subsidiary goals which each department must achieve if the plan is to succeed, and each department should in turn prepare a plan which will provide goals for each section and ultimately for each individual.

4 PROGRAM

From the preparation of the plan, thinking now turns to the details of implementation. The program lays down *when* all the individual elements of the plan are to be carried out and in what order. Intermediate goals are established to assist in the control procedure.

5 BUDGET

This is a statement of the implications of the plan in financial terms. It will be prepared in parallel with items 3 and 4. It will include estimates of cost (with separate statements of revenue and capital items), forecasts of revenue, of contribution (or perhaps of profit), and of the flow of funds. It will be integrated within the company's overall plan.

6 RESPONSIBILITY

The plan will make it clear which department or section is responsible for the various actions.

7 CONTROL

Arrangements must be made for measuring progress. It is necessary to compare results with intermediate targets (perhaps monthly) as well as the final target for the end of the year, and to compare environmental developments with forecasts. This feedback permits the review of progress, the taking of corrective action, and the revision of later targets if necessary.

PERIOD OF THE PLAN

It seems to be well established and good practice to make the marketing plan in two parts, the first a longer-range plan for a period of five or more years ahead. The period of time which the planner chooses (the planning horizon) depends primarily on the length of time which it takes for the major marketing decisions to mature. What is the life-cycle of a product? How long does it take to establish a new product in the market? These are the sort of questions to be asked. If today's decisions will largely determine the future action of the company in major areas for nine or ten years, then this is the period of time to choose for the longer-range plan. The long-range plan is normally a rolling plan, that is to say it is reviewed annually, amended, and extended forward one more year.

Consistent with this plan, supporting it and set out more fully, is the shorter-term plan for a period of one or two years ahead. This will be prepared in great detail, showing the amounts of different products to be sold, through what channels, in what territories, and so on, and will identify the nature and quantity of the marketing effort involved. In this chapter, the emphasis will be on the shorter-term plan. The longer-ranging plan adheres to similar principles, except that the detail is less and the link to corporate strategy closer.

Occasionally it is desirable to reinforce the main plan with a "project plan" dealing separately with some project of major importance. For example, the launch of a new range of products in a new market may involve substantial initial investment and it may be desirable to undertake detailed consideration in greater depth for a period of years of the implications of the project. Its supervision may therefore be more intensive and under separate control. The overall effect of the project will be incorporated in the main plan, but the separate project plan enables it to be controlled and executed separately.

DEVELOPING THE MARKETING PLAN

A plan is a complex array of interrelated ideas. It is not easy to identify the logical process by which such a complex is created. The following paragraphs set out, in simplified form, a possible procedure.

The initial phase is a review of the present and recent past situation in the market segments in which the company is interested. It considers the relative success of the company and its competitors, assesses the value of the different marketing tools used, and spots market trends.

This will require detailed analysis of each market segment, each major customer, each product, and each major application. The executive will bring to bear all the knowledge he can muster, seeking to identify economic trends, changes in relevant customer policies and practices, consumer tastes, possible competitive behavior, the trend of technological advance, and other environmental developments which might intensify the new opportunities and weaken the old.

This review also audits the marketing tools in terms of cost and effectiveness. It examines the work of the sales force and of technical service and reviews advertising, promotion, price, and product policy.

Out of this stage comes the determination of possible objectives. These usually fall under the following main headings:

1 PROFIT OR CONTRIBUTION OBJECTIVES

Although these are not solely the responsibility of the marketing department, the influence of marketing is so crucial that they must appear in the plan. Contribution objectives may be analyzed by products and markets at monthly or quarterly periods.

2 SALES OBJECTIVES

These must at some stage be analyzed in great detail not only for months (or quarters), product, and market, but also by territories and major customers.

3 COST OBJECTIVES

By type of cost (sales, advertising, technical service, etc., with perhaps further breakdown as in item 2).

4 SPECIAL OBJECTIVES

These will include goals for other policy areas. Currently the development of the company's image is an item which receives much attention, but the development of sales-force training, the updating of the product line, and improvement of delivery times are matters which may come in here.

All these possible objectives are tested for feasibility at a later stage, as strategies and plans are developed in detail.

THE DEVELOPMENT OF STRATEGIES

The word "strategy" is used to describe the basic approach to the deployment of the marketing tools which is to be adopted by the company. This is the grand design within which marketing tools are integrated. Ideally more than one possible strategy should be identified and evaluated.

The basic concepts of marketing strategy can be classed under the following primary headings:

1 MARKET IDENTIFICATION

Specifying the markets and segments which are to be developed. Often these will largely be current markets, but there will also be occasions when the company seeks to benefit from particular opportunities for expansion which market scrutiny has identified, such as different applications, growing industries, overseas markets, and particularly large customers.

2 ADDING VALUE TO WHAT IS OFFERED TO THE CUSTOMER

The primary object of the industrial customer is to enlarge profit by promoting sales or by using resources more effectively. Value can be added either by matching the product to customer needs in this way, or by providing technical or commercial service which is of value to him in relation to these prime objectives. Value can also be added, usually to a lesser extent, by satisfying decision-makers' other objectives as discussed in Chapter 2.

3 REDUCING THE PRICE AND COST TO THE PURCHASER OF THE PRODUCT

The price is what the customer pays for the product to the supplier. The *total* customer cost in obtaining the benefit of the product will include costs other than the actual price—costs of adapting his organization, training staff, or purchasing complementary items. Sometimes the product or service can be modified to reduce customer cost without cutting price (it will be seen that in this way the concept of cost reduction and value addition are interrelated).

4 BY IMPROVING AMONG THOSE WHO SWAY THE PURCHASE DECISION THE UNDERSTANDING AND APPRECIATION OF WHAT IS OFFERED

In the marketing strategy this is the function of communication in all its forms.

Clues to elementary strategies can be identified by considering the market analysis in Chapter 2, especially the principal diagonal in Fig. 2. In the buyer area, where competitive products are highly standardized (perhaps to national standards), competitive emphasis is likely to be on price and delivery. The latter implies regular contact between customer and supplier and good relations with the salesman. If the product is purchased in small quantities, and shows minor differentiation, the customer may wish to keep the cost of "searching" to a reasonable figure. For a small purchase of paint brushes, for example, he may prefer to buy a well-known make rather than to incur the cost of shopping around for and assessing lesser-known sources of supply in order to save a small sum. This indicates that in these particular circumstances promotion has a role in differentiating the product and reducing the cost of personal selling.

In the total involvement area, value added is emphasized even to the extent of providing specific products tailor-made to the customer's needs and backed with specialized advice. This will require contact at many levels from technical service man to top executive. Difference in price will be less significant, since the payoff to the customer comes from better sales and the more effective use of resources.

Other clues to marketing strategy can be obtained by considering the product life-cycle concept in Chapter 7. The object, however, must be to obtain an edge over the competition, and this requires the marketing executive to be constantly on the alert to seek even the smallest advantage. The best chance of such a creative advance comes about from conceptual thinking, that is to say, by understanding the basic underlying ideas of marketing and relating them to the market under study. Conceptual thinking is the springboard for the innovative jump from what is current good practice to new and better ideas.

THE ELEMENTS OF THE PLAN

As strategy has been finalized, so the elements of the plan will have been studied and details specified. They must be consistent with the strategy, of which they represent the development in depth, and this ensures that the elements are consistent with each other. They must also be consistent with the opportunities of the environment and with the resources of the company, and each should make its contribution in the most economical way.

In most industrial marketing plans, the following elements must be examined and decisions made on each—even if the decision is "no change":

Product line
Products to be introduced.
Products to be withdrawn.
Products to be phased out.
Products to be modified.
Products to be pushed intensively in present markets/applications.
Products to be pushed extensively in new markets/applications.

Pricing
Changes in the general level of prices.
Differential changes (i.e., raising some and lowering others).
Discounts and credit terms.

Direct sales
Changes in number and organization of sales force.
Remuneration, commission, expenses.
Recruitment, initial training.
Conferences, retraining.
Motivation and morale.

Indirect sales
(Essentially this is analyzed as in *Direct sales* above, and is frequently undertaken by the same sales force. It is, however, worth giving special thought to it, as the character of the work can be different.)

Advertising and sales promotion
Media advertising.
Direct mail.
Shows, exhibitions, films, symposia, seminars.
Public relations.
Literature.

Technical service
Presale surveys, testing, and advice.
Applications research.
Postsale advice, maintenance, customer staff training.
Provision of spares.
Number and organization of technical service force.
Remuneration, hiring, training.
Charges for service.

Physical distribution
Delivery time objectives.
Seasonal stock levels.
Location of stock.
Transportation methods.

Distributors
Policy on distribution.

Discount structure.
Cooperation and motivation.

Market research
Special studies.
Continuing environmental desk research.
Continuous monitoring of company progress.

Marketing organization and staff
Changes in organization.
Staff recruitment, training.

Because the marketing plan guides the company as a whole, its implications for other departments—R&D, engineering, production—must be identified and examined in consultation with these departments. In this process, staff at all levels should be involved, and it is becoming common to provide subordinate executives with information which permits them to determine their own objectives, which are then reviewed and discussed at a higher level. In this way the marketing plan leads naturally to a total company plan.

The detailed schedule above is, of course, only one way in which a plan may be drawn up. Each company's plan will show its own individual variations; for example, a company selling large items of capital equipment by tender would have to define the class or classes of customer from whom business would be sought and the timing of business in order to "balance" plant loading but might not be concerned with seasonal stock levels and might have no separately defined sales force.

The detail of the plan will gradually be completed in a way which will achieve the goals already set out. The process of analysis will often show that in certain parts of the plan there is more than one way of implementing the strategy, and each of these is examined for cost and effectiveness.

The strategy will be reexamined, molded, and developed in detail. The detailed goals will be modified as planning throws light on their feasibility until the marketing executive has a program of expected sales month by month (or perhaps quarter by quarter in some industries), showing what is to be expected from each representative's area, from each product, from each market, and so on. These month-by-month figures are the intermediate goals against which progress will be assessed.

SETTING OUT THE PLAN

The whole plan is now a substantial set of documents, and relevant parts of it are communicated to the different levels of operation in the company. The plan has, however, been built up by a long process of consultation and cooperation, so that its acceptance by major departments has been substantially ensured before its confirmation at board level.

The record of the plan comprises something on the following lines:

1 DESCRIPTIVE INTRODUCTION

(i) Review of company progress in past periods and assessment of results achieved.

(ii) Anticipated development in the economic environment, in customer and indirect customer behavior, and in expected competitor reaction.

2 STATEMENT OF MARKETING POLICIES

A statement of the main goals in terms of sales, costs, and profit (or contribution) and an outline of the strategy by which these goals are to be achieved, with particular reference to innovations.

3 DETAILED PLAN

A statement of the elements under appropriate headings (see pp. 48 and 49).

The following layout has been suggested for consideration as the planner's record of the basis on which the plan is developed.[12] The object is to show clearly the assumptions made about the future and their impact on each part of the plan.

Assumptions

PLAN ELEMENT	ECONOMIC ENVIRONMENT	CUSTOMER BEHAVIOR	COMPETITIVE BEHAVIOR	OWN COMPANY POSITION	SUPPLY OF INPUTS
Product line					
Pricing					
Direct sales					
(and so on)					

Under *Economic Environment* might be "mild deflation," with its concomitants of "some unemployment, interest rates up, price/wage freeze." The next column might indicate assumptions that customers were illiquid and inclined to defer purchases that made demands on liquidity. Competitors might be expected to meet this by cutting prices or by delaying introduction of new products. The *Own Company* situation might express comments on the domestic liquidity and profit situation and any other matter reflecting on the company's resource availability (e.g., new plant coming on stream).

Changes under any of these headings would reflect on many of the elements in the left-hand column. A change from mild deflation to mild boom would reduce downward pressure on prices but might encourage competitors to bring out new products. This would react on price policy, new product policy, and many other headings. Increase in prices of inputs might reflect not only on price but on investors' policy because of its effect on resources locked up in stock-holding.

4 BUDGET

From the elements of the plan flow the expected sales and prices, and concomitant revenue and cost forecasts, set out over months or other appropriate periods and broken down by responsibility centers. The budget figures also take account of cost trends and expected changes in efficiency.

5 CONTROL

The budget is a key element of the control process. It makes it possible to assess progress month by month, as results are compared with expectations, and helps to localize the sources of departure from plan. A certain variation is naturally inevitable, but the amount of permissible variation should be predetermined, and if this is exceeded the variation should be the subject of analysis and appropriate action. Predetermination of permissible variation levels is of great value. The executive today has so much paper flowing across his desk that he cannot scrutinize it all. If the amount of variation is predetermined, then he need only attend to those items for which the variance exceeds the norm. This "management by exception" reduces the day-to-day load and permits more time for the more important issues. Results which are unexpectedly favorable also deserve attention, as exceptionally good performance may indicate that some opportunities capable of further exploitation have been missed.

Apart from overall costs and revenue, it is also desirable to identify other statistics or ratios which help to assess the efficiency of the marketing operation. What these may be will vary according to the detail of the plan, but such factors as new accounts opened, sales cost as percentage of sales, inquiries received, proposals submitted, and proposals accepted may be indicators which in appropriate cases will show whether the company is on target and which may react before the financial accounts as a whole show any significant variation. They also show precisely where in the organization remedial action is needed.

The control system should also follow trends in the environment to check whether the basic assumptions and forecasts are correct. It is often more difficult to do this in precise terms, but assumptions about economic trends can be set out for comparison with appropriate published series (for example, unemployment, price index numbers, the index of production, and so on). Assumptions which are less easy to quantify, such as those relating to competitors' behavior, may be kept under systematic review. If there is a significant change (e.g., a new product introduced by competitors), this would normally be identified quickly, but the effect of small changes may not be noted for a very long while unless systematic procedures are adopted.

5

Marketing Research

Setting out to devise systematic plans and to carry through their orderly execution, the executive immediately finds a need for market facts and forecasts to help him choose the best courses of action. He keeps in touch with the market in many ways, both formal and informal. He has contacts through the sales force and direct with major customers and distributors. He tries to find time to read the business papers and the trade and technical press. He attends exhibitions, conferences, and seminars when commitments permit. Even so, these channels provide only a partial view of the changing environment, and this can easily be distorted and out of date. To provide an objective, fuller, and more reliable view of the market, industrial marketing research has grown rapidly in the United Kingdom during the last decade. It is now recognized as the prime method by which the marketing executive can increase his insight into the market and reduce the uncertainty of his anticipation of market developments.

For many years the importance attached to marketing research in the industrial field was slight as compared with that attached to it in consumer marketing. The Industrial Marketing Research Association was established in 1962 and today is a large and flourishing organization. Its membership (including associates and affiliates) amounts to nearly 1,000 at the time of writing, and the association is working to raise standards and to help management obtain full benefit from marketing research. The term "marketing research" covers not only the collection of data about the market, but also the careful analysis of the efficiency of the company's marketing tools.

BRIEFING FOR MARKETING RESEARCH

Despite the fact that marketing research has grown so fast, it is by no means proving an easy tool to use. Marketing research stems from the need for decisions to be made on the basis of facts, and its object is to provide the facts on which decisions are to be made. The marketing executive must first identify what the problem is that he has to solve and what facts he needs to solve it. Often in practice neither of these steps is straightforward. Some marketing men are very new to their job and may have been appointed without any special training and with narrow experience. Such a man has difficulty in giving a proper briefing to the market researcher and in the end may receive a report of only marginal relevance to the problems he faces, for which he may have paid $2,000 or more. In other instances, the executive has already decided what action he wishes to take and turns to the market researcher to "prove" that his proposed action is the right one. The sensible researcher will immediately make it clear that marketing research is only of value if it is impartial and objective, and that commissions can only be undertaken on that basis. In general, a basic requirement is a structural survey and forecast of trends in the market concerned. This would commonly comprise the following:

1 Estimated market size. Breakdown by: product group, intermediate customer, end-use and/or end-user, region.
2 Description of end-uses and schedule of main intermediate customers and end-users.
3 Description of buying decision procedures and influences.
4 Schedule of competing products, comparison of their specifications and prices.
5 Schedule of main competitors (or classes of competitors), showing size, market share, and marketing policies.
6 Description of distribution channels (where appropriate).
7 Government action (e.g., import duties, taxation).
8 Future trends in respect to these items.

The amount of detail and accuracy required may well vary. Increased detail and accuracy cost money, and after a certain point the extra benefit is small. A company with sales of $50,000 in a particular market may not be much concerned whether the total market size is $500,000 or $1,000,000. The difference would have no implications for its marketing decision, for in either case its share of the market is still only a small percentage. On the other hand, if present sales are $250,000, then the difference may well be material.

Once this basic data on market structure is available, specific marketing problems require different items of information which must be identified. There is often lack of clarity in defining the information needs of a company, and one of the benefits of preparing a formal market plan is that it sharpens recognition of these needs.

The marketing research worker should be capable of assisting the executive on this point, but the final decision on the information required is rightly a marketing decision. It seems that at present some research workers are finding it necessary to prepare their own briefs, and this is not likely to give the best results.

Deadlines should also be discussed. Work done under pressure will often involve extra cost, and in any case there is a certain time which is the minimum feasible for a satisfactory survey. Sometimes pressure of events makes it necessary to carry out work under time or financial limitations which involve a wide margin of error in the conclusions. In business, perfection is not often possible, but the responsible executive should be clear about the risks involved.

A study[13] in 1963 of the work undertaken by industrial market researchers in the United Kingdom indicated that the top ten functions regularly carried out by informants were as follows:

FUNCTION	PERCENTAGE OF RESPONDENTS REGULARLY CARRYING OUT THIS FUNCTION
Sales forecasting	76
Analysis of market size	70
Trends in market size	61
Estimating demand for new products	51
Competitive position of company products	48
Determining characteristics of markets	43
Determining present use of existing products	41
Studying economic factors affecting sales volume	38
General business forecasting	30
Evaluating proposed new products or services	30

There is a trend toward widening the range of market research work and exploring areas of increasing subtlety. Surveys to assess the effectiveness of advertising, the elasticity of price, or the nature of the company's image are becoming more common.

PLANNING THE SURVEY

The brief settled, the marketing researcher turns to the task of planning the survey. There are some phases which are the same in any survey which involves fieldwork, but others will vary according to the nature of the work. For example, the research executive will always need to start with a short period of familiarization, unless he is already acquainted with the subject matter of the research. He must "read himself in" to the problems, obtaining the necessary technical and general economic background.

He will then study the company's internal records. This is a very important step and the staff market analyst should ensure that appropriate records are kept within the company. The object should not be to increase the volume of statistical data, but to ensure that what is produced is useful and relevant, and that supplementary analyses can be obtained when required. He should try to make sure that data which is collected is classified according to sensible definitions, that the same definitions are used throughout the company and that, as far as possible, they are consistent with the definitions used by government and other outside bodies. For example, classification of customers by industry should be consistent with the national standards embodied in the Standard Industrial Classification. Likewise, regional data can often, with advantage, be classified consistently with the standard regions used for government statistics.

This preliminary study of the sales records of the company not uncommonly leads to a review of the research brief, and the questions to be asked may be modified as the nature of the company's problems is more clearly understood. Some market research workers, indeed, regard the internal review of sales data more as part of the problem definition than as part of the survey process.

There now follows a period of desk research, before fieldwork is considered. The researcher then has to decide whether fieldwork is necessary, the form it should take (mail, phone, or personal interview, or some combination of these), how many people are to be contacted, and who they shall be.

A general view of a typical market research operation is provided in Fig. 3—this depicts one survey actually carried out

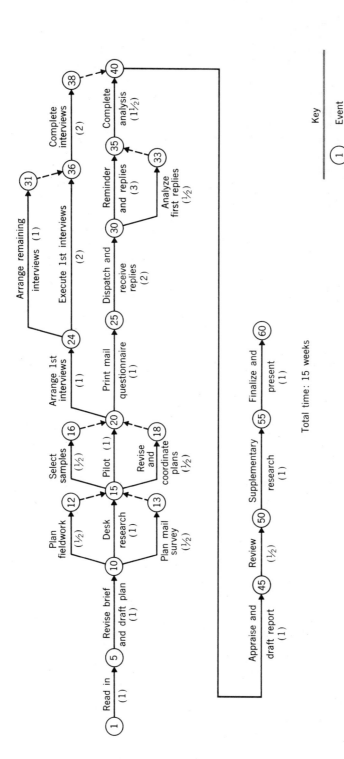

Fig. 3. Network of a marketing survey

in the packaging field. No two surveys are likely to be exactly the same, and in this case the researcher went through the following procedures, either by himself or with his staff.

After clearing his brief, he "read in" and carried out a study of the relevant sales data from the company's past records. Following this, he revised the brief in consultation with the instructing executive, spent some time on preliminary desk research, and consulted informed opinion—in this case, market researchers whom he knew to have some experience in the field of his operation.

In the light of this, he revised his plan and ended with the view that it would be efficient and economical to carry out his study by field interviews among major users and by a postal survey among minor users. These two operations were carried out in parallel.

After initial results were available, he prepared an interim report and discussed the matter with his client. Following this discussion, he decided to strengthen some parts of the study and for this purpose carried out some supplementary field and desk research. From this, he was able to finalize and present his report. This interim discussion is not always possible; often there is a firm quotation which cannot be varied.

The total time along the "critical path" shown amounts to fifteen weeks, but this can vary enormously. A researcher who obtains a relatively small query in an area known to him may well carry out a limited study by phone, desk research, and interview in a matter of a few weeks or even days. On the other hand, desk research can last weeks when it involves the tracing of historical data extending back over many years and complex statistical calculation. Time can be lost obtaining overseas statistics, having them translated, and finding out the basis on which they are compiled. Thus the diagram here is capable of endless manipulation and permutation.

SYSTEMATIC DESK RESEARCH

Desk research correctly handled can be a powerful tool. Government departments, official bodies such as the Monopolies Commission, research bodies, trade associations, universities, nationalized industries, and many other organizations are continually collecting information of one sort or another. Thus data which would be most expensive to collect is sometimes obtainable on very modest terms, the cost perhaps of a subscription to a journal, a fee for a special analysis, or a trip to a specialized library. A great deal of information is available in the

United Kingdom now, and painstaking desk research has sometimes revealed useful data on comparatively obscure products. However, anyone who has worked in industrial market research can generally point to areas where published data is inadequate.

Care must, however, be used in interpreting desk research information. Sometimes the analyst can be misled because the figures relate to only part of an industry and he mistakes them for the whole industry; also, such simple words as sales, exports, and production are full of unexpected ambiguity. Occasionally figures from responsible sources have been found to be wrong. Cross-checking with other sources and with related series is essential. When using statistics from a particular source for the first time, it is desirable to examine the method by which the data are collected—sample design, response achieved, and the questionnaire used. Sometimes figures which are widely quoted are based on small and unsatisfactory samples.

If, however, desk research does not reveal the information—and although it is a valuable introduction, it is rare for it to provide all the detailed up-to-date information which is required—then the researcher may well consider fieldwork information.

In planning a survey, "Who?" "What?" and "How?" are the questions. Who is to be contacted? A selection of the people who can help by providing information must be identified. Next the questions to be asked of them must be specified in greater or lesser detail, and the researcher must decide whether to use phone, mail, or personal interview or some combination. The choice of method depends upon consideration of a wide variety of circumstances.

CHOOSING THE RESPONDENTS

Whatever the method by which the study is to be carried out, it will be generally necessary for the research worker to collect the information from only a sample of the companies in the market. Sometimes the relevant population is small and an attempt can be made to obtain information from all of them, subject to the necessary cooperation being obtained.

There are two main categories of respondent. The primary respondent speaks from the immediate experience of himself or his company. He is able to tell about whether his company buys particular products, whether it is experimenting with new techniques, what type of equipment it operates, and so on. The secondary respondent speaks from his indirect knowledge of the experience of others. Intermediate manufacturers, for example, may express views on whether their customers are likely to require particular qualities in a product, on the trends in manufacturing practice within the industry they serve, and similar matters. In sampling primary respondents, the object is to select a sample representative of the whole industry under study, so that from the information obtained inferences are drawn about the market as a whole. If the number of establishments in that industry is large (as, for example, in agriculture, building, or small offices), then it is possible to consider adopting sampling techniques rather like those used for consumer surveys. These techniques are described fully in the basic textbooks on market research methods.[14] They are based either on probability theory or are quota samples or some combination of the two.

Probability samples (often called random samples) have the advantage that the possible error in the accuracy of their results can be assessed if all the rules are followed. However, even in the simplest case there are difficulties. Sampling frames, that is to say comprehensive lists of all the establishments in the population to be studied, are required as a basis for selecting a sample. They are often hard to obtain, rarely complete and up to date, and may require special compilation from a number of sources. Reasons of economy or shortage of time may make it impracticable to visit one establishment inconveniently located in the Highlands of Scotland or southwest England, although the application of the rules of probability might require it. Selected respondent companies may decline to cooperate and this spoils the sample.

Quota sampling, the alternative basic idea from consumer research, usually has the advantage of economy and speed but has not the same sound support from statistical theory as has the probability approach. Nevertheless, it is widely used in consumer studies and appears to give satisfaction. Defective sampling is only one source of error in the collection of survey data, and not necessarily the most important.

Suppose that desk research, analysis of the company's own sales figures, and some informal telephone discussions produce the following approximate picture of the market:

	SHARE OF THE MARKET (PERCENT)	NO. OF COMPANIES
Largest	33	3 largest users
Medium	33	c. 30 medium users
Small	33	200–300 smaller users

In these circumstances it is intuitively evident that it is important to secure the view of all the three largest companies. If they will cooperate, the cost will be small.

Similarly, it is possible to secure data which is sufficiently reliable by interviewing a high proportion of "medium" companies and a small proportion of "small" companies, although the number of interviews in the last-named group might be the highest. After collecting the data, appropriate "weights" in the statistical sense will have to be applied to the information collected from each group to compensate for the fact that different fractions of each group have been interviewed. Further improvement in sample selection can be obtained if available information permits the total population to be divided into additional groups or strata. In industrial research, this may involve ascertaining the amount of the product taken by different industries and then sampling those industries roughly in accordance with their importance in the total consumption pattern. An approximate idea of the relative importance of each industry is usually sufficient, but even this is often unobtainable. The usual problems of sample selection persist. In any case, however carefully the sample is designed, there may well be a percentage of respondents who will refuse or be unable to provide information, or whose information appears spurious and has to be discounted. Sampling in industrial markets is a compromise between what is theoretically desirable and what is feasible.

The sensible researcher will bear in mind the need for representation of all significant size-groups and all important or potentially important industries and will adapt his sample to ensure a reasonable cross-representation. He will then seek to support his conclusions by cross-checking the information in other ways; he may, for example, compare information from suppliers of a product with that from users.

When the object of the survey is to try to foresee technological and other trends, it is sometimes desired to obtain high-quality opinions rather than "facts." In such cases the object will be to seek expert individuals whose views have greatest value, rather than a statistical sample of primary respondents.

Apart from the selection of the respondent company, there is a need to select the right individual to meet within the company. In theory, the right respondent is the executive most able to give an authoritative answer. In practice it may be desirable to contact first a sympathetic executive in the respondent organization and obtain access to the authoritative source (or sources) through the beneficent assistance of an introduction by this intermediary. Not uncommonly it is desirable to meet several respondents in order to obtain authoritative information on all the aspects of a problem.

COLLECTING THE INFORMATION

Having designed the sample, how is the information to be collected? There are three primary methods, used separately or in combination: (1) telephone; (2) mail; (3) personal interview.

Combinations of these methods are common: for example, it may be economical to interview the most important respondents and to send a postal questionnaire to a sample of the less important. Group discussions—where a panel of users have come together to discuss a product—have also been employed.

TELEPHONE

The telephone is widely used in the initial informal inquiries and in approaching respondents with whom there is an existing personal relationship. It is less widely used in the more formal inquiry.

The phone offers an opportunity of speedy contact with the selected informant, but conversation must normally be short. It is thus suited for carefully planned inquiries where the informant either knows the answer without reference to any source or can obtain it quickly from a handy reference source, such as a file in his own offices. The phone has also been used as a way of reminding respondents who have not returned a postal questionnaire or in making supplementary inquiries from those who have already been interviewed. It has, in fact, a large role to play even in those surveys which would not be regarded primarily as telephone surveys. There are severe limitations, however, on the information which can be obtained from a respondent who has never been contacted previously.

Phone surveys can be inexpensive. They are certainly cheaper than actual visits, and some agencies have trained telephone interviewers in such main centers as London, Birmingham, Glasgow, and Manchester, who will telephone respondents in the area and thus reduce telephone costs to the minimum. Costs from $2.40 per interview upward are currently common in relation to telephone interviews in the United Kingdom.

POSTAL SURVEYS

This section might well be called "the use and abuse of postal surveys." Almost certainly this is the most commonly used method of collecting information—or at least of attempting to collect information—in industrial marketing research. It has advantages and disadvantages, including a most serious disadvantage—that of substantial nonresponse.

First, what are its benefits? It is, at first sight at least, simple to operate and inexpensive. The simplicity is somewhat deceptive, as the questionnaire must be very carefully phrased and worked out if it is to be understood easily and answered correctly by the respondent. Careful and systematic follow-up procedures are necessary to contact again those respondents who do not reply the first time, and perhaps also to follow up those who do not reply the second time if such steps are considered desirable and time permits.

The respondent to a postal questionnaire has time to consider his replies and to look up information when he needs to do so. He can also consult others.

Cost must be examined in relation to the number of completed questionnaires returned. If fully costed, this will rarely be less than about $3.60 each. Frequently, costing is not carried out within a company, so that many users are not aware of the true cost.

If the cost is looked at in terms of the value of the information received, it is clear that unless the survey is carried out carefully and receives a satisfactory response rate, money can be wasted. However, a *successful* mail survey can be much less expensive than a series of field interviews.

The problem of nonresponses is serious. It can mean that the expenditure is not only wasted but produces wrong or incomplete information. A study[15] among market researchers in the industrial field asking what proportion of replies they *normally expected to receive* produced the following information (incidentally, this was a survey among market researchers and economists by postal questionnaire which itself produced a response rate of 60 percent with one reminder). The table is based on thirty-three respondents who said they used postal questionnaires.

RESPONSE RATE (PERCENT)	PERCENTAGE OF RESPONDENTS
Over 80	3
60–80	15
40–60	24
20–40	21
Under 20	37

There is, however, no doubt that postal questionnaires do play a useful role. They often serve as a source of ideas which can be checked in another way. They can also serve to back up a main study of major markets with supporting evidence on minor markets.

There are three things which the researcher can try to

do about the nonresponse: (1) reduce it; (2) cross-check the results; (3) resample the nonrespondents.

Reducing nonrespondents is obviously the priority. What can be done to raise the response rate? The first and most valuable step is to send out a reminder. Phoning the respondent is best but works out expensive. Sending another copy of the questionnaire after a reasonable time also normally produces a fresh surge of replies. The time allowed before sending a reminder must be sufficient to permit the informant a chance to extract the information and prepare his reply, but not so long that he forgets all about the matter. For simple questionnaires two weeks is a common period before a reminder is sent; if the questionnaire is more complex, three or four weeks may be necessary. Some researchers will send a further reminder if a reply is not received to the first, but the extra delay involved often makes this impossible. Moreover, there is the occasional danger of upsetting a customer by "pestering" him.

There are a number of guide rules which researchers in general adopt as necessary to encourage and facilitate reply. These are briefly listed below:

1 CLARITY OF QUESTIONS

Questions should be clear, logically arranged, in the language normally understood by the class of respondent for whom it is designed, and unambiguous.

2 PRETEST (PILOT SURVEY)

For this reason, it is highly desirable that the questionnaire should be tested beforehand on a few typical respondents. This simple precaution almost always reveals faults even in an apparently straightforward questionnaire. The pretest survey also reveals not only ambiguities but shows whether the man who has to fill in the questionnaire actually has access to the information. It sometimes helps to identify questions which probe sensitive subjects and result in heavy nonresponse.

3 LAYOUT

The questionnaire should be laid out attractively and neatly. In the view of the present writer, the extra cost of printing the questionnaire is well justified because of the more favorable presentation which normally results. It also seems a reasonable courtesy to the respondent, who is being asked to give his time—and this is often valuable—that the small extra cost of printing the questionnaire should be incurred.

4 EASY TO ANSWER

In general, questions which are to be answered by a

"tick" in an appropriate box should make up the bulk of the questions.

5 LENGTH

Postal questionnaires should be short. A foolscap or A4 sheet, with a letter on one side and the questions on the other, is worth considering. The number of questions which can be printed on one side of a sheet with careful planning is surprising, but design and layout are important. Two sides of a foolscap sheet is common, and a few run to four sides.

6 COLORING

There is some ground for believing that questionnaires on tinted paper receive a better response—perhaps they stand out among the confusion of paper on many desks. Of course, this may cease to hold true if everyone sends out colored postal questionnaires, with the result that the respondent's in-tray looks as psychedelic as Carnaby Street!

7 STAMPED ENVELOPES

Most evidence indicates that sending a stamped addressed envelope for returning the questionnaire is likely to produce a higher response rate than sending a reply-paid envelope.

8 TIMING

Some seasons of the year are not considered good for certain industries because of seasonal pressure of work. Moreover, very few marketing research workers would send out a postal questionnaire which seemed likely to arrive on the respondent's desk on a Monday or a Friday. Both are considered bad days.

9 PERSONALIZATION

This awkward term means that a letter addressed to a respondent by name rather than as "Chief Purchasing Officer" or "The Sales Manager" pulls more strongly. Names can sometimes be obtained from the records of the researcher's company, from reference books, or by phoning the respondent company and asking the switchboard operator for the name of the executive concerned.

10 CONFIDENTIALITY

It is usually helpful to reassure the respondent that the information will be confidential within the marketing research department. This assurance must be fully respected. There are also occasions when it is considered desirable to tell the respondent that he can remain anonymous even from the market researcher should he so wish. To avoid a reminder, a *second* envelope is sent in which the respondent notifies that he has in fact replied to the questionnaire (which he has dispatched separately). To ensure that the respondent has complete confidence in the preservation of his anonymity, in some surveys it has been arranged for the completed anonymous questionnaire to be returned by the respondent to a neutral third party (perhaps a firm of accountants), a notification that it has been returned being sent to the marketing research department under separate cover. This device is cumbersome and is not often justified. Respondents do not always take advantage of their right to be anonymous when this is offered.

Efforts to raise the response rate are continuous. As an inducement to reply, some companies have offered to send respondents a summary of the replies to main questions. One marketing researcher sent inexpensive ballpoint pens to a random 50 percent of his selected sample of respondents and not to the others. The ballpoint pen group had a response rate of 5 percent above that of the other group.

Another questionnaire had at its heading a photograph of an attractive young lady, with the message "I will phone you tomorrow." She did phone for the answers to the questions, and a good response rate was achieved.

It must be confessed that not all of the rules set out above are supported by experimental evidence, and where there is evidence it is sometimes conflicting. The generalizations are not *invariably* true. For example, some long postal questionnaires have received high response rates, and unstamped envelopes have been more successful than stamped ones on at least one occasion when the figures were carefully checked (it is thought that the particular respondents were very status-conscious).

Finally, in addition to boosting the response rate, it is possible to resample a proportion of nonrespondents by phone or personal interview to find out the reason for their nonresponse and to try to check whether nonrespondents as a group are in some way different from respondents.

An alternative method sometimes used to test the representativeness of postal questionnaires returned is to check information from the returns against known national figures. For example, the respondent may be asked to indicate the numbers of persons employed; the returns can then be classified by industry to test if industries are represented in their appropriate proportion. Control questions can be inserted solely for the purpose of collecting information which (after the sample has been raised) can be compared against already existing information from published sources or former studies. If the comparison shows sufficient agreement, then the confidence in the results of the questionnaire is increased.

More and more postal questionnaires are being used (or so it seems), and every care is necessary to maximize response. Unless the respondents are individuals known personally to the researcher, or there are some other particularly favorable circumstances, it is a creditable result to receive a response much in excess of 40 percent.

PERSONAL INTERVIEWING

Interviewing is probably the method of collecting information most likely to produce accurate information from the respondents. It is only the face-to-face meeting between the interviewer and the respondent which provides a satisfactory opportunity to explore complex problems in depth. There are few marketing research departments which do not require this type of fieldwork from time to time.

Interviewing is expensive. The actual cost depends upon such factors as the length of the interview, the quality of the interviewer required, and the distances to be traveled between interviews. A typical figure at present is $12 to $24 per interview, while higher figures are mentioned sometimes, and even up to $60 where there are a few very high-level interviews. In order to keep costs to the minimum, visits must be carefully scheduled.

Nonresponse is lower than with postal surveys and is sometimes negligible. The interviewer can ask more questions and can seek clarification in depth. He can explore the implications of the respondent's thinking.

Interview situations vary from those in which the interviewer has a highly structured questionnaire, which he follows implicitly with little or no authority to vary it, to those where the interviewer has little more than an *aide-mémoire* of headings to be discussed.

The former type is used where there are a very large number of interviews to be carried out and where the information sought is capable of classification into clearly defined headings. The points about questionnaire design and pilot work, made in relation to postal inquiries, apply here also, but questionnaires can be longer and probe more deeply. The interviewer does not need to have technical or economic qualifications, and part-time interviewers can be used satisfactorily providing they have reasonable intelligence and training. This type of approach is often not possible in industrial research.

The alternative is a brief to the interviewer which has either a check list of points to be examined or even just a broad list of areas to be discussed. This might apply, for example, when the market for a possible new product is being discussed. Obviously it requires greater skill in the interviewer, who has to probe in depth in an area which his respondent may never have considered. He may also have to interview a number of different people in the course of one inquiry at a company and build up his information, not in the sequence which logic dictates, but according to the train of thought of the various executives. He must be alert for the odd remark which may indicate that there is something deeper of relevance which needs exploration.

This is the technoeconomic equivalent of the depth research of the psychologist used in consumer motivation research. The interviewer needs considerable sensitivity to the respondent to be able to obtain from him the maximum cooperation. He must endeavor to create an atmosphere where there is a sense that respondent and interviewer are working together toward a common goal and build up in the respondent trust and even enthusiasm for the research.

If an interview can be obtained, much more information will be given to a live interviewer compared with that which will be passed on to an unknown inquirer through a postal questionnaire. Respondents frequently become interested in the subject of the survey and will give as much assistance as is within their power, providing blueprints, samples, and analyses and enlisting the aid of more expert colleagues.

Market research workers, where they are able to do so, may promote a better relationship by indicating that they will offer reciprocal benefits to the respondent, perhaps by sending him some of the information collected which is of special interest to him yet not prejudicial to the sponsoring company. Alternatively, they may offer to assist with information on those occasions when the roles may be reversed and today's inquirer becomes tomorrow's respondent. It is important that relations be good, as it is not uncommon that toward the end of a survey it is necessary to reinterview earlier respondents to obtain further information in the light of facts revealed during the survey subsequent to the first interview.

In planning an interview, it is desirable to insert questions which to an extent cross-check information given earlier in the survey. There are a number of ways in which errors may arise in the interview situation. The respondent may be deliberately misleading the interviewer (although this is probably rare); he may not know the answer but may be anxious to conclude the interview and is thus saying the first thing which comes to mind. Or he may be too anxious to help. If cooperation between the two parties is good, the danger arises that the interviewer, by his form of words or by a change of tone, may affect the respondent's answer.

In one instance[16] a respondent was asked how many vehicles he had in his fleet.

> *Respondent:* Twenty.
> *Interviewer:* Twenty?
> *Respondent:* Well, eighteen then.
> *Interviewer:* Eighteen?
> *Respondent:* Perhaps fifteen.

A count showed that he had twenty!

Tests of the validity of respondents' replies take a number of forms. One is the "ratio" technique. The respondent, having been asked about his purchase of a particular product, is then asked about his output of the equipment or goods in which the product is used. This establishes a ratio which can be compared with that for other firms in the same industry. Alternatively virtually the same question may be asked separately later in the interview in somewhat different words, for example, by asking how much of the product per unit of output is used.

Industrial marketing research can be carried out either by the company's own staff or by the employment of an agency, and these two methods are not mutually exclusive. Appointing a marketing research manager in a company has the advantage of bringing in an individual of logical, scientific, and quantitative ways of thought who can provide an independent view of all those matters with which the marketing department is involved. He may do some survey work with his own resources, but he will also be responsible for placing the company's work with agencies and will be better able to close the gap which very often exists between the problems of the marketing manager and the terms of reference laid out in the brief to the research agency. The number of agencies is growing, and the selection of a suitable agency is not easy. Some specialize in particular fields, while others adopt a broader policy.

Industrial marketing research is still in its early stages of development. The range of tasks which it is asked to tackle is increasing all the time. Sensibly used and clearly directed to provide the right information, it is a powerful tool for the marketing executive. At this stage both the marketing executive who uses the results of research and the market researcher who collects the information have much to do to raise the value of their joint efforts.

Business Forecasting

Planning, as discussed in Chapter 4, begins with a forecast. Forecasts are the basis of every business decision, whether it be to erect a plant, recruit staff, or purchase equipment, since each decision implies some view of the company and its market. The forecast may be implicit only, but this chapter is concerned with clearly stated forecasts giving a quantitative opinion about the future.

Short-term and long-term forecasts present somewhat different problems.

Short-term forecasts tie in with the company's plans for the next few months in relation to production, purchasing, stock control, and finance.

Long-term forecasts are more concerned with capital investment, manpower planning, and corporate strategy.

Many companies make regular long-term forecasts for a period of from five to seven years, although a minority whose products take a long while to come to fruition forecast for ten to twelve years. Very often these are rolling forecasts, that is to say they are revised annually and extended forward a further year. For special projects forecasts may be made for longer periods.

Long-term forecasts are more concerned with the trend than the actual level of demand at a particular time and thus differ in emphasis from short-term forecasts. Some companies find it desirable also to make medium-term forecasts for two to four years ahead. This is the period in which the state of cyclical fluctuation in the economy is important; the difference between "go" and "stop" in some industries can represent a 30 percent fluctuation around the trend.

LONG-TERM FORECASTS

The long-term market forecast is an anticipation of developments substantially outside the company's control. The word "forecast" here implies the best possible view of the future market size after taking account of both statistical and other information and exercising personal judgment. It differs from a sales target or forecast, which is to a lesser or greater extent dependent on the company's own endeavors in increasing or holding its share of the market.

In practice, it is sometimes difficult to separate the market and sales forecasts. Where the company is the sole or major supplier of a product for which there is no close substitute, the market and the sales forecast are not distinguishable.

The market which is to be forecast should be clearly defined, and it must, at least as a first step, bring in all competition widely interpreted. An oil company, for example, may well first forecast the market for energy (including coal, natural gas, hydroelectricity, and so on) before forecasting its own share. A company operating in a local area may well forecast the total national market before turning to its own particular segment.

Accuracy in forecasting is often higher in basic product groups, such as energy and iron and steel. It is lower for products which are susceptible to innovative competition either by the discovery of new applications or by the development of new competitive products.

There are also occasions when it is difficult to identify the error in a forecast. If capacity is related to a forecast of sales and sales threaten to fall below the anticipated level, it is sometimes possible to intensify the search for new applications for the product and thus to boost sales. Under such circumstances, the forecast can be considered self-fulfilling. Perhaps the forecaster's true objective is to provide management with an indication of the highest feasible figure.

MANAGERIAL IMPLICATIONS

The relation between the forecast and the plan is not one-way only; there are logical implications in both directions. Initially, the plan is derived from the forecast. But the reverse relationship has its own special significance in that the plan is now consistent with the particular view of the future set out in the forecast. If, as the forecast is reviewed annually, it is modified, then it is possible to adapt the plan in a logical and controlled way to match the company to the new situation. This is not, of course, an argument for indifference to accuracy in forecasting. It is, however, an argument for not explicitly rejecting forecasting because inaccuracy may arise.

In some companies, senior managers now prefer a "range" forecast, rather than one specific figure; the market for the product in 1975 is not indicated as 100,000 tons but as 80,000 to 120,000 tons.

This approach has much to commend it. It is more realistic. Although the forecaster may consider 100,000 tons the most probable outcome, the range gives an indication of the magnitude of possible error. In choosing between alternative strategies, executives can examine their implications in relation to the upper and lower limits of the range.

A particular plan which may seem to be the best for the "most probable" market may be so severely damaging at the lower figure that management may prefer a plan which is rather more defensive, giving reasonable protection in the poor market and a satisfactory (though perhaps not the theoretical optimum) result in the most probable situation. This type of approach is likely to be developed in greater detail in the future, as the computer provides greater facility in calculating the implications of alternatives. It would be feasible to attach probabilities to different figures and to work out the most appropriate management decision on a probabilistic basis.

Range forecasting may also reduce the tendency to timid decision-making, which sometimes flows from the need to express the forecast as *one* figure. The forecaster who is under pressure to report to management one figure as *the* forecast may be inclined to advance what he considers a safe forecast —a figure which is rather low. This means that the sales plan is also low. Goals may then be achieved and exceeded, to the great satisfaction of unsuspecting managers. If he were to advance a figure which proved too high, goals might not be achieved, and this is sometimes regarded as proof of culpable inefficiency on the part of the forecaster! Yet overachievement may signify that the company had not exploited its opportunities to the full and can be as harmful as underachievement.

A forecast should be as objective and as neutral as human ingenuity can make it, and the forecaster should not feel impelled to lean toward conservatism—or the other way. By permitting the forecaster to state a range, he is given a margin of protection and has no need to provide another unseen margin.

If no indication is provided about the range of uncertainty in the forecast, some executives provide their own safety margin by mentally discounting the forecast. Such discounts may well be too wide, particularly when formal forecasting as such is new to the company and the forecaster has not yet established the confidence of management.

THE APPROACH TO FORECASTING

While forecasting has departed from clairvoyance, it is hardly a fully fledged science. Statistics generally play an important role—particularly for products such as basic materials which have a wide range of potential uses—but the judgment of individuals remains important. Judgment tends to be particularly important in industries with a high incidence of technological innovation and product obsolescence. Even in forecasts which are bespattered with mathematical formulae, there are often important judgments incorporated, perhaps introduced by such a phrase as "it seems reasonable to suppose that. . . ."

Forecasters should support all their calculations by a wide and imaginative awareness of the implications of change. Such change may flow from technological developments (very important in industrial markets), from changes in consumer habits which at first sight may seem remote from the industrial market until deeply examined, from new discoveries (natural gas in the North Sea), or from changes in economic or political circumstances. It often takes time before such developments are reflected in official statistics in such a way that they assist the long-term forecaster. One of the crucial problems in forecasting is attempting to identify those changes which represent turning points, either replacing growth by decline or introducing a new acceleration of growth. Only an inquiring and original mind can identify the embryonic ideas of today which become the norms of the future.

The nature of forecasting is such that there is no unique technique. Basically, however, most of the following elements may be found in a closely integrated long-term forecast:

1 Background assumptions.
2 Past statistics and their extrapolation.
3 Explanatory analyses (which may have a substantial statistical content).
4 Circumstantial and cross-checking evidence.
5 Personal judgment and intuition to modify and integrate.

Background assumptions are generally a major conditioning influence. Such issues as "Will there be a major war?" "Will there be devaluation?" "Will England join the Common

Market?" "Will the space race continue?" may be crucial, and the answer given may make a great difference to the forecast. Such issues need clear identification in advance, and the assumptions made should be clearly specified.

The other elements are discussed below. They may be applied to any of three main approaches to the problem of making long-term forecasts, and these approaches may in practice be combined or used in parallel to cross-check and buttress each other.

The first approach is to treat the market as a whole and to set out to forecast it as one entity without breaking it down further. Most weight is given to this approach when the market is very wide and the product concerned is so fundamental that there is hardly any change in the pattern of consumer or investment demand which does not affect it.

The second approach is to analyze the market into different major segments, which are then forecast separately. This approach is emphasized when the demand comes mainly from a small number of industries, from certain end-uses, or from certain applications. It is also important when the demand pattern is changing, because some parts of the market are developing faster than others or because of changes in processes or products of intermediate manufacturers.

Sometimes this approach may be used for important parts of the total demand, with the residual demand treated as a whole as in the first approach.

In using segmented forecasts, the analyst must usually take the further step of forecasting the change of demand for the output of the different industries, etc., into which he has divided his total market. This may involve another cycle of forecasting, in which all three possible approaches are considered in relation to the forecasts for each segment.

Finally, there is the possibility of looking at each customer individually. As a systematic approach to long-term forecasting, this applies when demand is wholly or very substantially in the hands of a few big customers. The forecaster is then in the position of having to forecast the sales of each customer, the consequential volume of product demand, and whether or not his company will win the business or some share of it.

It will be seen that the methods of calculation and estimation discussed in the following pages may be applied to any of these three classifications, but there will be differences in its importance and in the nature of the data to which it is applied.

EXTRAPOLATING PAST STATISTICS

The scrutiny of past data, the identification of a trend, and the extension of that trend into the future—this is a common ingredient of a market forecast. The data extrapolated may be the sales of a product or it may be some other statistical series which is considered to influence those sales, for example, the Gross National Product or the output of a customer industry.

Extrapolation may best be described as a useful walking-stick but a bad crutch. Where past sales data exist, it is of value to attempt to identify the trend and to extend it forward. Extrapolation indicates what will emerge if the pattern of development which has operated in the past continues into the future. It thus offers at least a comparison with any alternative approach. Extrapolation is sometimes called a naive method in that in its crudest form it involves no understanding of the pressures at work which mold demand for the product. This is a fair comment. The present argument is that extrapolation is useful as one step, a first step, in building up a total forecast. Examples can also be quoted where the cold emotionless mathematics of "naive" extrapolation have been more successful than the judgment of individuals.

Where the intention is to take past sales and to extrapolate them forward to forecast future demand, the past data need careful scrutiny. The figures are only relevant if they do in fact measure demand. This is different from sales if past demand has not been fully satisfied, as for example when power cuts have reduced sales of electricity below what customers were prepared to buy. Changes in definitions or in units of measurement must be identified and suitable adjustments made to convert them to an appropriate common basis; different nitrogenous fertilizers may have different percentages of nitrogen, and to measure the pattern of consumption they can be converted to a common basis of nitrogen content. Trends may often be more clearly and logically defined when different major market segments are examined separately: how is demand developing in the coal industry? in steel? and so on.

This book is not primarily a statistical treatise, and therefore the present chapter treats statistical aspects of forecasting superficially. The reader is referred to the more specialized books for further reading.[17]

Three main classes of trend are commonly distinguished by statisticians:

LINEAR TRENDS

These increase or decrease by the same fixed quantity each year. The following would be an exact linear trend, but no real-life set of data is likely to fit the rules of mathematics so neatly as the data below.

Total United Kingdom Sales of Product X

YEAR	TONNAGE SOLD
1963	70
1964	100
1965	130
1966	160
1967	190

Each successive year is a precise 30 tons above the sales of the previous year. Naive forecasts would be: 1968—30 tons more than 1967; 1972—5 × 30 tons more, i.e., 340 tons. If the figures are plotted on ordinary (arithmetic scale) graph paper, they lie in a straight line (see Fig. 4). The straight line is the simplest way of representing a series of annual figures and is consequently often used. But there is seldom any reason why the sales of a product should follow this pattern, and it is generally worth examining whether other trends "fit" better.

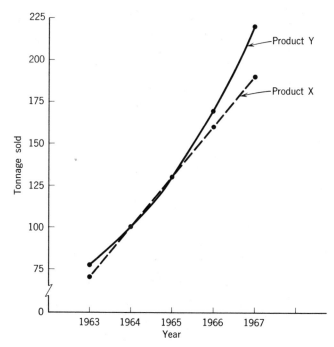

Fig. 4. Linear and exponential trends: arithmetic scale

These increase or decrease by the same percentage each year, as in the example below:

Total United Kingdom Sales of Product Y

YEAR	TONNAGE SOLD
1963	77
1964	100
1965	130
1966	169
1967	220

Each successive year's sales are 30 percent more than those of the previous year. The naive forecast for 1968 would be the 1967 sales multiplied by 1.3, and hence for 1972 the forecast would be obtained by multiplying the 1967 figures by 1.3^5, i.e., by 3.71, giving a forecast of nearly 820 tons.

On semilogarithmic graph paper (which has one of its two axes on a logarithmic scale), this series would lie on a straight line (see Fig. 5).

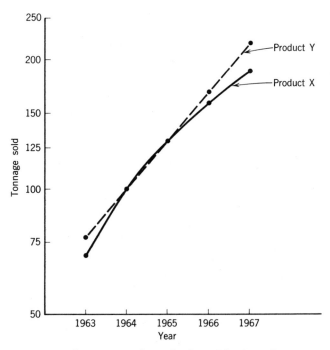

Fig. 5. Linear and exponential trends: logarithmic scale

There is much to be said for plotting long-run series of sales figures on this type of paper. It is simple to use, and the percentage change in such a series is more important than its absolute amount. To say sales have risen by 30 tons means nothing: 30 tons on 30,000 (0.1 percent) is negligible, but 30 tons on 300 (10 percent) is significant.

TRENDS WHICH TEND TO FLATTEN OFF TOWARD AN
UPPER LIMIT

There are a number of mathematical formulae to describe different ways in which growth can flatten off toward an upper saturation level—a ceiling which is the absolute maximum. Each of them has somewhat different characteristics, and they are on the whole rather complex to handle. It is sometimes possible to make an estimate of the saturation level *separately,* and this is of great help in cross-checking the reasonableness of the extrapolation. These trends do present difficulties both mathematically and logically.[18]

In a real-life situation, the past history of the sales of a product frequently does not fit very neatly to the mathematician's formulae. Most examples show rather uncertain cyclical elements and some irregularities as well. Examples of exponential growth are illustrated in Fig. 6.

Usually the first step in identifying a trend is to calculate a simple moving average of the annual figures (a three- or five-year moving average is widely used) and to plot the trend and the original data on a graph. Five years is long enough to eliminate most short-term variation, and also smooths the United Kingdom economic cycle of stop-go, which seems to have a similar length. It is then usually possible to see by inspection whether there is a reasonably well-defined trend and into which of the three categories above it may fall. More exact tests can be found in the specialized literature.

Statisticians are apt to argue that to extrapolate into the future it is necessary to deduce the mathematical formula which is most consistent with past figures and then derive the forecast in accordance with that formula. There are times, however, when the forecast is only one part of a wider study, and graphic work with a ruler or freehand (particularly on linear and exponential curves) may well be considered adequate.

The relationship between the individual past figures and the plotted moving average should then be scrutinized. It will often help toward a deeper understanding of the factors influencing the changing size of the market.

Some curves show a "step" where the trend appears to move from one level to another, and it may be that the period prior to the step is now irrelevant and should be ignored in

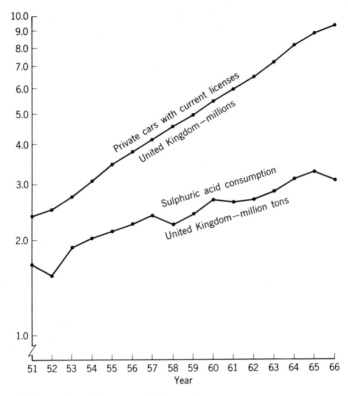

Fig. 6. Examples of exponential growth

extrapolation. Investigation into the market circumstances at the time of the step helps to check this. Sometimes the past figures lie close to the trend; at other times they may be well dispersed about it. This gives some clue to the inherent variability of the market and may indicate the degree of uncertainty in the forecast. On the whole, simple extrapolation seems to be most meaningful for raw materials and basic industrial products which have a wide range of uses, so that if one use is lost, another may be expected to arise.

EXPLANATORY ANALYSES

Explanatory analyses of market change often take the form of a simple model. It is convenient to use the term "model" for any attempt to answer the question "What causes change in the size of this market?" and to set out the answer in a formula. To take a very simple example, if it were thought that the demand for coffins depended on the number of people who died, then a simple model would be:

number of coffins required = number of deaths.

It will be seen that this has shifted the forecasting problem from the number of coffins to the number of deaths. This implies that the latter can be forecast with greater confidence—otherwise there will be no gain. The term on the left (number of coffins) is called the dependent variable because it depends upon the term on the right, which is the independent variable (in this particular model the number of deaths). This principle is utilized in many forecasts. The dependent variable, whether it is total demand, demand from a segment, or indirect demand for a major customer's product, can be treated as being primarily determined by one or two or occasionally more independent variables. For example, the demand for a product might depend largely on the level of the national income, its price relative to other products, and the rate of technical change.

The national income may be forecast by considering its past trend and the comments of various specialized organizations (such as the National Institute of Economic and Social Research). Prices may be forecast by studies of the cost structure, trends in the cost of various inputs, and the possible effects of improved efficiency. Technological advance cannot be measured directly, but if development is reasonably continuous and smooth it may be possible to treat it as if it advanced by more-or-less regular annual increments and use time (the number of years) as a substitute for direct measurement.

Thus the forecaster can set up an equation expressing demand as a function of these three variables and by the fairly simple statistical technique of regression analysis deduce a relationship which he expects to continue throughout the forecasting period. He applies his equation to the separate forecasts for his three independent variables and thus derives his forecast for the product under review.

When studying demand as a whole for basic materials, it is common to compare the demand in a country with the national income of that country. Fig. 7 shows the relationship between the Gross National Product of the United Kingdom and the sales of iron and steel products over a series of years. While there are residual unexplained differences, much of the change in iron and steel demand can be explained by growth in the Gross National Product, and this must therefore be taken into account in forecasting.

In other models, the demand for an industrial product may depend upon the demand for particular categories of consumer goods, and the forecaster must perforce study the con-

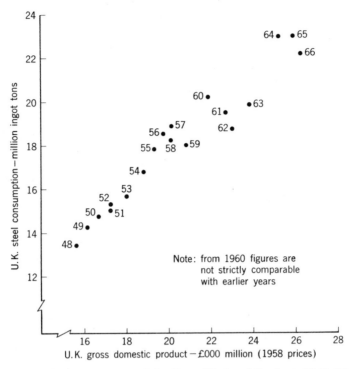

Fig. 7. Steel consumption and the Gross National Product, 1948–1966. (Statistical sources: *Iron and Steel Annual Statistics; Annual Abstract of Statistics.*)

sumer market for this product. A forecast of the demand for vehicle components depends upon the final demand for the vehicles plus a replacement market in existing vehicles.

Major categories of capital goods often show a long-run trend which moves with national income. They may react very strongly to shorter-term fluctuations in the rate of national growth. A particular type of capital good may be affected in part by this general pattern for capital goods and in part by a longer trend reflecting technological change peculiar to the product concerned. The demand for consumable goods and minor items of capital equipment will be affected by the output of the different industries served and it may be necessary to study separately the trends of sales to major customer industries and treat the balance as moving with the Gross National Product.

Thus the general principle behind model-building in the present context is to find a small number of factors which are thought to explain most of the market variation and for which some reasonable forecast is feasible and then to fit them to the dependent variable by a simple equation.

Sometimes the formula is derived by technical considerations rather than by statistics. If it is known or anticipated that on the average the demand for brickwork for houses and bungalows will be 6,500 bricks per 1,000 square feet of floor area, then a forecast of the number of houses and bungalows which will be built can be turned into a forecast for bricks. Here a technical coefficient has been used to obtain a measure of demand for one product from a forecast of the demand for the product which incorporates it.

Such procedures are common. They are used because sufficient data for a reliable regression analysis are not available or because, although the product is new, a technical coefficient can be derived from the knowledge of engineers or research workers. It is also suitable when it is known that a change in products or processes is occurring which will noticeably alter past relationships so that historic statistical coefficients will no longer be relevant.

CIRCUMSTANTIAL AND CROSS-CHECKING EVIDENCE

Technical change of this type is only one of the circumstances where the assistance offered by statistics may be limited. Sometimes the statistics do not exist—no one has bothered to collect them. Sometimes the product is new, or new to this country.

There are various lines of thought which prove of value in limiting the range within which the "correct forecast" lies. The phraseology here is carefully chosen!

One line of approach is to "ask your customers"—either the major ones or a sample of them. Customers may, of course, be in no better position to make the forecast. Sometimes it is possible to work with them to explore the factors which affect their demand and with their aid to build up a view of their market. Where capital equipment is concerned, some customers will reveal their future plans, although even these are liable to change as a result of economic or other developments.

Sometimes the object is to obtain supplementary information in order to modify a forecast undertaken by methods mentioned above. In almost every forecast it is necessary to consider the question "Is technological change likely to affect the size of my market?" The more sophisticated customers may help to answer such questions as "Is propane replacing acetylene?" and "To what extent is demand for industrial lubricants likely to be reduced because improved products last longer?"

The customer is not always, of course, the only or necessarily the best man to ask. It may be that a research association or the indirect customer can be of more help.

With new products it is sometimes possible to carry out a technoeconomic study in conjunction with customers to ascertain what benefit the new product offers in comparison with existing methods in different industries and applications and thus to make an approximate assessment of the potential market. Sometimes this has been done in such a way that a view was formed of the possible sales at different price levels.

Overseas comparison can be helpful, largely as a check, or perhaps in desperation. When as a basis for forecasting a comparison is made between the United Kingdom Gross National Product and domestic consumption of a product, the cautious forecaster wonders whether this calculated relationship holds for other countries. If study of other countries shows a similar relationship, he considers his forecast that much stronger.

In certain areas of technology, some executives seem to have developed a working rule that the United Kingdom is always a more-or-less fixed number of years behind the United States in adopting new ideas. The time-lag is a subject of dispute and no doubt would vary industry by industry. It does represent a useful line of approach when there is little else on which to form a judgment.

In making intercountry comparisons, geographical, climatic, and cultural backgrounds need to be considered to decide whether the inference is reasonable. The relative carbon dioxide consumption between this country and France is affected by the fact that the Englishman drinks more beer, but also by the fact that the English brewing process has its own special characteristics.

In forecasting new products, unless they clearly replace products which have become obsolete and are to be withdrawn, there is a period of time which inevitably elapses before the bulk of potential users adopt the product. Even if the product offers benefits, unless these are abundantly self-evident and clearly advantageous, there will be a period of consideration and assessment. For capital goods, existing assets would commonly be required to yield at least a reasonable working life before new improved equipment is installed. These are factors in the forecast.

PERSONAL JUDGMENT AND INTUITION

When statistics prove of little avail, personal judgment takes over. In some cases the role of personal judgment is substantial, and it becomes extremely important that it should be objective and dispassionate. Some individuals are neither cautious nor optimistic by nature, and sales staff sometimes have a reputation for volatility. There is much to be said for placing the long-term forecasting operation in the hands of an individual who is not in the day-to-day battle for order-winning. With some degree of detachment from immediate problems, he is better placed to resist being led astray by the mood of the moment. He is less likely in times of boom to take the view that the sky's the limit and in times of setback to forget that this too can be temporary. It is no easy task to distinguish significant longer-term developments from the continual short-term to-and-fro of the tides of business.

The forecaster must, however, be willing to review his past forecasts impartially. If the trend of events calls the original view into question, he must be prepared to reexamine it without feeling emotionally committed to his former view.

Finally, the growing interest in sensitivity analysis should be noted. Where a model is developed, the accuracy of the forecast will depend on the accuracy of the view of the independent variables' future behavior. If the demand for a basic product depends upon the Gross National Product, then the question which a manager is tending to ask is "If the GNP forecast is 5 percent wrong, how far is our forecast astray?" In other words, how sensitive is the forecast to the assumption about the GNP? If the forecasting technique is very complex—and some models of increasing complexity are beginning to appear on the business scene—this is one way in which the manager can cut through the mathematical theory to identify the crucial assumptions to which he should give his own attention.

Judgment may be used simply to modify forecasts produced by primarily statistical techniques, for example to decide whether the pace of technological change may be accelerating. An interesting example of a more substantial use is in the Lockheed Aircraft Corporation.[19] After the standard analyses were complete, the company was faced with a special problem. The number of major customers was small, so that much depended on whether these specific decision-makers would accept a proposed aircraft. Accordingly, the company set up a small group of executives unconnected with the preliminary work on the aircraft concerned, fed them all possible information and said, in effect, "If you were Air France, etc., what would your decision be?" Their replies guided Lockheed to their forecast.

SHORT-TERM FORECASTING

In short-term forecasting, some matters which are of little or no significance in the longer term come to the fore. Short-term forecasting is concerned with the months and quarters immediately ahead; seasonal variations in product demand and the cyclical variation of the economy have thus to be reflected.

Valuable statistical techniques have been developed. The traditional method of calculating a moving average month by month over a series of years, extending this forward, building in seasonal variation factors, and garnishing the result with market knowledge, still has much to commend it. It is found in almost any introductory textbook on statistics.

For products which sell in bulk (as opposed to major capital goods), a technique honored with the rather horrifying name of exponentially weighted smoothing averages is increasingly used and has been widely adopted. Despite the rather forbidding name and the rather complex mathematics needed to substantiate it, its practical application is simple. The basic rule for making the forecast for a month ahead is:

1 Take the forecast made for last month.
2 Calculate the size of the error (i.e., last month's actual sales minus the forecast).
3 Adjust the former forecast by adding a proportion of the error if it is positive (or subtracting if it is negative) to give the new forecast.

Additional allowance needs to be made for any trend in the data and for seasonal variation, but this too is straightforward. The proportion of the error to be added needs to be established by experience, but figures in the region of 0.2 to 0.3 seem to be commonly used.

Where many hundreds of forecasts need to be made each month to cover all of a company's products, a computer can produce all the necessary information very quickly.

The alternative approach is the grass-roots approach, in which the salesman with his local knowledge is asked what he expects his customers' purchases to be.

This is still a valuable method, and even when the statistical methods already mentioned are used, the salesman should be asked to comment on the results. He may know, for example, that a particular company is at that very moment finalizing the decision on a new purchase. Where the purchase of products is lumpy, so that there are extreme variations from month to month in the value of orders booked, statistical methods offer little. This can apply to large capital equipment. Forecasts then still depend heavily on close knowledge of what is happening in the customer company, modified by some awareness of the state of the economy which can lead to changes in customers' best-thought-out plans.

Product Planning

Product planning has become in recent years one of the most crucial areas in determining the success or failure of an enterprise. Technological advance, new methods in industry, and more rapid change in the patterns of final consumer behavior have reacted on industrial markets, and products have become obsolete at a faster rate than ever before. Yet, at the same time, many companies have been unsuccessful in launching new products to replace the old.

Thus the problem of the business executive in product planning is like the classic problem of Odysseus trying to navigate the narrow passage between the whirlpool of Charybdis and the monster Scylla. Too far in one direction, and profits are sucked down by the Charybdis of product obsolescence; too far the other, and the profits are snatched away by the Scylla of new product failures.

From a great deal of discussion on this subject certain common lines of thought have emerged. There is disagreement on detail and some confusion of terminology, but the main core of ideas has achieved a wide measure of acceptance. Nevertheless, detailed application of these ideas must differ from one company to another. It will depend upon the type of customers and structure of the market, upon the technology of the industry, upon the economics and other characteristics of the production process, and upon the traditions and attitudes of the people in the company concerned.

The overall purpose of product planning is to ensure that the product range is composed of those products which make most profitable use of the resources of the company in relation to the opportunities of the environment. It is this which brings it within the basic concept of marketing on which this book is based.

To maintain an appropriate product line over time, it is necessary both to adopt new products and to drop old ones. The process of developing new products means searching out ideas, examining them for their suitability, and developing from such embryonic ideas as are suitable products which will achieve success in the marketplace. There must also be review of the product range to examine whether current products are pulling their weight or whether the company is struggling along, committing to low-profitability products financial resources and executives' time which could be used elsewhere to greater advantage.

WHAT IS A PRODUCT?

The marketing man views the product not as a piece of hardware, but as a device by which the resources of a company are turned into customer-satisfying benefits. It is useful, but not easy, to try to analyze the customer implications of the product by dissecting it into more fundamental elements.

The following is a suggested approach to the problem of product analysis. It divides the product concept into five elements which can often be distinguished from each other.

BASIC CORE

The innermost core of the product concept is the statement of the main need which it satisfies and the service which it supplies to customers. It indicates the way in which this particular product sets out to serve the company's product mission. Thus a fork-lift truck might be described as a materials-handling device for relatively small loads.

PRIMARY DIFFERENTIATION

In general, there will be a number of products having the same "core," and the primary differentiation distinguishes the different ways in which various products satisfy the same class of need. How does the fork-lift truck differ from the conveyor and from overhead handling equipment? Considerations such as load-carrying, flexibility, ease of control come to the fore here. Different products also make different demands on a customer in terms of staff skills required, ancillary equipment, and investment.

SECONDARY DIFFERENTIATION

This separates one model from another. The normal technical specifications are a relevant basis for secondary differentiation of products—capacity, mode of holding the load, turning circle, and so on. Differentiation can also be achieved by variations in certain additional features (optional extras) which offer benefits required in some applications but not others.

TERTIARY DIFFERENTIATIONS

These are matters which do not affect the applications to which the product is suited. They may make its use more convenient to the customer (for example, ergonomic considerations in engineering products), or they may make it easier to open, measure, or dispense. They can relate to the external appearance of the product (aesthetic features, packaging, and labeling). Even in industrial marketing, such factors can help to create confidence in buying decision-makers, and help give an edge over competition.

SERVICE

Both commercial and technical services, although not part of the hardware, add extra value to the product (see Chapter 12).

This analysis is probably best suited to an engineering or other fabricated product; for other types of product it may require modification. The basis is the idea that the product is specified implicitly or explicitly by the market and the customer. As the product concept is elaborated in detail, so is it focused more sharply on particular applications by particular classes of customers. In turn the customers' own requirements are better understood and reflected back with increasing sharpness to define the product ever more precisely. The ability to provide what the customer wants on acceptable terms to some extent depends on the state of technology at the time, and advances in technology increasingly make it possible to offer better value.

Sometimes finding out what product innovation the customer wants is not difficult. There can be sources of dissatisfaction with existing products which can well be remedied, resulting in an improved product. It becomes more difficult to identify customer needs which can be expected to emerge in the future but which the customer has not yet recognized. The marketing man must then try to stand in the shoes of the customer of tomorrow and to think through the problems he will face so that his needs may be anticipated even before they have become clear to the customer. This requires information, thought, and insight.

THE PRODUCT LIFE-CYCLE

A familiar and very valuable tool in developing an effective product policy is the idea of the product life-cycle. The underlying hypothesis is that products are in the market for a span of years, during which total market sales pass through the successive phases illustrated in Fig. 8. These are initiation, growth, maturity, saturation, and decline. This description may not be applicable to all products in all industries, but it is certainly widespread. The length of the cycle varies from industry to industry, and the tendency over the last quarter of a century or so has been for this cycle to shorten. It may be that those industries which do not appear to be affected by this phenomenon either have no life-cycle, or else that the cycle is of such a length that it stretches beyond the time-span of even the longest of the corporate plans. Nevertheless, let the producer beware! Advances in technology and changes in consumer habits and fashions are increasingly dethroning well-established products in the most unexpected way.

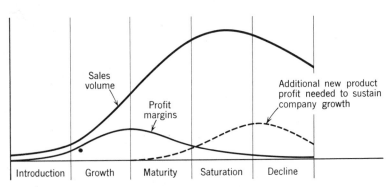

Fig. 8. The product life-cycle. (Source: Management Research Department, Booz, Allen & Hamilton Inc.)

Essentially, the hypothesis is this. In its early days after the product is launched into the market, growth of sales proceeds gradually. This is a difficult time and if not carefully handled can be long drawn out. A high proportion of the products which are launched fail to achieve success at this stage, and this is one of the problems of product policy.

If the product survives the period of infancy, the growth of the market accelerates. Expansion comes about as a result of such factors as better knowledge of the product by potential customers and a widening of markets and applications. The marketing effort of the innovating company operates to promote market growth, and price reductions may support this effort.

For most products, sooner or later imitating competitors enter the market with what is essentially the same product (perhaps with minor variations). In addition, the market growth rate slackens as unexploited potential diminishes. Eventually the market reaches its saturation level. By this time there may be little difference between competitors' products to base a choice upon. A newer product may now enter the market, and the original product, now obsolescent, will begin to decline in importance.

This pattern shows a number of variations in practice and it is perhaps as well to mention the most important of them.

At the saturation stage, if there is no better product forthcoming, the product demand may well rest on a plateau for a while, perhaps growing with the growth of the economy as a whole but not capturing new markets. However, there are some instances in which, even after reaching apparent saturation, renewed expansion has been achieved by giving fresh thought to the product. This phenomenon of "regeneration" is discussed more fully later in this chapter.

Finally, when decay does set in, the product does not necessarily lose its entire market at the same time. While the later innovating product may gain the main markets, there may be segments for which the existing product is still preferred and may continue to offer profitable sales for some time, although this may not be of much interest to the bigger company.

One feature which is not uncommon in industrial markets is the phenomenon of a "foothill" in the early stage of the cycle, i.e., a small spurt in demand, followed by a limited decline. After the foothill, the main pattern of the cycle reasserts itself if the product is successful.

This foothill probably arises from the fact that potential customers make limited purchases for the purpose of testing the product—thus causing the spurt—and there is then a lull while they are forming an opinion of the product.

A product may also show very fast growth rates in the first stage of the cycle, because the users of the product which it supersedes have hitherto been consciously dissatisfied. When there are explicit complaints about an existing product, these contribute to a clear specification of customer requirements to be met by the new product, and if it does in fact succeed in meeting this specification then there is a valuable basis for successful sales. Under such circumstances, a company may phase out the old product rapidly and leave the market that much clearer for the new.

In certain markets, the growth of sales follows a wave-like pattern: a surge of sales, followed by a slowing down before a new surge. This would match a market in which growth depends on finding new applications; each surge represents a new application which opens up.

Associated with the cycle of demand is the change in financial returns from the product, illustrated by the cycle of net profit in Fig. 8.

At the beginning of the product's life-cycle, net profit margin is commonly low despite the favorable price. This is a result of high costs associated with low volume and initial teething troubles in production, relatively heavy demands on technical service, and initial publicity. Later, with extra volume, increased experience, and the decline of these initial expenses, lower costs give a wider margin despite possible price falls.

Price reductions to help market growth and to meet competitive pressures are common over the life-cycle. As cost reductions taper off, falling prices force down the profit margin. This often happens before total market sales decline, and at this stage an innovating company may seek to bring out a further new product to maintain and expand sales and profits.

The net profit margin thus signals decline in advance of the fall of sales. The concept of net profit is, however, somewhat unsatisfactory for this purpose, because the margin may well turn upon the convention which the company's accountant has adopted in allocating the initial capital investment and the overheads of the company.

Alternatively, therefore, it is suggested that if no new capital investment is called for, the assessment of the product's return should be in terms of the "contribution" which is being made (see below, under "Reviewing existing products," for a discussion of this term), or if fresh capital investment is required it should be in terms of the net cash flow (see Chapter 19). The executive should regularly review the contribution from the product, and a decline in contribution is an early warning of the time when the introduction of a new product will become necessary.

STRATEGY AND THE LIFE-CYCLE

As the product develops over its life-cycle, changes in strategy become necessary. Some of these changes are sufficiently common (but not universal) to justify special comment here.

When the product is launched, the company has usually spent heavily on development and perhaps on research also, and the future of the product is somewhat problematical. Capacity too may be relatively limited. In general this leads to the company seeking a relatively high price, which implies that it must find a market segment which obtains an appropriate benefit. (Other approaches are possible but rare in industrial marketing—this is discussed in Chapter 16.)

At the same time, the fact that the product is new implies ignorance at all levels in customer companies and perhaps even prejudice against the product. There is thus an educational task for the innovating company, through public relations (often very successful with new products), the sales and service force, and different forms of advertising and publicity. Sometimes, even before the product is formally on the market, it may be tested with customers, and the success of these tests may enable sales to be made to the "guinea-pigs" and provide information to help sell the product elsewhere.

As the sales rise and competitors follow with the same or similar products (as commonly happens unless effective patents or other barriers keep them out), prices may well fall in real terms.*

In certain types of product greater secondary differentiation develops and the combined effect of this and price decline is to aid the market expansion.

Promotional efforts tend to emphasize more the supplier or the supplier's brand, and the educational effort of the early phase fades away. The need for technical service may also be less as customers are now well informed about the product. Expansion of production capacity can run beyond the growth of the market as demand moves toward saturation, and product regeneration policies seek to maximize the market and to extend the product's life.

This is the point where an innovating firm may bring out a newer product. This further reduces the demand for the

---

* "In real terms" means after discounting the effect of any decline in the value of money which may have taken place. Here and elsewhere in this book, the term "price" or "price change" is to be interpreted in this way, unless the context makes it clear that the contrary is intended.

aging product and intensifies pressure on price. By this time there will often be greater standardization of product, or major buyers may determine their own specifications. It is sometimes said that at this stage the product tends to become like a "commodity," with customers buying against specifications and primarily interested in price. For some products this point is never reached, but the pressures are frequently in this direction. More firms may by now introduce new products and de-emphasize or withdraw the old one, but suppliers with low overheads may be inclined to continue even at low prices.

PRODUCT DECISIONS

If the view is accepted that for most products (except perhaps a favored and diminishing minority) the life-cycle is limited, then this has implications for management action.

Clearly, it is necessary to carry out a policy of planned readiness to introduce a new product as the old one becomes obsolete. In fact, a planned product policy will aim to achieve a balance between:

> Products in the pipeline of development;
> New products not yet making much contribution;
> Developing and mature products making the main con-tribution and carrying a deficiency on others; and
> Decaying products which are candidates for withdrawal from the range in the near future.

This is a planning task of no mean difficulty and a challenge to the skill of the manager. It requires forecasts of the length of cycle of the product to anticipate the date on which it will be timely to introduce the next new product. The profits of the company are maintained and expanded by in-troducing new products when the profits from the present ones decline, and this involves maintaining a sort of "product calen-dar" to show when new products must be ready. All departments are then geared to match their work with this requirement.

REVIEWING EXISTING PRODUCTS

Quite apart from developing new products, which is discussed in the next chapter, a successful product policy re-quires the regular and systematic review of existing products.

If the product is prospering, then it is necessary to consider whether it should be exploited more fully. If the product is not so successful, then the company may be concerned either to regenerate the product or to eliminate it.

With the prospering product, the company may wish to reinforce success by cultivating the present market more intensively, by exploiting those areas of the market which have unrealized potential, or by seeking new applications. This may require more active market research and market development work or modification of the product's secondary or tertiary characteristics to match a particular need. Inevitably there comes a stage where the regular financial analysis of product results shows that the return from some is beginning to flag. These products have survived the agonies of product launch and have been successful in the market; now comes the first hint that they will not be earning their keep much longer. Can such a product be regenerated and given a further boost to its sales and returns?

Clues that regeneration may be possible include such things as declining product sales when no more advanced product has entered the market and market research which indicates potential customers who, while apparently able to benefit from the product, are genuinely deterred by price or who find it in some ways unsatisfactory.

In such circumstances, there is a chance that the product may be given a further lease of profitable life. It may be modified, that is improved in a way which gives it a boost across the full span of the market, or it may be adapted, that is to say adjusted in a way which strengthens it in a particular market segment which is ripe for exploitation.

Regeneration can be achieved in a number of ways, separately or in combination. Market research clues may suggest ideas for improving the product for existing classes of customers or may identify areas for further exploitation. Ideas from an industrial designer have helped to revive sales for a fabricated product in a surprising way. Value analysis has an important role: it may show how costs can be reduced without loss of efficiency or appearance. Marketing should be represented on the value analysis team of the company to ensure that its discussions about the product focus on the customer's needs and that unnecessarily strict specifications or irrelevant features do not add to the product cost without adding meaningful customer benefits.

But product regeneration must be handled with care. It is not a substitute for new product policy, but a complement to it, and a company should plan and control product regeneration to ensure that it does not become a device for keeping in the range products which have become obsolete but which no one has had the courage to drop. This means having clear target figures in the market plan against which results can be checked.

This brings into focus the next major issue in product planning—the retirement of obsolescent products. This can be an issue which raises strong emotional reactions in a company. Whenever the suggestion is made to remove products from the line, there is almost always some objection, and dealing with this requires judgment, courage, and determination from management. It is remarkable how often when a company in difficulties is taken over by a successful bidder or when it calls in a "company doctor," one of his first steps is to eliminate lines of products which are offering little return. Obsolescent products distract executives and representatives from the profitable work of exploiting the worthwhile products and tie up capital and other resources which could well be spent on digging out new, better, and more profitable products.

The test of whether a product is to be kept in the range must, of course, depend very much on the financial return from it—not only today's return, but the return which is to be expected over the next few years. For most products, the starting point of the calculation is the "contribution" to overheads and profit which the product is making at present, or in the latest period for which figures are available. On this basis, and a realistic appreciation of trends in development, a view is formed of what is likely to be its contribution in the years ahead. The meaning of "contribution" is discussed below, and it is as well to make it quite clear that the contribution would not be so important if the question were one of *adding* new products or of incurring capital expenditure on current products. What is suggested here is that, in considering whether existing products should be kept in the range or dropped, the key financial calculation is the product's contribution. This figure is then to be interpreted by the executive responsible, who will also take account of other factors, such as the effect on other products in the line or range.

The product's contribution is defined as the difference between sales revenue from a product and those costs which arise from manufacturing and marketing the product and which would not arise if the product were dropped. These costs, if precisely calculated, would commonly include direct labor and materials, variable overheads, variable selling costs (salesmen's commission), and other variables such as royalties, stock-holding costs, and freight. They are sometimes called avoidable costs or out-of-pocket costs.[20]

In practice, some companies find it sufficient to approximate to the contribution by deducting from sales revenue only direct labor and materials. Other variables are small and often make little difference to the final decision after marketing "imponderables" have been taken into account.

It should be noted that for the purpose of calculating the contribution, general administrative overheads are not charged to each product.

If a whole line of products is under review, then sales, service, clerical, and administrative staff may be reduced if it is dropped. These costs accordingly become "avoidable" and are also deducted in arriving at the contribution. There may also be specific programed costs which are incurred for a particular line by management decision: attendance at an exhibition relevant to that line but not to others, literature, or market and product development costs.

Contribution is an important concept. It is referred to again in Chapter 15 and is considered in depth in more specialized textbooks.[21]

The example in Table 4 sets out details for an imaginary company manufacturing and marketing five products.

Table 4 Contribution by product

(1) PROD-UCT	(2) PRICE $	(3) UNIT SALES (x1000)	(4) REVENUE (x$1000)	(5) VARIABLE COSTS (x$1000)	(6) CONTRIBUTION (x$1000)	(7) RATIO*
A	288		1,440	1,080	360	0.25
B	216	6	1,296	480	816	0.63
C	192	3	576	360	216	0.37
D	144	5	720	600	120	0.17
E	144	2	288	360	−72	−0.25
		Total	4,320	2,880	1,440	0.33
		Less General overheads			960	
		Profit			480	

* Contribution as proportion of revenue (also sometimes described as price/volume or P/V ratio).

It will be seen that although A provides one-third of the revenue, its share of contribution is only 25 percent. B provides less than one-third of revenue but over half the contribution. Even for C, the contribution ratio is higher than it is for A. E is not covering its variable costs and its future comes into question. Even D is not doing well, and if the common method of allocating overheads in proportion to revenue had been adopted here, D would be showing a loss.

Several questions immediately suggest themselves. First,

can B be pushed more strongly and can resources allocated to other products be diverted to making and marketing it? This possibility should be explored. One word of caution is necessary. If a common facility used by several products creates a bottleneck, it may be necessary to consider contribution in relation to the use of that facility.

For example, if both A and B are made on the same machine, so that production of A competes with production of B, the position may then be as in Table 5.

Table 5 Comparative contribution and machine time

(1) PROD-UCT	(2) REVENUE PER TON*	(3) CON-TRIBUTION RATIO*	(4) CON-TRIBUTION PER TON†	(5) TIME TO PRODUCE 1 TON (UNITS)	(6) CON-TRIBUTION PER UNIT OF MACHINE TIME†
A	$288	0.25	$ 72	1	$72
B	216	0.63	136	2	67

*From Table 4.
†Col. (4) = col. (2) × col. (3).
  Col. (6) = col. (4) ÷ col. (5).

Clearly, unless and until this bottleneck is cleared, it will be worth pushing A rather than B, assuming this can be done without affecting price levels. This analysis should be extended to other products if scarce resource bottlenecks exist for these. In complex problems of this type, linear programing may help to find the best solution.

E is a strong candidate for phasing out (although some further comments are made later in this chapter). D is making a contribution to overheads, but a low one. If there is nothing else upon which the resources used for D can be employed, then on financial grounds alone D is worth keeping in the line. If it is dropped without a replacement, $120,000 in contribution is lost but general overheads are unchanged.

A company as a whole must, of course, cover its full overheads and yield a surplus if it is to trade and be profitable in the long run. If this is not happening, there are many other matters to be examined, such as the need to reduce costs or to identify and bring into the line more profitable products. When, however, the company is engaged on a systematic reexamination of its individual products and not actually contemplating additional investment, then the contribution is the item to be scrutinized. Where the contribution is negligible or nil, the first presumption is that the product should be phased out. Where the contribution is low, then the possibility of replacing it with more profitable products should be considered.

Under what circumstances should a product which is not expected to make a contribution be retained in the range? Clearly, if its contribution can be improved by regeneration or by some other means (perhaps by the simple process of raising the price!), then the product may be saved at least for the time being. Moreover, a new product will often not contribute at the beginning of its career, and this may have to be accepted for a while, if its future return has been assessed and will justify present losses.

The relationship between products in the same line needs consideration. These products may be competitive (if one is bought then another is not), they may be complementary (a buyer requiring one product is likely to require another), or they may be neutral. For example, different grades/sizes and finishes of photographic paper may be competitive up to a point, so long as a reasonable range is provided. In providing minor hand-tools a line may have to provide all sizes within certain limits in order to satisfy buyers.

These considerations must be evaluated and an attempt made to quantify them. A salesman may well be selling non-contributing products when he could be selling contributing ones (with little more effort). Every noncontributing product sold means that the other products must recover the resulting shortfall even *before anything is available toward overheads*, let alone profit. The difficulty is that salesmen's successes are generally measured by turnover, but marketing results should be measured on an operating basis by contribution and on the longer-term basis by profit.

The analysis can be carried further and contribution measured for different markets and different customers. It may be that a company is keeping a noncontributing product in its line to maintain the goodwill and therefore the business of a particular customer. Yet if that customer's entire business is examined, it may not produce a contribution.

If the salesman is provided with sufficient motivation and shown how other products will serve his customer better, he will often, when it comes to the crunch, be able to sell the new products to the customer. In one instance, a company ceased to manufacture certain products but continued to supply them by acting as a distributor for another supplier.

Finally, there is often one product in the line which makes no contribution but is supposed to support the company's image. If it does do this, any loss should be charged to the P.R.

budget and the P.R. man can then decide if it does support the image to a sufficient extent to justify this cost.

The analysis of contribution can, of course, be carried further and the contribution of different markets and different customers can also be examined. A noncontributing product may sometimes be justly regarded as an "investment" in long-term market or customer development. The danger is that this view may too easily be adopted as a way of avoiding unpalatable decisions. The marketing man should be cautious in the extreme about carrying products and customers which are making no contribution and from which none can be expected in the near future and none too keen on those making low contributions. The more poor relatives there are in the family, the harder do the other members have to work. The policy should be to ensure that the company devotes its resources to those products which, over their lifetime, give the best contribution, and that additions and deletions should work to this purpose.

Developing New Products

What is a new product? Newness is a relative term and it is as difficult to define the difference between a "new" product and a variation on an old one as it is to define the difference between hot and cold. The extremes are obvious, but there is no border line. Very few products represent a fundamental departure from the past. Perhaps the most substantial changes are exemplified by technological advances such as the development of the first wholly synthetic fibers, or of the transistor. From the customer's point of view, these largely represent better ways of doing something which has already been done before by offering improved or additional qualities. Nylon is a textile for the provision of apparel with its functions of warmth, propriety, and adornment, to mention one primary end-use. The transistor superseded the thermionic valve and made electronic equipment cheaper, compact, and more versatile, with advantages to ultimate users seeking to satisfy their needs for entertainment, for communication, and for more efficient industrial operation.

These new products represented major technological advances. Far more commonly, new products involve the use of established technological knowledge to produce a product which is new in the customer's terms. New models of typewriters over the years have offered additional or different features without a substantial change in the basic machine; even the biggest change, the electric typewriter, has not involved a technological advance comparable with those mentioned above. Nevertheless, to the customer it was a new product offering advantages not available before. It must also have involved the manufacturer in considerable development and production problems.

Many products are only minor variations of existing products to improve operational efficiency, to overcome difficulties which have been found in use, or to adapt for a new application. For example, a maker of a commercial vehicle might alter the type or location of switches or handles. Many companies would not regard minor variations as creating a new product and would delegate authority for them to a product manager or other appropriate middle executive. This is a convenient arrangement, although such delegation needs to be clearly defined and controlled.

Nevertheless, an attempt must be made to give at least a broad indication of what is implied by the concept of newness in the present discussions. A useful approach to this is suggested by the analysis of the product in the preceding chapter.

Firstly, any product with a basic core differing from those of established products in the company is new. In fact, this change in the core of the product concept is what is commonly implied by the term "diversification" in business discussions. The product is so different from existing products that it represents a change in the purpose of the company. Most companies certainly treat the introduction of a product with different primary characteristics as new, but there would probably be less agreement on whether this term should be applied to secondary variations. In companies where such changes involve considerable costs in capital investment, retraining staff, and so on, the safest policy is to treat secondary product variation as new product development and to handle it in accordance with the general company arrangements for new products.

Tertiary differentiation would not normally be regarded as new product introduction, and the authority to deal with these may be decentralized. However, it is essential that some record be kept of them, and some simplified basis for centralized approval should be adopted within the company. Moreover, if these small changes are not introduced in a coordinated way, there can be problems in keeping catalogs up to date, in ensuring that distributors have the right replacements, and so on. However, as long as these changes have been carefully checked, do not require significant capital expenditure, and have been the subject of proper interdepartmental consultation, the benefits to be obtained from more complex procedures are probably outweighed by the cost involved and the clogging of communication channels.

New products, for the purpose of this chapter, include products new to the company, although they may be already established in the market by another company. A company which for the first time brings out a product in the home market is referred to as an innovator, and the companies which follow it are imitators.

The fact that one company is already manufacturing and selling the product apparently successfully does not *necessarily* mean that another company which imitates it will be able to do the same. There may be differences between the skills or the established markets of the two companies which make the comparison a misleading one. Or it may be desirable for the imitator company to offer a product which incorporates advantages that the innovating company's product does not have. The role of an imitator can often be an advantageous one, particularly for the smaller firm, but it still requires management skill in its application.

THE BASIC APPROACH

How then is a businessman to devise and carry through successfully a policy of new product development?

Any systematic approach must have certain elements which have to be applied in different ways according to circumstances:

1 *Product guidelines.* A broad indication of the general class of products which is considered to be appropriate to the company's long-term strategy and present market situation.
2 *Search procedure.* Arrangements for the seeking of product ideas which are consistent with these guidelines.
3 *Screening and development procedure.* A formalized and controlled system by which ideas are developed, screened from time to time, and if found satisfactory carried forward until they are ultimately marketed.

PRODUCT GUIDELINES

If a company had to examine every possible product before it selected one, the problem of deciding which was the best product for it to launch would become impossible. So from the very beginning of thinking about new products, a company will find it necessary to indicate in broad terms those categories of products which have a reasonable probability of being suited to market needs and to its own capabilities in the years immediately ahead. This ensures that even at the earliest stage, when expenditure on the development of the product is lowest, time and money are allocated only to products which have some justification for consideration. Moreover, when the company is actively searching for new product ideas, the establishment of guidelines which answer the question "What sort of product are we seeking?" is essential to direct the executives concerned.

The use of product guidelines is sometimes criticized on the grounds that it may exclude products which the company could in fact market with success. This is possible, but it is unlikely if the guidelines are drawn up after careful study. Moreover, the object of new product development is not only to seek products which are profitable in themselves but to sort out the few which are the best, in terms of profit and risk, and which also contribute to the long-term development of the company.

The value of product guidelines is illustrated by the story of one group of companies in which it was customary to establish such guidelines for each member company. The objection that this unduly restricted these companies was met by allowing each managing director to spend up to a certain maximum sum annually on products of his own choosing outside the guidelines. Experience of these discretionary products was such that the authorized expenditure became known within the group as the "managing directors' folly."

The guidelines themselves must be consistent with the overall corporate strategy of the company concerned. This strategy is the starting point from which they are developed. They may be broad, leaving a wide field for exploration, or narrow and precise. Some companies have very strict and exact ideas of their product needs at a particular time, for example, when it is necessary to replace obsolete items in the product line. On other occasions the guidelines may be very wide because of difficulty in defining what precisely will be most compatible with the company's logical development. Wider guidelines permit more product ideas to qualify but consequently involve more cost in developing accepted ideas and in the stricter screening required later. The following paragraphs indicate some of the factors which may be relevant to the determination of product guidelines.

CORPORATE OBJECTIVES

The corporate objectives will have indicated what business the company wishes to be in and whether products are to be directed toward diversification or otherwise. They will also indicate the status which that company seeks to have within that industry—to emphasize innovation and pioneer new ideas, or to emphasize imitation and adapt existing ideas to limited segments of the market or to producing cheaper versions. If these points are not in corporate objectives, then they must be considered for the purpose of the guidelines.

MARKET CONSIDERATIONS

Even if it wishes to remain in the same business, the company may have reasons for wishing to develop certain markets and avoiding others. If present markets are growing and have much untapped potential, then the aim will be to exploit this opportunity. On the contrary, if the present market is unattractive, then the need to develop alternatives must be specified. One company which suffered severely from loss of markets when a major defense project was cancelled specified that, in order to spread its risk, new products should be suited to general industrial purposes rather than defense. Similarly, a company which has become heavily reliant upon one customer may seek products which will offset this.

Marketing skills will also be relevant to the specification of product guidelines. If the present sales force can carry more products without loss of effort on present lines, then it might be desired to develop products which are of interest to the company's present customers. The company may also have an image or name in the market which it is anxious to preserve or develop, and this may affect the view which it takes concerning the type of products it wants.

PRODUCTION CONSIDERATIONS

Here again many points may arise. Is the product to be based on the use of present skills and equipment? Or is the company keen to develop new skills? Is there some plant which is underutilized, the capacity of which the company should wish to exploit? Has it control over supplies of certain raw materials? Some companies are best able to produce standardized products which are made in bulk, others are by past skills and experience better placed to make smaller quantities to customer specification.

R&D FACTORS

Particular skill in certain aspects of R&D and a high efficiency in developing products of technical originality and sophistication within the field of their experience is another characteristic which it may be worthwhile exploiting. Another company had recently taken on a number of science graduates as part of its longer-term planning and was anxious to employ their skills at as early a date as possible. Other companies may have little skill in this field and may therefore be interested in products which have already had all the R&D problems solved, or in minor variations of these.

SERVICE CONSIDERATIONS

This is a consideration which has probably not been given all the attention in industrial marketing which it deserves. Some companies are, for reasons of location or of staff, particularly good at offering pre- and postsale technical service. They may therefore wish to build on this factor.

FINANCIAL AND RISK FACTORS

At this very early stage it is difficult to be precise in defining desirable risk levels and the financial return which is sought, for the simple reason that until some study has been given to the product, it is not normally possible to evaluate the risk involved and the return to be expected. Nevertheless, some companies indicate the turnover level which the product may be required to achieve. Large companies with heavy overheads may require a reasonable probability of achieving a certain minimum figure. A smaller company may set an upper limit in order to concentrate on markets in which larger companies are not likely to compete. Alternatively, the financial guidelines may set a limit on the amount of new capital investment required. Other companies require products which are patentable and therefore difficult for competitors to copy.

CONSIDERATIONS OF TIME

Sometimes a company—which has perhaps been slow to wake to the importance of product planning—may require new products urgently. With no time to develop a product, there is an immediate need for a ready-made product, perhaps through a licensing agreement for a product which is successfully marketed overseas. This may need to be backed up by the longer-term development of products for the future.

THE PRODUCT SEARCH

The product guidelines have now indicated the general class of product which is required and thus opened the way for a search for suitable products. The product search seeks to bring forward as many eligible products as possible so that, by a process of sifting, the best may be determined. Much of the searching is continuous, but sometimes this may be supplemented by intensified search in depth when circumstances require such action. In the latter case it is usual to take extra care to direct the search by specifying relatively narrow guidelines for the product sought.

The basic concept of marketing is that ideas come forward from insight into the market. This does not mean that the task of identifying new product possibilities can be put on the shoulders of the customer. The innovating company seeks to anticipate his needs. Nor does it exclude seeking ideas from other indirect sources and examining their suitability for the markets with which the company is concerned.

Many product ideas are devised from the study of evolutionary growth and change in the company's established markets and its natural extensions. Existing products are progressively modified to exploit technological advance, to meet changes in customers' markets, technology, and products, and to develop new applications. A somewhat different situation arises when a company seeks to change direction and switch from its traditional product mission because of prospective market decline.

In the evolutionary situation the company will look first to its contacts with the market for ideas about changing requirements: the sales force, the service force, formal market research, distributors, and others. Its internal departments—R&D, engineering, design—will be familiar with its market and contribute to the pool of ideas with suggestions arising from their own work. Indeed, ideas can come from employees at all levels.

However, no one organization can assume that its own staff will have the monopoly of ideas, and the search will extend outside the company, particularly when the guidelines stress diversification or change in the primary characteristics of the product. Nor is it easy to develop feasible ideas which match both the market and the company concerned. Trade and technical literature, scientific journals, research organizations, and universities will justify continuous attention. Patents, new and established, can be examined with a view to acquiring licenses, and the search can be extended overseas to the USA, Europe, the USSR, and Japan through specialized consultants.[22]

The search then produces a large number of product ideas—and it is surprising how many ideas can come forward from a conscientious search. But at this stage these are often no more than rather rudimentary concepts of what the products should offer. If they are more fully developed ideas from outside sources they may not be suited to the company's market and capabilities.

The concepts should be expressed as precisely and clearly as possible. From the point of view of the marketing man, the question "What is the primary additional benefit which we propose to offer to potential customers that they are not already enjoying?" should be clearly answered. Sometimes at this stage this may in fact be all there is of the product concept.

For example, a perfectly good product concept may be "A device to permit telephone operators to call numbers by pressing buttons rather than dialing and thus to increase the speed and accuracy at which numbers with many digits may be called." The concept may describe specific modifications of existing products: a variation of a lubricant or plastic to offer advantages under a certain range of conditions (for example, conditions of heat, cold, atmospheric pollution, or fungal growth), in certain markets or applications.

THE SCREENING PROCESS

Once a product concept has qualified by satisfying the guidelines, the company begins spending money and allocating resources to its development and examination. Yet at this stage it may have less than a 1 percent chance of becoming a successful product. The next steps are designed to build up information about the proposed product and use this information to decide whether or not to continue with it. Evidently, it is an advantage to eliminate unsuitable ideas as early as possible before any substantial expense has been involved.

The company has also to move from the concept to a fully developed product. There may be occasions when this is a simple task, as when the company plans to produce under license a product which has already proved itself elsewhere. There are, however, many occasions when the product has to go through stages of refining the concept, developing the specification, adding to its definition, and planning production and marketing. These can involve years of time and trouble.

The object of the screening process is to permit all these developments to take place in a controlled way. At certain predetermined stages in the development of the product, all the information must be brought together in order that a decision should be made about its future. This decision may be:

To authorize the commencement of the next stage of development;
To drop the product; or
To refer the product back for further consideration.

The number of times a product is screened during its development and the exact point at which those screens are inserted will vary with the type of business. The example below suggests four screenings, but it is clear that some companies operate with fewer, and other companies with more. More screenings are probably justified when development time is long and costs are high.

The process of screening is illustrated in Fig. 9, which also shows the two main lines of development: within the firm (perhaps involving R & D, production, engineering, and design) working on problems of developing the physical product, and in relation to the market obtaining information and planning marketing.

The four stages are:

1 Preliminary analysis.
2 Commercial analysis.
3 Development.
4 Testing.

PRELIMINARY ANALYSIS

The first stage is a brief and inexpensive review—"quick and dirty," as some executives prefer to describe it. The market assessment indicated is based on desk research, with perhaps some telephone inquiries among informed opinion. The object is to obtain a view on such points as:

How significant to the customers is the benefit offered by the proposed product?
Within what range is market size likely to be?
Is it growing/about the same/declining?
Is the market difficult to enter?
How quickly are competitors likely to copy the product?
What is the character, and what is the severity, of the competition?
Are customers likely to accept the new product quickly/hesitantly?
Can it be carried by our present sales force?

The production feasibility assessment will be similarly concerned with possibilities. Typical questions will be:

Is this consistent with our technical knowledge?
Can we develop an appropriate product to embody the concept?
Can we purchase the necessary raw materials or components?
Is this consistent with our labor skills?
Have we the appropriate type of fixed equipment?

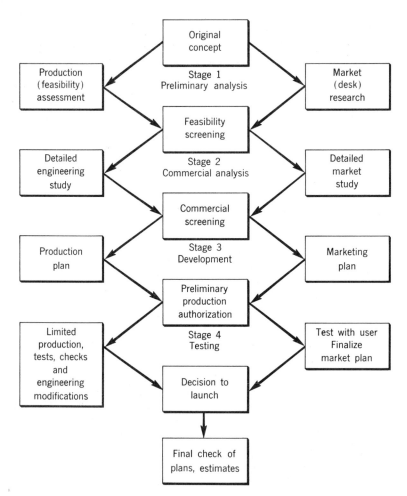

Fig. 9. Screening new products

These lists are illustrative and will differ from company to company.

One useful approach is to allocate scores to each of these items by subjective judgment. Each would be allocated as follows:

Highly unfavorable	−2
Unfavorable	−1
Neutral	0
Favorable	1
Highly favorable	2

A check list of the points considered relevant can be built up and by adaptation over time can become most valuable. The overall total scores for all the different items can be established and are an indicator of the merit of the product concept. Some of the items listed may be more important than others, and a weighting scheme is sometimes used. Several authors have recommended such schemes as this either for the preliminary analysis or in the commercial analysis stage.

The overall score is useful as a guide, but sometimes the information on a particular point will be such as to preclude the product completely, if, for example, it is likely to require an expertise which the company does not have and might find difficulty in obtaining.

Experience will show where the cutoff point between acceptable and nonacceptable ideas should be, and products falling below this will be excluded. Assuming that a satisfactory flow of initial product ideas has been achieved, as many as two-thirds of them may be eliminated at this stage.

COMMERCIAL ANALYSIS

Products which pass the first stage satisfactorily will now go forward for more detailed treatment, and the expenditure on them begins to mount sharply. This stage is one of the most important, and many companies may wish to subdivide it. The objective is to move from a concept of the product in broad terms to a fully developed and detailed specification, supported by forecasts of expenditure and revenue in considerable detail, an assessment of the risk involved, and a calculation of expected return on a discounted cash flow basis.

Market research has a very important task to perform here. It must evaluate the market, segment by segment, to produce a detailed "customer specification," setting out performance characteristics which this product should meet. By examining the value of the product to each segment, market research will prepare estimates of possible sales at different price levels. It must form an opinion of the speed at which demand is likely to build up and the possibility of competitors copying the product or reacting in some other way. A rough marketing plan may now be prepared, together with supporting costs.

Those responsible for production are also examining their problems, and preparing details of costs and investment requirements. Together with the marketing department's calculation, these are the basis for the view of expected commercial results on which authorization for the next stage is decided.

The number of products which reach this stage is now a modest figure—perhaps 10 to 15 percent of the number of starters. Many different departments of the company are now involved in some way or other. The production department is involved in the detailed plan of the process by which the product is to be made: blueprints are prepared, sources of supply for equipment, components, and raw materials are explored. Prototypes may now be produced. The marketing department develops its marketing plan, with literature and other promotional material being designed, arrangements for recruiting and training new salesmen or retraining existing salesmen, the training of servicemen, settling of discount arrangements, and the outlining of other marketing details. Careful management control is needed to ensure that this stage is completed smoothly and expeditiously.

By the end of this stage, the commercial assessment will be reviewed in the light of this considerable volume of work. Estimates are now much firmer.

The design of the product is now frozen, that is to say no material alteration can be introduced after this date (although engineering modifications are, of course, still possible). Freezing the design is an important step; instances have been reported where product development has dragged on interminably because there always seemed room for improvement. In one company, a certain product was first devised for mechanical operation, then electrical operation was considered better and seemed an idea worth adopting, until somebody else had the even better idea of an electronic product. After seven years there was still no new product, and the existing product was becoming increasingly obsolete and sales were sharply declining. This should be avoided by writing a freezing point into the product-planning system, after which point the product must stand or fall on its frozen merits. Further bright ideas can be the starting point for the next new product.

By the end of the development stage the field has narrowed considerably. In the next stage—that of testing—prototypes are tested and checked, and engineering modifications made. In consumer products this would be the point for test marketing. This is not normally possible for industrial goods, but at the preproduction stage it may be possible to place samples with users for field testing.

Following this stage, estimates and plans will be checked, and the decision whether or not to launch made. Sometimes this is a very gradual process. Phased marketing, whereby the most promising market sectors are attacked first and subsequent extension of the marketing program is based on review of results, leaves considerable flexibility in the hands of the marketing manager.

FOLLOW-UP

Systematic arrangements will be made for monitoring the sales and contribution from the product, so that any necessary action can be taken. This follow-up is important and an integral part of the job of new product development.

ORGANIZATION OF THE PRODUCT FUNCTION

The importance of product planning to the company as a whole needs little emphasis. Indeed, it is often in the long run the key factor in success or failure in industrial marketing. The right new product opens up new applications, new customers, new markets; the obsolete product loses them.

The life-cycle concept, discussed in Chapter 7, implies that a company must plan for its new products while current products are still prosperous and must try to foresee when current products will require replacement. There will be a timetable indicating approximately when such a product will be required.

Coordination and control are therefore essential, and a common device is to establish a special new product or product planning section, which is responsible for the entire product program of the company. In smaller companies the new product function may fall on the shoulders of one executive specially designated for this purpose. His task is to keep the range of products up to date by bringing in the new and dropping the obsolete. This is a high-level responsibility, and the location of this section is discussed more fully in Chapter 18.

For a major new product, once the preliminary stage of screening is complete, the actual process of development is controlled by a special task force (or working party or project team, according to the terminology preferred). This is responsible for screening at each stage and for authorizing budget and timetable for the next stage. The working party may vary in composition, with different departments being represented as the product progresses through the various stages. At first the product planning section may lead the working party, but as the final stages near, the product manager or other line executive will have increased responsibility and will take over when the working party is wound up.

9

Communication in Industrial Marketing

However good the product, however excellent the technical service, however prompt the delivery, the world outside the company will remain indifferent until these advantages are brought to its attention. And even when they are brought to the notice of prospect companies, their claims compete with a host of rival claims for the attention of busy executives. The average executive has an established set of ideas, knowledge, opinions, and prejudices which affect the way in which he will react to information put to him. The message must reach him with credibility and impact. It is not a passive supply of information but a force designed to modify his ways of thinking and behavior.

This is the task of communication. Communication for present purposes may be defined in the words of a well-known author on this subject as follows: "The word *communication* will be used here in a very broad sense to include all the procedures by which one mind may affect another."[23]

The term "communication" is not used at this stage just because it is more pretentious than such words as "promotion," "advertising," or "salesmanship." Its definition is more extensive than any one of these terms, and it opens up a wider range of possibilities for original thinking about how a company may put forward its ideas in the industrial market. There are very many media through which this can be done. Research and careful thinking may well produce an original, economical, and effective blend of communication techniques. Buying decision-makers and influences can build up their ideas about the company and what it has to offer and are influenced, logically or otherwise, by messages through all sorts of channels. It is easy to overlook some of these.

Personal representation is very often the centerpiece of the communication strategy, with other methods supporting it. These other methods seek to make personal selling more effective, efficient, and economical.

The concept advanced here is one of a total communication strategy, designed not only to provide a natural path to sales, but to help the customer make the right purchase, obtain full benefit from his purchase, and to develop and nurture an enduring relationship between supplier and customer.

DEVELOPING COMMUNICATION OBJECTIVES

General objectives will often flow in a straightforward way from a clearly defined strategy. They will be subordinate to marketing objectives and perhaps limited by the resources which the company is able to devote to communication.

If a campaign is concerned with introducing certain new products, then the communication objectives must be directed toward executives concerned with decisions of this nature. It will be designed to bring home the limitations of existing arrangements and to educate them in the benefits the new product offers. It must also, at appropriate stages, educate them in the use of the product and help overcome the problems of initial adoption and installation. Later, as the product matures, emphasis may well switch to unexploited opportunities in new markets and new applications and may give more weight to increasing company or brand awareness.

In the short term, general objectives may include:

Developing a new application.
Introducing a new product.
Widening the market for existing products.
Exploiting seasonal or other short-term possibilities.
Promoting inquiries and creating interest.
Reminding to buy, stock, and use.

Medium-term objectives are:

Developing understanding of the problems which the product aims to solve.
Educating customer's staff to get full benefit from the

product (by using it efficiently or by utilizing its advantages to promote sales to indirect customers).
Correcting false impressions.
Building more sales by wider usage.
Strengthening links with customers.

In the long term, primary objectives could be:

Projecting the company's image.
Strengthening links with customers which will resist minor inducements from competitors.

But before an advertisement is inserted in the press, or mail sent out, or a salesman calls, four basic questions must be answered:

1 To whom shall we communicate?
2 What is the general sense of our message to be?
3 Through what channels (media) shall the message be conveyed?
4 With what frequency, magnitude, and timing?

The company can communicate with the market in many ways. The range and subtlety is such that a full consideration of the communication possibilities and their interrelation in a particular marketing situation is a very time-consuming operation. But care spent on planning—if time permits—is well worthwhile. After careful research and thought about the possibilities of different media in relation to the different targets for the company's communications, ingenious and original approaches can often achieve surprising results for relatively modest expenditure. Whereas in the consumer field the marketing man is generally at work on a large canvas with a broad brush, the industrial marketing man is frequently working like a miniaturist with tiny painstaking strokes on a small area. His target may be only one firm, but the buying decision may result from pressures from numerous people, and to achieve the required total effect sought, each of these may require a number of communications, differing in nature over time and coming through different channels.

In first approaching the development of total communication strategy, it is desirable to leave on one side specific questions such as "How shall the sales presentation be made?" or "What is the role of advertising?" and to determine the general purpose of communication in relation to the different categories of people making and influencing the buying decision.

The role of personal communication is almost always highly important in industrial marketing, but it is one ingredient of a series of interwoven communications to people inside and outside the companies in the target market.

For the purpose of the current analysis, general communication theory may be adapted to the following plan:

1 The *information source* which selects a desired message.
2 The *transmitter* which changes the message into a signal.
3 The *communication channel* which carries the signal.
4 The *receiver* which turns the signal back into a message.
5 The *destination* (or audience) for which the message is intended.

The selection of the message and the destination is the responsibility of the marketing department. The marketing manager may decide that he wishes architects to be informed about a new product and will decide which points must be put over. The advertising agency, or perhaps the company's own specialist, is responsible for the signal, that is to say, for the copy for the advertisement and generally also for the choice of channel (for example, the journal in which the advertisement is inserted). In practice, of course, there will be interchange of ideas, but the underlying logic of the relationship is clear. The signal is received by the readers of the journal—the architects—who in due course should turn it into a message to their clients in the form of a recommendation or specification of the product. The receiver and destination may often be the same group.

In communication theory, there are three levels at which one may consider the communication problem:[24]

Level A: How accurately can the symbols of communication be transmitted?
Level B: How precisely do the transmitted symbols convey the desired meaning?
Level C: How effectively does the received meaning affect conduct in the desired way?

The level A problem is the technical problem which the marketing executive must often take as outside his province, except that it may influence his choice of media. He is concerned with Level B (for example, he trains salesmen to efficiency as communicators), and above all with Level C. To this he adds concern for the cost. He has choice of combining a number of channels for his different purposes, and each combination has its own cost and its own effectiveness.

This is not intended to be an account of the theory of communication, and the reader is advised against interpreting it as such. Nevertheless, it is a helpful way in which to see the role of the various elements in marketing communication.

In communication theory, "noise" distorts or confuses the communication. In marketing, the channel or medium can itself have an effect on the signals on their way to the receiver. Some channels are suitable for certain types of marketing communication because they reinforce the authority and credibility of a message; other channels have the reverse effect.

Finally, it is as well to remember that the market receives information about a company from third parties—competitors, for example! Work which has been carried out among farmers and physicians reveals that there are reference groups of individuals who are widely regarded as leaders in their calling and whose views carry special authority among their colleagues. It is hard to say how common this phenomenon is, but where it exists it offers an interesting opportunity for a special angle in marketing strategy.

CHOOSING THE TARGET

The first question is simply "To whom is the communication to be addressed?" In Chapter 2, the process of making the buying decision was considered and the range of decision-makers and decision influences was discussed. The question is therefore partly answered already. The communication is with those who will decide or can influence the decision.

Sometimes there may be a very large number of people involved, each with the same role (as users, for example), or a large number of categories of people with different roles (buyers, specifiers, and so on). Role differences arise because the individuals concerned have different degrees of authority in the decision-making process; they may apply different criteria and may be accessible through different communication channels.

Consider the case of a company making a component. Its market for this component is (say) ten original equipment-makers (OEM's). In each of these companies, the number of people concerned with the initial buying decision in an official sense may be eight to ten: buyers, accountants, technicians, policy-makers. In addition, there could be a larger number unofficially concerned, including perhaps foremen and people on the shop floor. Each of these customers sells its equipment in turn to other companies, who are indirect customers for the component manufacturer.

What possible lines of action are open to the component manufacturer? He may:

1 Communicate with the original equipment manufacturer.
2 Communicate with the indirect customer as well as the OEM.

If he adopts the first possibility, he must decide who are the target employees in the companies concerned. (It is assumed that the planning process has already determined the market or segment at which the company is aiming.)

His object is to achieve maximum leverage from the communication expenditure, that is to say, the most favorable relationship between the cost of promotion and the benefit accruing from it. One way of approaching this is to identify key targets, people who have decisive influence in the final buying decision. A key target is not easy to identify. The test is the importance of the individual's role in the buying decision. This influence may derive from formal authority or from the logic of circumstances, as for example when shop-floor workers resist using a particular product. Influence may also be external to the company (for example factory inspectorate, political and public opinion, and trade unions).

The concept of a *key* target audience is often a useful one in ensuring that a communication campaign is effectively aimed. A key target audience is a group whose views predominate over those of others in making a buying decision. Such predominance can come from:

Formal authority, generally in a line capacity, perhaps as director or senior manager.
Specialized knowledge, such as may be exercised by a technologist in specifying a product or the expertise of a commodity buyer on price movements.
The logic of circumstances, as already described.

Key targets may sometimes be outside a company; the authority of an official inspectorate is an example. They may also change from time to time; as one group accepts a product or company, another group which is not yet "sold" may move into a key role. For example, the OEM mentioned above begins to use the component, and his sales force may have to offer equipment incorporating the new component side by side with the equipment incorporating the former and established component. Sales of the new component may depend on how well the OEM's salesmen do their job, and this may depend on whether they are fully briefed on the new component and have confidence in it. Thus the OEM's salesmen may become a key audience.

The original manufacturer may, however, find little reaction to his direct appeal to the OEM until he has created acceptance among end-users. He may therefore decide to put the emphasis of his campaign on "back-selling."

Sometimes it is possible to identify points of support and of resistance. A product may offer advantages attractive to one group of executives—for example, packaging which adds appeal may attract marketing executives—and this can be capitalized in promotion. Conversely, there may be points of resistance—perhaps from specialists who feel that the use of a new product may harm their status—and this may need attention.

The cost and availability of communication channels is also a relevant consideration. It might be desirable to communicate with all the millions of final consumers, but the cost can be prohibitive. In that case, a possible strategy involves communicating with the executives within the original equipment manufacturer's staff, and points of support may be found in the sales and marketing departments.

Perhaps it is possible to summarize the factors in the choice of key targets as follows:

1 The influence of the target group concerned in supporting or resisting a favorable buying decision.
2 Their present knowledge and attitudes and the extent to which these require modifying to produce the desired buying behavior.
3 The probability that they can be inspired to favor the product, bearing in mind:
   (a) their degree of commitment to other products/suppliers;
   (b) the benefit which is being offered.
4 The cost and feasibility of communicating with them with credibility and impact.

During the development of the communication campaign, the emphasis may shift from one target to another. First it may be necessary to persuade top management that there is a problem to be solved, then to show the technical specifier that the particular product is technically able to solve the problem, and so on. Any analysis of the market is something which is not static but is shifting as the market situation varies and as competitors react.

THE CHOICE OF MESSAGE

An approach to this aspect of communication policy can be adapted from the principles of a well-known book on advertising by R. H. Colley, [25] who writes:

> All commercial communications that aim at the ultimate objective of a sale must carry a prospective through four levels of understanding—from unawareness to:
>
> *Awareness* The prospect must first be aware of the existence of a brand or a company.
> *Comprehension* He must have a comprehension of what the product is and will do for him.
> *Conviction* He must arrive at a mental disposition or conviction to buy the product.
> *Action* Finally he must stir himself to action.
>
> This formula, perhaps in different words, is as old as advertising, selling, and other forms of persuasive communication.

It has sometimes been suggested that for many purposes of consumer marketing this procedure is too logical, and that there are other routes by which the consumer arrives at the action point. This question is outside the present field. In industrial marketing, it is certainly helpful to widen the analysis quoted above. It is rare, for example, in Britain for a domestic company to be completely unknown. Frequently, however, it may not be sufficiently well known that the company manufactures certain lines of products, or it may not be known or appreciated that the product is capable of use for certain purposes.

A product may claim to solve a problem, but customer executives may not even be aware that the problem matters. For example, they may never have thought about the effect of noise on efficiency and the loss which it might involve, yet an understanding of this may be a prerequisite of purchasing products which deaden noise.

Market ignorance may be of a large number of different things:

The company which is marketing the product.
The need that the product aims to meet.
The existence of the product.

The fact that the company makes the product.
Applications for the product within the prospect company.
How the product is used to best advantage.

But if ignorance of these matters gives a zero score, existing attitudes can sometimes justify negative scores. Having become aware, perhaps only somewhat vaguely, of the product and of what it offers, executives may have overrated the problems and difficulties of obtaining the benefits of the product, or have wrongly assessed those benefits in relation to those of competing products, or they may wrongly consider that the benefits are insufficient to justify the cost and financial risk implications of using the product. Thus at any point of time the marketing man may be faced with a set of existing attitudes in his audiences. Yet each of these audiences has a part in the complex procedure determining the purchase of the product. To play that part in a proper way, each must have the "right" information and the "right" attitude. What "right" means has to be determined by the marketing executive from knowledge of how the buying decision is made.

The task of persuasive communication is to shift these individuals from their present knowledge and attitudes to the right ones—those appropriate to the buying behavior sought.

This may involve one step only, for example a mail shot to small builders with an offer on special terms of some well-known item of equipment. More commonly, there is a series of steps to carry the target audience to the requisite state of mind. Consider the example of an imaginary new product to control or reduce noise in factories. One decision-making group is the directors of companies engaged in an identified noisy industry. Information gathered prior to the campaign indicates that few of this group are aware that this is a problem deserving consideration, and fewer still have heard of the product. If they become aware of the problem, it is likely that they may find it hard to appreciate that it has the substantial effects on productivity which the suppliers of the product claim.

The first step must be to bring home the basic problem and its economic implications. This may require a campaign of an educational nature directed to this group and to informed opinion generally. Secondly, gradually developing in emphasis, the work of XYZ Inc. in this field is to be brought out. Thirdly, the campaign is to show the value of XYZ's new product in reducing noise and finally to win approval of a study of the costs and benefits through a survey of the plan of specific customers.

It may be objected that not all directors in the target

market segment will have the same attitudes and ideas. This is true. If it were possible to quantity precisely, one would like to specify as in Table 6.

Table 6 Attitudes of directors/senior executives in target industries

	PRESENT ATTITUDE	REQUIRED ATTITUDE*
Aware of problem	10%	75%
Aware of XYZ's work	8	60
Aware of XYZ's product	5	50
Would approve survey by XYZ	4	40
Could be expected to approve installation after survey	?	20

*This is the target to be achieved at the end of the campaign.

Similar analyses are desirable for other buying influences.

It may be premature to expect that as fully quantified an approach as this can often be obtained at present. Discussion shows that some approximation to this principle increasingly underlies many efficient approaches to marketing communication.

CHANNELS OF COMMUNICATION

Clearly the development of the necessary attitudes and understanding can be a substantial task. To carry it out, the industrial marketing man has a rich variety of communication channels available to him. Very rarely will any one channel be used to the exclusion of all others. It will be necessary to use a variety of channels not only because of the different decision-makers and influences who have to be contacted, but because frequently it will be advantageous to address the same group of individuals through different channels. The different channels have a different quality of impact, and thus will reinforce each other, and the variety of approaches will give a freshness to the message.

The *total* concept of communication which is here advanced is designed not only to promote sales in the limited sense, but, applying the service concept of Chapter 1, to help the customer to benefit from his purchase and thus repurchase the same and other products from the company.

A company is constantly communicating with its market in a wide variety of ways, if communication is used to refer not only to an oral or written message in its everyday sense, but to any symbol or act of behavior from which the market may draw inferences about the company or its products, or its service, or any other matter relating to it. Some of the communications which pass between the firm and the market are never consciously considered as having marketing implications by the originating company. Yet they may well have such an effect, if not in the short term, then cumulatively over time. Under the total communication concept, the company aims to bring all its communications under conscious control, to organize them so that they are mutually reinforcing and to ensure that all messages shall be consistent with the marketing needs of the company—or at least not antagonistic to them!

The following list of possible channels is reasonably comprehensive. Some are obviously particularly suited to the short- and medium-term objectives of the company. Others are appropriate to the longer-term objective of projecting the company image. Not all are relevant to every firm. This list is essentially a check list to ensure that no possible approach is omitted from consideration.

Check list of communications channels

Personal communication:	Sales force and technical representatives.
	High-level contacts.
	Technical service force.
	Switchboard operators.
	Distributor sales force.
	Customer sales force.
Media advertising:	Television.
	General press.
	Trade and technical press.
	Direct mail, including letter writing.
Literature:	Sales literature.
	Technical literature and reference material.
	Price lists and catalogs.
	Calendars and diaries.
	External house journal (prestige or technological).
Exhibitions and similar occasions:	Trade exhibitions.
	Distributor-sponsored exhibitions.
	Company exhibitions.
	Demonstration visits to company plant and laboratories.
	Demonstration visits to user/customer plant.
	Films.
The product:	Physical appearance.
	Name.
	Packaging and labeling.

Public relations:	Press releases and relations.
	Speeches and writings by company executives.
	Symposia and seminars.
Background material:	Company's name.
	Letter-heading.
	Vans.
	Staff uniforms.

The roles of the main channels are discussed in later chapters. It will be noted that this list includes more than is commonly included in the promotional approach to marketing communication. It aims to include virtually all the company-controlled sources from which inferences may be drawn, in accordance with the definition of communication adopted. Some of the items listed may be regarded as more important in consumer than in industrial marketing. For example, the name of the product, the design of the pack, the name of the company, and the appearance of the product are frequently regarded as having implications only in consumer marketing. Nevertheless, there have been occasions when each of these has had an important role in the industrial field.

A product designed to be used as a material in putty manufacture was developed on the basis of polybutadiene rubber. Experience with the product has been described as follows:

> To say that we met sales resistance from putty manufacturers is an understatement. Many, even the biggest manufacturers, told us our putty was no good and they had no intention of changing their formulations which had remained unaltered since great-grandfather started the business.
>
> So, once again, we decided that marketing and technical pressure must be kept up in order to bring this project to a profitable conclusion. It was now realized that maybe the thought of incorporating a "rubber" was not acceptable to the putty manufacturer. "Rubber" is an unfortunate word to use in many contexts since the layman thinks of it in terms of an elastic insoluble black lump. Rubber to the putty manufacturer also meant "Thiokol" which was expensive or "Butyl" which gave very difficult mixing and a tough unworkable putty. Our new approach was to sell an oil-modified polybutadiene in attractive kegs and call it Unipol 31. In this form it did not resemble rubber. The material eased many of the mixing problems of the putty manufacturer. Unipol 31 in this form has attracted quite a demand. . . .[26]

Because communication is concerned with the effective use of the product, it is often helpful to include instructions on or enclosed with the pack. This particularly concerns minor maintenance goods which may be used by inexperienced workers. Packaging can assist ease of identification by the storeman, thus facilitating the use of the product and consequently helping sales. In an experiment in the USA products normally enclosed in brown kraft cartons were sent in white packs. It was found that this resulted in greater care in handling and unpacking.[27] These matters may sound trivial. It is, however, often difficult to put one's finger on all the factors which influence sales. Attention to these small matters will often cost relatively little and may make that slight difference in securing useful marginal sales. They reinforce main selling tools, or at least do not run counter to them, as they may do if neglected.

THE COMPANY IMAGE

Many of the tools of marketing communication are passive rather than active in relation to the marketing process. That is to say, they are not directly concerned with influencing buying behavior in relation to specific purchases but provide a background against which the more active tools of advertising, sales promotion, and personal selling can positively motivate buyers and users. What is active and what is passive can vary, and it is sometimes possible to convert a tool which is commonly passive to an active role in a particular set of circumstances. Such matters as the company's letter-heading, its vans, and certain types of press work (to quote a few examples) are commonly background communications to the company's general public relations concern with the image of the company.

The word image occurs often in marketing discussions. It has been defined as the complex of "knowledge, feelings, ideas and beliefs" about a company which are commonly associated with its name in the minds of customers or other groups of individuals.[28] It is the personality which the company is seen to possess. Different groups of individuals may have different images for the same company; buyers, the trade unions, the government, all may see the company in different ways from each other. It can affect the relationship between employees and management, the ability of the company to attract the right type and quality of recruits, and it may even have political significance and affect the company's valuation on the stock market.

Levitt[29] has indicated in an experiment carried out on purchasing executives and others how the reaction to a salesman's presentation can be influenced by these initial ideas about a company, a favorable image creating a more receptive customer. The same experiment also indicated that this advantage could be lost if the salesman's presentation was poor. This example not only illustrates the benefit of a good image, but also the importance of integrating all aspects of the company's communications scheme into an efficient whole.

SUMMARY

In concluding this section, it may be useful to recapitulate the series of steps which it is suggested is likely to be appropriate in developing both communication objectives and specific communications. The model is this:

1 Marketing strategy and selection of market target.
2 Derived broad communication objectives.
3 Schedule of groups who make or influence the buying decision, with particular identification of key groups.
4 Schedule of current attitudes and knowledge.
5 Schedule of attitudes and knowledge appropriate to the "right" decision.
6 Choice of desirable and feasible communication targets.
7 Specification of steps in communication campaign by which (6) is to be achieved.
8 Choice of channels (media) and identification of interrelation.
9 Determination of message, timing, channel, target interrelationships.
10 Turning the message into a signal (e.g., writing the copy).
11 Transmitting the signal (e.g., having the advertisement published).
12 Review of results.

Although this order seems the logical one, there will be feedback at some stages. When channels are examined and costed at (8), it may be found that targets at (6) are too ambitious. Cost and effectiveness must also be assessed, and it is worth noting that it is generally cheaper to maintain than to establish knowledge and attitudes.

Throughout, one is not dealing in general with exact figures. What is being sought is to raise the probability of purchase (or other appropriate action).

It is sometimes convenient to divide the campaign into two parts: the preparatory promotion campaign, primarily through impersonal media, and the selling or negotiating campaign, involving face-to-face communication by personal representatives with prospect companies. This is generally convenient, provided the overall interrelationship is not forgotten and is reflected in the planning arrangements.

Finally, the possible reaction of competitors must be assessed. This can sometimes be beneficial. For example, when there is widespread ignorance about a product, informative communication by several firms can expand the total market. This may happen through a joint trade promotion or can come about by normal competitive action at the early stage of a product's life-cycle. At later stages, as specifiers and others are well informed on the product, customary brand or company competition takes over.

10

Personal Representation

Personal representation is a key area in industrial marketing. The heading "personal representation" is preferred to "selling" or "salesmanship" because it emphasizes the wide range of face-to-face communication between supplier and customer, and the fact that this relationship usually involves much more than achieving a sale in the short term. It often involves cementing and maintaining a long-term relationship between the two parties, and the representative who forgets that his object is to serve the customer may well harm a relationship which can be as valuable an asset to his firm as a major item of capital equipment.

The term also emphasizes the fact that to the customer the salesman is often the representative of the supplying company in a very full sense. He is the prime contact between his firm and the customer—sometimes almost the only one—and he is apt to be charged with the faults of the company, and the company with the faults of the representative. The actual placing of some orders is not through the salesman at all, but by phone or by post. However, if the company has done its marketing correctly, and the salesman his work to the same standard, then the actual order which follows is a direct consequence of these efforts.

THE VARIETY OF REPRESENTATION

There are some situations in industrial marketing where a *formal* sales force is only part of a wider network of personal communication between the two companies. This applies particularly where the purchase of the product has implications of product complexity and commercial risk for the buying company. New and additional capital equipment can involve not only heavy expenditure, but a change in the way in which the company operates. It may mean replanning production, retaining staff (perhaps making some present skills obsolete), even reorganizing the management structure. Something similar may be involved when a component which represents an important technological advance is to be adopted as standard by an original equipment manufacturer.

This is the total involvement section of Fig. 2 (see Chapter 2 under "Making the buying decision"). These purchases imply high cost, high risk, and high innovation. There are therefore many people involved in the buying decision, many questions raised, and many problems to be solved. The product will require careful adaptation to match the buying company's vector of needs, and ample service will need to accompany it. Selling and marketing become fused together. At appropriate stages in the negotiations, many different members of the staff of the supplying company will make contact with their opposite numbers in the prospect company.

At the other extreme is the salesman who calls on many customers to make small sales of a standardized product, for example a man calling on small builders to sell paint brushes. Here the product and its brand name are well known, the sum involved in the average purchase is modest, no service is required, and the degree of innovation and risk to the purchaser is nil. The time required to complete the sale is small, there will be only one person involved in the buying decision, and he meets only one salesman from the company for a short period.

It is not hard to identify circumstances which are different again from both of these—the representative calling on architects to seek specification of a product, or calling on retail shops to seek the right to survey and bid for an illuminated sign. In neither case does the sale *automatically* follow from the call, but in both the representative's task is an essential prerequisite to securing the order, and the link is close.

With this range of circumstances, there corresponds a range of titles for the man whose prime job it is to be responsible for commercial contacts with the customer: salesman, sales engineer, technical representative, marketing engineer, account executive, and others. Each company must analyze its own particular market to decide the role of the sales force and the key ingredients to success in building sales. This determines the type of individual required for the job, and what his technical knowledge, intellectual ability, and general background must be in order to carry out his task effectively. The cost of the representative must also be consistent with the amount of business he can be expected to generate.

Personal selling is in many ways the most efficient, and certainly the most flexible, of the means of communication available to the industrial marketing manager. The salesman can and often must help the buyer and other executives of the prospect company to clarify their problems, and from the armory of products and services which his company has to offer he can identify that combination which most aptly meets the needs of the customer. He can adjust the appeals which he makes to the problems of the company he is dealing with and to the personal attitudes of the people he is meeting. He can identify not only the present needs of his customers, but will seek to anticipate future needs and when they will arise. As a result, he will plan to call on the customer at the right time and feed back information to his own company to assist in the development of new products to satisfy the needs which, from his observation, he anticipates will emerge in the future.

Representatives are, however, expensive. At the time of writing the salary, and commission where paid, of industrial representatives working in the home market varies from an upper level above $9,600, for a senior representative selling technical products, to something not far short of $3,600 for representatives selling simple standardized products. In addition to this is the cost of pension and other benefits, and of traveling and expenses. These can add as much again to the cost of the salesman to his employer. Finally, there are the overhead costs of managing, training, and administering the sales force.

THE JOB OF THE SALESMAN

Like the other members of the staff of the company, the representative should have a written job description which will make clear what he is supposed to do, to whom he is responsible, and the extent of his own authority. While the nature of his job may at first sight seem self-evident, there are a large number of details which need specifying. For example, what is the responsibility of the salesman in such things as credit control, prospecting, service, dealing with complaints, making returns to head office, collecting market intelligence, and so on? Many of these points are not always sharply defined, and by default may not receive the attention they deserve, or may receive too much, so that other matters are neglected.

The basis of the job description is an analysis of what

it is the salesman has to do in the course of his duties and his relationship with the rest of the company's organization. Commonly such factors as the following will be covered in the course of this analysis:

Basic sales function
Classes of products to be sold.
Classes of companies to be called upon.
People to be seen (functions, knowledge, status, whether individual or group presentations).
Nature of "sale" (e.g., is it a straight sale, request for survey, specification, negotiations?).
Degree of authority with salesman (may he vary price or agree allowances for below-standard products?).
Assistance to distributors.

Technical functions
Keeping customers informed of new products.
Assisting customers to define requirements (e.g., by survey).
After-sales service: to what extent does the salesman need to analyze technical problems himself and perhaps make minor adjustments?
Training and instructing customer's staff.

Commercial functions
Collecting market intelligence on customer plans and competitors' actions.
Identifying need for new or improved products.
Checking credit status.
Planning or recommending marketing action within his territory.
Attending exhibitions, tying in mail shots, organizing film shows, seminars.

Administrative responsibilities
Filling out orders.
Keeping records and submitting returns.
Training new representatives.
Planning his activities for coverage of territory.
Requesting specialized service for customers.

Preparing a job description for the sales force requires a careful scrutiny of what is done and what should be done. It will be carried out in consultation with the sales force, but it may be worth seeking specialized advice so that the analysis is objective and not restricted by preconceived ideas. Once the analysis is complete, it should lead on to a written description of the job. From this follows the specification of the man to fill the job: what specialized knowledge, intellectual qualities, emotional and physical requirements, education (both general and vocational), and experience are required? What age, family, background, mobility are preferred? In selling, personal qualities are of great importance, and the individual's own motivation and commercial attitude, enthusiasm, and determination are key requirements.

In most industrial marketing situations, four considerations come to the front in the work of the representative. These may be described as:

1 Selling skill.
2 Diagnostic skill.
3 Technical background.
4 Organizing ability.

Selling skills have not always been regarded as important by many companies concerned with industrial marketing in Britain. This point of view has been consistent with a general attitude toward marketing which is now at last passing. There is increasing awareness of the value of skills in understanding and dealing with people which lead to efficient, economical, and successful selling. This may sometimes need to be supported by some technical background, although often the value of technical knowledge has been overrated and the value of sales ability underrated. Sometimes new men, less talented technically but better equipped in selling skills, have moved products which the existing sales force had found hard to sell. Even in high-level selling, when director meets director, or a group of executives negotiate around a table, a key factor in success is the ability to understand the natural human reactions of the man on the other side and to match arguments and presentation to them.

Diagnostic skill is the ability of the representative to assist the customer in identifying and analyzing his problems more sharply, so that suitable products may be recommended. In many cases the customer himself may not have identified the problems clearly and sharply or may even have misunderstood them. The representative may carry out a survey to identify the customer's needs for his products and to recommend what grades, qualities, or types of product should be used. Often this will show how a more advanced or better selected product will give greater efficiency. The analysis may go further and identify trends in the customer's market and anticipate the nature of his market requirements in the future. If the salesman passes the information back to his company, it will help in the identification of new products. The salesman's diagnostic skill may often be the trigger which sets the buying–decision-making wheels in motion in the prospect firm and improves the match between what the customer wants and what the firm offers.

The need for technical background in selling some

products is self-evident. This may not mean that every man in the sales force needs to meet this requirement. It may be that there should be different classes of representative with different levels of skill and that technical support should be available on request.

The need for technical skill takes many forms. It may be part of the diagnosis which permits the salesman to make the correct prescription. Where products are made or modified to individual customers' needs, the salesman must work with the customer's technicians to determine the specification. The technical ability required will aim to assist the customer in getting the full benefit from his product and will often be different in orientation from that of the technician employed elsewhere in the company.

A product which is complex to design and make is not always technically complex to sell, install, and use. The representative's requirement for technical knowledge needs sharp identification.

Finally, administrative and organizational ability is necessary. The representative must be aware that his time is expensive and aware of the need to organize his work to ensure proper contact with his customers and economic use of his time. Even the less well paid, making regular calls on customers in a market where most orders are small, must plan to maximize call time and reduce traveling time. He must ensure that the time in social exchanges is not disproportionate and must make proper reports and keep efficient records.

SELECTION

Selection is a matter of finding the right man to match the specification. When the emphasis is on personal characteristics, the task of finding the right man is difficult enough, but when it requires both selling potential and some technical background it is even more difficult.

Applications may be sought from outside the company through the general or technical press. Where a specific technical qualification is necessary, professional societies may circulate vacancy notices to their members. Many companies welcome applications from salesmen of competitors, distributors, or other companies selling to the same market. There also seems to be increasing interest in recruiting salesmen who have been trained by well-known consumer-goods manufacturers, and this seems a reasonable step where empathy is the key to sales success.

Junior salesmen are often recruited from within the company. Some firms who consider they require technical background rather than technical expertise seek men who, after starting technical training, have felt the appeal of a commercial career. These can have sufficient technical knowledge plus the necessary personal qualities.

In industries where the technical content of the sale is high, it will often be necessary to recruit men from outside with a degree or other appropriate qualification and to train them for the sales force. Not every man has the potential to become a good salesman, any more than everyone is suited for accountancy or law. It is important that the individual concerned is keen to sell and suited to sell. He must be commercially minded and adept at understanding and dealing with people. Sometimes a suitable man too young to enter the sales force may be taken on and employed in some other capacity before becoming a salesman. This can be a useful device to match personal qualities with the necessary background. In larger companies, sales force recruitment is regarded as a continuous process and the company is always interested in suitable applicants, even though there is no current vacancy.

The personal qualities needed in selling are difficult to assess, and whereas for many occupations selection is largely by selection tests, in industrial selling such tests are rarely used. The interview as a method of selection is more justified in selling than in other occupations, for the interview situation is, in fact, the one in which the prospective candidate will work. Selling himself is the first part of the total job of making a sale, and this is a skill which should be shown at an interview. It is also an opportunity to explore the value of his previous experience and to check his qualifications for the post. There are both good and bad interviewing, and any executive who undertakes the responsibility of selection by this method should ensure that he is well acquainted with the principles of interviewing.

Most companies require two interviews: a preliminary short-listing by a middle manager (perhaps the field sales manager in the area concerned); then, for those short-listed, a second interview at a more senior level. Some companies require more than two interviews.

While the development of selection tests for industrial salesmen is still in its infancy, there are signs that such tests may have more to contribute in the future. They will not take the responsibility of selection off the shoulders of the sales manager, but will provide additional information. The appropriateness of any test for a particular industrial market needs to be checked when it is brought into use.

SALES TRAINING

Whereas in the past there has been little formal training for industrial salesmen, recent years have seen rapid growth. Larger companies can devise schemes of training specially adapted to their own needs, either using their own specialized staff or employing consultants. Introduction is preceded by a careful study of what the training needs are for that particular company. Smaller companies may have little choice but to send their men on external courses, where they will work with men from other companies. This is not necessarily a bad thing so long as the interests of the participants in the course are not too widely diffused and so long as the methods used give each individual time to examine the problem of adapting the techniques taught to his own work. Such outside courses cannot, however, focus as sharply on the needs of specific companies as can custom-tailored courses. Moreover, they can only deal with the selling skills and not with other aspects, such as knowledge of the particular market, particular competitors, or particular products.

Sales training is, however, a continuous, not a once-for-all, process. The opening stages may well be a period of classroom work, associated with planned field training, but later stages will often put more responsibility on the shoulders of the sales manager or field sales manager whose regular supervision of the sales force involves an element of built-in training. This is not restricted to the regular sales conference with its opportunities for case-study work, role-playing, films, and other formal procedures. It is day by day on the job, and the executives who have to undertake this responsibility may well be given some training in the art of training—not to make them specialists but to provide some background.

In addition to selling skills, salesmen's training includes product and applications knowledge, customer and market knowledge, the planning of the salesman's work, and company policy and procedures. It is also worth considering whether he should not be given some wider insight into the principles of marketing so that he has a better understanding of and sympathy with the company's policy decisions in relation to, for example, the introduction of new products. Training and retraining is now recognized as important in all branches of industry and at all levels. The sale is the point at which all the previous operations of the company reach fulfilment. The introduction of sales training in a firm is a recognition of this fact and not a criticism of past sales efforts. Almost all representatives will gain from systematic training; the best gain only a little, but others will gain more.

SALARIES AND INCENTIVES

The variation in salesmen's earnings is considerable, as has already been noted. Sometimes the higher earnings are for men with special technical qualifications, but high earnings are also sometimes achieved by salesmen working mainly on commission whose results come from their own skill in dealing with customers and putting over the product. Some managements fear that the relationship between the representative and his customer can be so strong that if the representative leaves, customers go too.

Very many companies today pay entirely by salary. They do this for a combination of reasons. Partly they find it the way to attract the right class of individual—often a man with high professional qualifications who seeks a career in the industry who may well, in due course, move into a higher managerial post. From his viewpoint, rewards by career development are more appropriate than commission. He seeks a post with prospects, superannuation (pension or retirement benefits), and similar rights. Mortgages are more easily obtained against salary than against commission, and he is guarded against fortuitous fluctuations in income arising from causes outside his control.

To pay by salary only is also often logical. The "sale" may be made by the combined efforts of a group of people and not that of a lone individual. It may well be difficult or impossible to decide what part of the success in achieving a sale is attributable to one or another person. Conversely, a representative may do his job well, yet no sale is completed. For example, he may successfully obtain the right to bid, but the company's bid is not successful. The representative must also spend his time cultivating new accounts for future business and must not seek short-term increases in sales which could damage relations with a customer who might afterward feel the victim of a "hard sell." The representative's function is very often to create a durable relationship with the customer to the benefit of both parties. He is a consultant to the customer as much as he is a salesman.

Other companies consider that absence of commission blunts incentive. When sales depend more specifically on the efforts of the salesman and where the order is placed after a short period of negotiation, the case for such financial incentives is strongest. Usually they are only a small part of the man's income, between 10 and 15 percent; the salesman relying entirely on commission is rare today.

There are many ways of setting commission for financial incentives. The simplest is to pay a certain small percentage on all sales. An alternative is to pay commission on all sales over quota. This "bites" at the point where the effort required in getting sales is greatest, and on those marginal sales the percentage rate can be made attractive.

A sharper incentive is provided by paying a lump sum when the quota is exceeded; but once the lump sum has been achieved, there is then no more incentive. This is suitable if the company can clearly identify an appropriate feasible quota but, having achieved that, wishes the salesman to spend his time prospecting or advising present customers.

The arrangements suggested above all imply that the test of success for the salesman is the volume of sales. This may not be so. It may be that the correct test is the volume of profit or contribution generated. This may not vary directly in proportion to sales, because some products contribute more than others, or because the salesman has some authority to vary price and may be tempted to cut prices too quickly if sales volume is the crucial test.

Often the sales manager may have a series of tasks which the salesman is required to work toward. There may be some products, perhaps new products, on which a certain level of sale is specially required to meet the company plan, or it may be desired to achieve a balance of sales between different parts of the range. It is difficult to reflect all these variables in an incentive scheme. Point systems can be operated in order to encourage a balanced pattern of achievement, the salesman being rewarded according to the total points accumulated. These more complex schemes raise greater difficulty in implementation.

Commissions and similar incentive schemes must be substantially accepted by the sales force to be successful. This means they must be carefully discussed before introduction and the salesmen satisfied of their fairness. Difficult problems— such as arise when representatives in different territories both have a hand in producing business—need to be clarified. The scheme should be well understood, and the salesman should be able to assess what he will receive from a sale. It must, of course, be administered efficiently and commission paid promptly.

Such companies are now experimenting with the use of competitions as short-term incentives. These are less acceptable in industrial marketing than in consumer marketing, particularly for older or highly qualified salesmen. There may be some areas in which suitably planned competitions have something to offer.

The absence of a direct monetary incentive scheme

implies that the salesman's work is recognized financially at the regular review of his salary. In order that this appraisal be fair, there should be a clear understanding of what the salesman is expected to achieve and understanding of the basis by which achievement is to be measured.

Whatever remuneration method is adopted, it should seek to attract and keep salesmen of appropriate quality, provide sufficient incentive to encourage them to carry out the tasks required of them with skill and diligence, and be consistent with the economic use of the sales force.

Material and monetary awards are not the only incentives, and sometimes not the most important. Some individuals appear to have a limit beyond which financial incentives seem to have little effect. Motivation must be reinforced from other sources. The average representative spends only a small proportion of his time in the office meeting his colleagues in the sales force and in the company generally. He can easily feel that he is not part of the team, that his efforts are not adequately supported and his problems not full appreciated. This can have a demoralizing effect, leading to loss of drive and perhaps to unnecessary labor turnover.

It is, in fact, very easy for the salesman to find himself in the position that the bulk of the communications from his head office are queries open to the interpretation that something has not gone too well and that he is being called on for an explanation—"This account is lost," "That customer has complained," and so on. Often the good work which he has done may not seem to call for specific action from the head office, so he hears no more about it.

Regular contact seems to be the method by which interest and motivation can be raised and maintained. With smaller sales forces, the sales manager can regularly spend some time in the field with his men, as part of the normal routine, not only to improve selling efficiency but to promote mutual understanding. If the sales force is too large for him to do this personally, the work must be delegated to field sales managers. The general sales manager works closely with them and treats attendance at local sales meetings as an important part of his functions.

Regular newsletters to salesmen, if well done, have been found to be of value not only in passing on routine information about organization and marketing changes, but also in reporting sales successes of individual members of the sales force and their contributions in other ways to the company's work. Where the representatives are requested to pass back information about new and competing products, then it is useful if they can be told how some of this information has been applied in practice. This underlines the value to the company of a task which some salesmen find irksome. Sales conferences can also be given a democratic atmosphere when common problems of the salesmen are discussed. Individual salesmen are encouraged to express their views on their problems and how they are approached and to discuss how they make their presentations and demonstrations. This passes good ideas from one man to another and generates team spirit and cooperation in the sales force.

OTHER CONTACTS WITH THE CUSTOMER

The salesman will rarely be the only contact with an important customer, although he will be the prime one. Where the product represents a major innovation in the customer firm, there will be continual close contact with a large number of people meeting on both sides (called "total involvement" in Chapter 2). In any company, senior management will often find it well worthwhile to make arrangements for personal contact with customers' senior staff, at least in the case of major customers and those with good potential. This may be used to enlarge the representative's circle of contacts in the buying company and to help him to meet decision-makers whom he might otherwise find it difficult to reach. Such meetings may serve to show customers the interest which is taken in them and to improve relationships on a broad basis with the companies visited. The meeting may be a formal visit to the customer's office, at an exhibition, or some other avenue of interest to the customer's executive. Where a company is supplying a customer regularly with components or parts on a long-term basis, there may be regular contact between a plant or factory manager of the supplier and senior executives of the customer which are an important link in maintaining the long-term relationship.

The service force, the sales office staff, the switchboard operator, and others will also have to deal with customers and prospects from time to time. They need guidance and training. Service can be a valuable link with the customer, reinforcing the salesman, meeting other people in the company, and often being in a position to identify a customer's need for replacement equipment and to make recommendations about the replacement which might be selected.

Delay or lack of consideration at the switchboard can also lose orders and even customers. In the sales office, too, any member of the staff (particularly in the small firm) may find himself dealing with a customer or a prospect on the phone or face to face. Even if he is not an expert salesman, he should be commercially minded, keen to promote sales, and aware of the importance of tact, consideration, and need for accurate recording of details and quick action by follow-up.

11

Sales Force Economics

Where the market for a product is concentrated in a small number of companies, each representing a large amount of business, the personal contact with the buying companies is conducted through a few executives. Each of these is, in effect if not in name, an account executive in the best sense of the word, combining and consolidating the promotional work of his company and directing it toward the executives of the target companies. He will call in other members of the staff of his company to work with him and to cooperate in making presentations to clients, as necessary. Where, however, the market is more dispersed, the sales force in its traditional sense appears. Even if this is only small—perhaps six members—the question immediately arises: "How shall the force be organized?" This requires careful consideration so that the sales force approximates to the optimum relationship between increasing marketing push and keeping costs down.

PRINCIPLES OF ORGANIZATION

There are, in fact, four main approaches to the problem of organization, and it may well be possible and desirable as the sales force increases in size to combine more than one of these in order to achieve the best results. The four approaches are:

1 Specialization by class of customer.
2 Specialization by type of product.

3 Specialization by territory.
4 Specialization by function.

The basic principles of marketing immediately suggest that, other things being equal, the first approach deserves most careful consideration. Each representative specializes in serving a particular class of customer (or other market segment) and thus gains expert knowledge of the industry concerned, its technology, the way in which the buying decision is made, its growth prospects, its customers, and all other matters which throw light on its present and future needs. This type of specialization may well be regarded as the ideal form for the sales force handling industrial products. The representative becomes personally acquainted with a large number of individual decision-makers in customer companies and can explore their particular problems in subtlety and depth. He knows not only who makes what decision, but also what influences him, and when the decision is made. The salesman is able to feed back to his company information which enables its management to adapt and improve its products and to permit better planning of advertising and promotion generally.

One writer speaks of this system with great enthusiasm.[30] He cites its advantages as follows:

1 The salesman lines up his calls by industry or trade channel, rather than territory; a practice to which we have given the name "industry marketing."
2 By thus specializing in an industry, the salesman becomes virtually a "partner" of the customer, so much so that he can quite literally forecast the future sales and marketing strategies both of his customers and of his own company.
3 With that close relationship, the salesman deals with the top customer-management levels where basic company policy is made.

There are, however, certain problems which the industry approach presents. The representative concerned has to be acquainted with all his company's products; and where they differ in type of technology, this may require a width of knowledge which is not obtainable at a cost proportionate to the potential business.

The industry approach is also less valuable where the products concerned are standard and technically fairly simple. Buying firms are well aware of possible applications, and understanding the individual industry does little to advance sales. Sometimes there are only one or two people involved in making the buying decision, and the potential business from each customer is small. This points to a territory type of organization, which reduces the amount of traveling between calls and maximizes the face-to-face time. The representative concerned need have little specialized technical knowledge but should be good at dealing with people.

Specialization by product is most appropriate where the products concerned are diverse and require different technical knowledge, and where the key decision-makers in the prospect companies differ from one class of product to another. Under these circumstances, the sales force will be organized according to the class of product, or (which is analogous) there will be separate sales forces for different products. This type of organization is very common—in fact it sometimes exists where there does not seem to be adequate reason for it. It perhaps originates from the fact that in many companies different plants produce different products and the tendency, therefore, has been to develop distinct sales forces for each class of product, without serious examination of the alternatives. Sometimes its roots are historic: companies with independent sales forces have merged but the former selling arrangements have continued. It can mean that one purchasing officer will have several representatives for the same company calling on him.

The territory form of organization is the most widespread and is often found associated with one or another of the two principles already mentioned. The major advantage is that the area to be covered by the representative is smaller and it reduces the time spent traveling between calls. If there is need to visit an account urgently, the representative can quickly be on the spot. From the representative's point of view, not only is traveling time reduced but nights away from home are also reduced.

Territory organization may well be coordinated with one of the two forms mentioned above. For example, the sales force may be divided first into sections concerned with different industries (or products) and subsequently these sections are subdivided into territories.

Where industries are localized in a particular area, the salesman responsible for that area in any case automatically tends to become a specialist in the local industry, and this can provide a convenient amalgamation of the industry and territory principles—always provided that the other industries in that area, including new and developing industries, are not thereby neglected.

Finally, it is worth considering the possibility of specialization by function. This is a more controversial issue and less widely adopted. The principle is that a total selling job may require a different type of representative at different stages. For example, specialization may be achieved by separating development work from the regular work of the representative and placing this in the hands of a specialized representative. Development work here means something beyond the normal job of prospecting; it is concerned with developing the market for new products or for new applications of established products. This may mean that a few major customers have to be introduced to the product, and considerable time may be required for working with each of these few companies to overcome technical, production, and commercial difficulties. In addition, there may be a problem of price negotiation which is not within the responsibility and competence of the regular representative in many sales forces. For this reason some companies will place this work in the hands of a very small number of specialists with special status. Once the initial development work is done, the selling operation for what is now a standard product passes over to the main sales force. The existence of a separate force such as this may sometimes cause resentment among the other sales staff.

In other cases, the negotiation may pass through a series of stages which involve a number of meetings over several months and at different levels. For example, a particular market may be such that it is necessary to make a large number of calls to identify a genuine prospect, using the word "prospect" to mean a company which at the particular time has a need for the product concerned. Once prospects are identified, then there is a further meeting or series of meetings, and at a certain stage technical advice is required.

This situation might be met by a sales team of a senior representative, technical representative, and junior representative. The junior has the prime task of identifying prospects. Once they have been identified, the senior representative moves in to undertake further discussions, perhaps at a higher level. The technical representative is called in when required and may be concerned in supplementary discussions with the technical staff of the prospect. Finally, there may be a major meeting to complete the transaction, which may involve a number of executives.

This arrangement may be amended in other circumstances to a ratio of one technical representative to two or three or more nontechnical representatives, depending upon the requirement of the market concerned. The whole team is coordinated by a senior representative or, if it becomes larger, by a field sales manager. Such arrangements make the best use of the time of the more costly representatives by delegating work which does not require their attention to subordinates.

Many of the more fully worked-out ideas about the economics of the field sales force were developed in connection with the selling of consumer goods to retailers. This means that the ideas as they stand initially are out of line with what is feasible in a large number of industrial selling situations. They require adapting, to a lesser or greater degree. The scalpel-sharp calculations of the leading mass-selling consumer-goods manufacturer must be replaced by a more flexible and rather more rough-hewn approach to match the realities of the industrial market.

Nevertheless, the basic problem of deciding how to obtain value for the money spent on the sales force remains, as do the consequent questions, such as: "How many salesmen should we have?" "How often shall they call?" "How much time shall we spend with this customer?" These underlie all well-founded approaches to sales.

The elementary ideas described in subsequent pages apply most effectively to those products which are reasonably standardized and are sold to horizontal markets. The salesman's key job is then to cover the territory regularly and efficiently. Where the market is partly like this, but also contains a few large customers, the ideas are capable of adaptation; for example, one solution might be to give the work with the larger customers to specialists and to give the smaller customers to the route salesman.

As a preliminary hypothesis, the amount of business produced depends upon:

The number of calls made.
The proportion of calls identified as current prospects (that is, potential buyers at the time).
The number of prospects who place an order.
The size of the order.

This hypothesis will frequently require amendment or elaboration. If, however, the above description forms a reasonable model of the market, then it suggests some interesting lines of thought. It suggests the direction in which increased efficiency might be sought and also indicates that nothing is to be gained by improving in one element at the expense of another.

For example, suppose that in one month a salesman:

Makes eighty calls;
Identifies 75 percent as current prospects;
Successfully makes a sale to 60 percent of these; and
Achieves an average order size of $360.

The total value of the sales obtained is therefore $12,960.

However, if small improvements can be made under

each heading, sales will be increased provided that improvements in one item are not offset by decline elsewhere. This is important; for example, extra calls must not be sought by unreasonably reducing the length of calls with important customers and losing business as a result. However, if the number of calls rises to 90, identified current prospects to 80 percent, conversion of prospects to 67 percent, and the average sale to $384, then the total sales are now $18,432.

The increase under each heading is moderate, but the total overall improvement is great. The sales manager can decide that at a particular time one of these elements may promise more potential improvement than the others and may focus attention there. He can do this by a combination of methods: comparing the performance of different salesmen, from market analysis which pinpoints possibilities more closely, or from a "work study" type of approach. Thought on these lines may help to focus on priorities which offer the quickest possibilities of improvement.

Other markets may require somewhat different models. If, for example, the sale consists of negotiations involving several calls, the model will need to reflect this.

The general point is that progress is most likely to be achieved by analyzing the total selling task into its elements, measuring each of these, studying their possibilities, focusing on those elements which offer most opportunity for improvement, and then measuring again to assess progress.

TERRITORY PLANNING

The object of territory planning is to ensure that all worthwhile customers are called upon regularly at proper intervals of time and with minimum traveling between calls. This has been brought to a fine art by some of the larger consumer-goods companies selling branded products which are in regular demand. The problems in industrial marketing are different, but this does not mean that it is never possible to learn anything from those companies. Much can be learned, provided it is adapted to the more flexible approach required in industrial markets. It is first necessary to outline briefly[31] the principles which are used in consumer goods and then discuss the problems of adapting these ideas.

The accounts to be called on are classified into three (or perhaps more) groups, according to their importance as measured by potential business:

A. Accounts to be called on weekly (these are large accounts).
B. Accounts to be called on biweekly (medium accounts).
C. Accounts to be called on monthly (small accounts).

There may be some shops smaller than C accounts which are not called on at all as the amount of business does not warrant the cost involved. These are supplied through wholesalers.

The next stage is to draw up a plan which will ensure that the salesman covers the entire territory over the twenty working days in a lunar month, calling on each customer the correct number of times.

As a first step, each salesman's territory is divided into five segments, each of which has in it one-fifth of the sales work-load for that territory. These segments may not be of equal *area*, but the time involved for the representative in covering them (including traveling and time with the customer) is equalized as far as is possible (see Fig. 10).

Each segment is then to be visited on a particular day of the week, segment A on Mondays, segment B on Tuesdays, and so on. This is the first step in balancing the work-load over the twenty days. As there are four Mondays in the lunar month during which the whole cycle of work is to be covered, the next

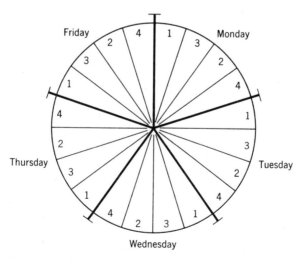

Fig. 10. Territory planning. (Adapted from J. O'Shaughnessy, *Work Study Applied to a Sales Force*, British Institute of Management, 1966.)

step is to consider Segment A and to split up the work in this segment over *four* days. This means that all the A accounts in that segment are to be visited *every* Monday (these are the big accounts), the B accounts are to be visited every other Monday (half of them will be visited on the first and third Mondays and the other half on the second and fourth Mondays), and finally, the C accounts to be called on monthly are shared equally between the four Mondays. This procedure is repeated for every other day of the working week. The work is in this way spread as evenly as possible over the whole twenty days of the cycle.

The problem of adapting this procedure to the industrial marketing situation is twofold. First, there may be certain customers who are so important that they *must* be called on at the time which suits their convenience. For example, it may be that the representative has been trying to meet the commercial director of an important customer, and when the chance comes it is not to be missed. The second is that the representative may be called away on a "fire alarm" call, an urgent message that a customer has a complaint, and this must be attended to.

In the first instance it will be necessary to estimate the proportion of time which is required for those special accounts and for problems which require priority attention. To measure this may require some records to be kept for a trial period. The sales manager must then consider whether, in the light of the tasks which he wishes the sales force to undertake, this is the right proportion. It may be too low if he wishes them to spend more time nursing the "special," or it may be too high and he will seek ways of relieving the salesmen of some of this load.

For example, in one company analysis showed that the main reason why a representative was interrupted in his routine calls was to attend to technical problems, and that in well over two-thirds of the cases his action on arrival at the customer's plant was to phone the head office for a technical service engineer. In general, a telephone call to the customer would have revealed the nature of the inquiry, the technical help could have arrived more quickly, and the routine calls would have suffered less interruption.

It should be noted that in territories with an efficient plan, the representative will be in the near vicinity of a customer requiring special attention within a few days and can thus by arrangement call on him with minimum interference with regular calls. There may also be a case for considering whether the area sales manager should not follow up some of these special calls when the representative is not in the vicinity.

The remaining accounts may be classified into two or

three groups, according to the frequency with which routine calls should be made, for example:

A	(medium accounts)	Four-weekly.
B	(smaller accounts)	Eight-weekly.
C	(very small)	Only if these can be fitted into spare time when the representative is in the vicinity or in response to an inquiry.

Analysis of salesmen's records, or special studies, will reveal the extent to which, on the average, time must be devoted to these prior claims. Suppose it is found that 40 percent of the time must be devoted to them. This means that in a period of four five-day weeks, eight days will be required for specials, and the remaining twelve will be available for systematic calling. The salesman does not, of course, know in advance which days will be required for specials, but he estimates that in most weeks he will have three days available for regular calls.

The calls can then be identified by setting A and B accounts on a map, using different-colored pins. If it is desired that the salesman travels around his territory each week, the territory is divided into three areas (each representing one of his days for systematic calling) and each area into four groupings of customers to represent one week's load. The actual day of the week on which each customer-grouping is visited is not necessarily a predetermined part of the plan; it can be scheduled nearer the time to fit in with the requirements of the specials.

Time allowed to cover each group of customers can well err on the side of generosity. The margin uncommitted can then be used for prospecting and for the C accounts.

Another alternative which has been tried is for the representative to spend one week on routine calls and the second on the priorities. This is suited to circumstances where, once interest is aroused in a prospect company, several subsequent calls are necessary to complete the deal. The free week is thus spent on developing the leads produced in the routine calls.

When schemes such as this are being introduced for the first time, it is best to experiment in one territory; it is rare to get the plan just right the first time. The actual detailed planning is left to the salesmen concerned, in order to promote flexibility. The sales manager would receive a regular forecast of calls to be made.

This planning procedure will show whether the territory size is appropriate for the representative. If all accounts cannot be called on with proper frequency, then it is a sign that the work-load may be too heavy for one representative and either the territory size must be reduced or the smaller accounts dropped or visited less often. Alternatively, it may show that the territory is too small and too much time is spent on visiting C accounts. Once the system is operating, it is not uncommon for a salesman making regular calls to find a buyer saying: "I thought you'd be around about now. I've got this matter I've kept to discuss with you."

Finally, a cautionary but true story told by a sales manager who thought all his salesmen were diligently occupied— until he stopped at a gas station and the man who filled his tank was a member of his own sales force.

The second element in the formula in the preceding section was the proportion of calls which are current prospects. This issue is more important in some types of business than in others. Larger accounts must usually be visited consistently, but various methods have been adopted to make other calls more productive. The identification of leads by mail shots or by advertising may help to reduce wasted time. The use of a junior representative for this sort of work can save a senior's time. The collection of information on one visit can help choose the time for the next which most closely matches buying plans.

Preliminary inquiries by telephone have also been successful in some cases. In fact, some companies are experimenting in saving the salesman's time by actually completing the sale or taking repeat orders by telephone. Views on the value of this vary at present. Some buyers are affronted, while others regard it as a method which economizes on their time. Part of the difficulty in formulating a view is that telephone selling is still in its infancy and requires different techniques from face-to-face selling. Sales managers are watching these developments with interest.

The importance of training in salesmanship in making sure that as many calls as possible produce as big an order as possible has already been mentioned. Remarkably few industrial salesmen are provided with efficient visual aids to support their presentation. A few managers plan a proper presentation kit for each man, at least in respect of those lines which are being most strongly pushed at any time. A good folder of well-mounted photographs, case histories, and other material, with notes to remind the salesman of the selling points and answers to objections, can help gain and hold the prospect's interest and provide visual support for the salesman's verbal presentation.

Desk-top projectors can show moving films which can add punch to a presentation; they are particularly useful for showing equipment actually operating. The salesman will need training in the use of such aids.

Sales manuals are also not commonly provided to representatives in industrial selling, yet some companies have found them a valuable tool. It gives the salesman background to help him sell successfully. Companies have different ideas about what should go into the manual, and the following is an illustration:

1 Background information about company policy.
2 Methods of making presentations, dealing with common objections, and closing sales.
3 Information on customer benefits from company products.
4 Information on competitors' products, prices, and policies.

If the customer is really important, there must be a group presentation, which requires specially prepared aids and can well be rehearsed in advance, with a critical group of executives playing the role of buyers.

THE PROBLEM OF SMALL ACCOUNTS

One source of dispute in many companies is whether or not small accounts should continue to be visited by salesmen. The argument is that small accounts, even if not economical at the present time, may one day grow into big profitable accounts. This problem can be approached by examining the economics of calling.

The real cost of a representative has been discussed at the beginning of Chapter 10.

What is the cost of an individual call? Suppose that in a particular company a representative costs in all (salary, commission, superannuation, and expenses) $12,000 to keep on the road. After deducting holidays, bank holidays, sick leave, and time necessary in the office for conferences and administration, he may be making calls on customers for 225 days in the year. If he is averaging two calls per day, giving some 450 calls per year on the average, each call costs $26.

Assuming that it is necessary to call on an account four times per year to keep it active, then the account costs $104 annually to service. If the contribution (and the word "contribution," rather than "profit," is the right one to use for marginal accounts) which the supplier earns on each $100 of goods sold is 50 percent, then he must expect to receive $208 worth (i.e., twice $104) of business from the company concerned to break even. The value of this business will then cover the cost of calling—but no more. The $208 provides $104 to cover direct production costs and $104 to cover the cost of the representative's calls.

Clearly there is no point in calling on a company simply in order to break even, so the executive will set a higher minimum level. He might very well decide not to call regularly on a customer who was unlikely to place at least $384 of business with his company annually. This does not necessarily mean that this level will be obtained every year, but that it can reasonably be expected taking one year with another.

The simplicity of this analysis has, of course, to be modified in a particular case. If a company seeks about one-third of the market for its products, any company averaging $1,200 of purchases in its class of goods is worth regular attention. The total amount of business which a prospect company places and the average share are not always sufficient criteria. Even if 33 percent is the share of the overall market a supplier holds, there will be some buyers from whom it can expect a much higher share of the business on the average, and others from whom it will expect less. This can be taken into account in planning calls and modified from time to time as circumstances change. There will also be occasions when the representative, after visiting the specials and A and B accounts in an area, will have time to visit the only other accounts locally, even though they are small. The opportunity cost (to use the language of Chapter 15) is nil, because otherwise the time would have been unused.

It may be necessary to take a firm line with the sub-economic accounts and reduce them to the level of C accounts. It is true that one or two of these will grow, but to visit regularly many such accounts against the day when one may grow incurs a loss which the company has to carry today. If these outlays are to be genuinely recovered in the future, the losses of today must be recouped with compound interest. Finally, the possibility of keeping in touch in other ways and reducing the call frequency should be examined.

Often a careful survey of all possible customers, present and prospective, in a territory may reveal that a representative is conscientiously calling on some small and uneconomic accounts but frequently omitting some which offer more potential.

Cost per $100 of turnover or contribution is a key yardstick in assessing performance. As a measure of efficiency, it has the limitation of any other average. Average cost can be low because the territory is being "creamed" and some worthwhile but small accounts are not being properly covered. The real test is the marginal one: the smallest group of accounts regularly visited should be economic when cost and return are compared, and those accounts which are not called upon should be subeconomic by the same yardstick. If there are accounts not being visited which could potentially yield a contribution after allowing for the cost of calling, then it is of advantage for them to be visited, even though the cost/turnover ratio for that group of accounts will be above average. If in reducing time spent on subeconomic accounts the salesman directs his attention to these better accounts, a double benefit is achieved.

RECORDS AND RETURNS

The concept of control in the industrial sales force, particularly with the senior representative, is one to be used with care. It is rarely the case that the stick is a better producer of results than the carrot, and the objective must be to create a team relationship in which the enthusiasm of the sales manager communicates itself to the salesmen and the search for more and more profitable sales becomes a joint effort.

This does not mean that the sales manager does not require information and does not follow up the salesman's progress to commend achievement and amend weakness. It does mean that he tries to involve the salesman in the process of examining problems and to decide by joint collaboration the means of solving these problems. In the last resort, the sales manager may have to take more drastic action; he may, for example, have to install plans and procedures which are not well received to begin with, but (except in real emergency) this should follow a period in which the salesmen have had explained to them the nature of the problems and are given an opportunity to discuss and put forward their own proposals and to comment on those of others. The examination and consideration of these comments must be real and not a facade—this is easily detectable and results in harm, not benefit.

Making returns is not popular with anyone, and salesmen are no exception. The best salesman is not necessarily the best at making returns. Yet the information is needed for marketing action, as well as for sales force planning. Returns should be collected only on information required for management action and which cannot reasonably be secured otherwise. Call reports, plans for forthcoming calls, and customer reports are the chief information required from salesmen. Where calls follow a regular pattern and there are a number each day— say four or more—it may be possible to present the form in such a way that much of the required information can be completed by a check in the appropriate box. Details of companies seen, people met, sales achieved will have to be written in if required, and fuller supporting information supplied on those few calls that really justify it. Where calls are less frequent and each account more important, then more detailed reports will be required indicating matters discussed, sales made, customer's buying and other plans, competitive action, reasons for failure to get an order, and the follow-up progran. The representative must be guided to provide material *relevant* to decision-making and planning.

When a prospect is called on for the first time, a special report giving much fuller information about the company may be required, and the salesman is expected to update this systematically. Information of this sort is transferred to a customer record in the office to provide a comprehensive picture. Many salesmen also find it worthwhile to keep their own record cards, which include not only details of past calls and commercial details to be followed up, but personal details about the interests, attitudes, and prejudices of the decision-makers he meets. Consulting these documents before the next call enables him to plan the call properly: the objective of the call, whom he seeks to see, what points he wants to make, what objections and complaints to prepare for, and how to match what he says to the man he is meeting. Some companies also require completion of a regular intelligencee report at monthly intervals.

Even when the salesman's job cannot be planned in much detail, it is still worthwhile over a period of, say, six months to prepare an analysis of calls made in relation to business received from different sizes of accounts, to see if the overall pattern of calls is consistent with the importance of different customers.

Records are, in fact, the only basis other than personal contact on which the sales manager can assess the performance of a representative in those circumstances in which the link between the individual's efforts and sales achieved is not a close one in the short term. Particularly when a salesman is building a new territory or developing a market for a new product, the results of his efforts in terms of turnover may not appear for some time.

Analysis of the records provides much information which can be used in evaluating salesmen and improving their performance. Some of the factors commonly examined are discussed below, and in most companies standards of performance become established. These standards will require adjustment to allow for differences in the product sold, territory differences, and customer differences. The number of calls made is one common test, and allowance must be made here for different distances between customers in various parts of the country, and for differing times required with particular customers. Thus small variations are inevitable, but big differences and trends require examination.

The average success rate and average sale per call are also useful indications of performance. A figure that is too high may be as significant as one that is too low. It may be that a salesman's territory is too big; he can then concentrate on the bigger and better accounts and leave somewhat smaller (but still potentially profitable accounts) unexploited. If several salesmen are doing this, then a reapportionment of territories and the employment of additional salesmen may be justified. Before taking this action, the sales manager will explore the potential among the small customers to ensure that the extra business will cover the cost. He will be examining the relationship between accounts called on and the total worthwhile accounts—a study of value in itself.

Quotas, where feasible, are part of the armory of assessing a salesman. This does, however, judge him on short-term results. Quotas for this purpose commonly include a moderate incentive element, sufficient to imply full extension on the part of the salesman. Setting industrial quotas is not easy and usually involves a study of area potential—with particular reference to major accounts—and a comparison with past sales. Where incentive payments are related to quotas, these will commonly begin at something less than 100 percent of quota. It goes without saying that the quota cannot be settled without full consideration of the views of the salesman concerned.

Where the salesman has other objectives to achieve, performance will also need to be assessed against these. They can include such tests as new accounts opened and level of expenses.

12

The Role of Service

In marketing in general, but in industrial marketing in particular, the customer's need to "solve problems" is not always completely met when he has purchased a product from a supplier. A shrewd supplier can very frequently increase greatly the value of his product to the customer by providing service which helps the customer solve those related problems which require solution before he realizes full benefit from the product in terms of extra sales, extra profit, and higher productivity. In some industries, service has in fact become one of the keys to successful long-term competition.

The principle is that service, by improving the value of the product to the customer, will lead to returns to the supplier in extra sales or better prices or a reduction in other marketing costs. Clearly, for the operation to be economic these returns must exceed the cost of providing the service. This is very often the case; sometimes, indeed, the cost of service is a relatively small addition to the costs of the product.

Broadly speaking, one may distinguish two classes of service:

1 Commercial and financial service.
2 Product support service, of which technical service is the typical example, but which includes some service which is not technical in the customary sense of the word.

COMMERCIAL AND FINANCIAL SERVICE

The two main commercial services which a customer commonly seeks are "delivery" and "finance."

Delivery can mean one of two things: prompt delivery for items required urgently, or planned delivery at a particular time for items which must tie in with the customer's own operational timetables (like ready-mixed concrete).

Prompt delivery depends upon the size of stocks held by the manufacturer or an intermediate stockist and whether or not they are held convenient to the purchaser. Holding stocks is expensive, and the decision on the size of stock-holdings depends upon the importance which the customer places on this factor.

In many routine products, stocks will usually be on hand at the time of the order, or a further supply will commonly be scheduled for early production. Where economies of long runs are not great, smaller stocks will generally be carried, but where long runs are clearly more economical, then the economic solution will be to carry more stock rather than be forced into emergency short runs. This problem would appear to be capable of solution by operational research techniques, although it has some aspects which differ from those present in the stock-control problems which relate to purchases of supplies.

Good organization is important. Frequently, a review of stock levels will show that some lines are overstocked and others persistently understocked. If the proportions are adjusted, if better forecasts are introduced of short-run demand by, perhaps, exponential smoothing techniques, and if production schedules are carefully planned, delivery problems may be eased. In addition, communication with the sales force may require attention. Embarrassment and bad feeling can result when representatives make delivery promises which cannot be implemented. Even if there is no firm promise of delivery by a certain date, departure from past practice may cause consternation and difficulty when the purchaser has had no intimation of it.

Nevertheless, when all is said and done, there is a balance to be struck between the cost of carrying stocks of finished goods and the danger of losing an order for a product, perhaps related orders on other products, perhaps even a customer. Policy depends on the importance of these matters to the customers and the value of the business of the customer concerned.

When scheduled delivery is what matters, close working

with the customer can result in a supplier–customer "team" planned as a unity so that the production by the supplier is tied in closely with the requirements of the customer, to the benefit of both. This can reduce the amount of stock which both carry, with consequent saving.

A related problem arises when the runs are short and the product is to some degree adapted to the requirements of individual customers. For example, if glass containers are being produced, many customers will have, for promotional or other reasons, special requirements. Customers' demands will have to meet different deadlines, which are known by the sales or marketing departments but not always by the production department. In order to match output to customer requirements under these conditions, scheduling of production may with advantage be taken over by the marketing department. The lines of communication are reduced and the marketing department, aware of both customer priorities and of production limitations, carries full responsibility for meshing output with demand.

Finance is another service which is sometimes the key to sales. It is frequently impossible for the individual company to provide as much finance as customers reasonably need. To do so may well be directly uneconomic and may also mean that the supplier may himself run short of liquidity. While there is little that the supplier himself can normally do, the possibility of providing customers with information on credit sources and perhaps even on occasion developing a special working relationship with some finance house may be worth considering. There are, of course, special arrangements for exports.

PRODUCT SUPPORT SERVICE

Companies provide many different advisory services for prospects and customers to help specify the most suitable grade or model of a product and to obtain fullest value after purchase. Commonly referred to as technical service, there is in fact a wide range of services which have these overall purposes. This includes design service (provided perhaps by packaging manufacturers) and systems analysis (provided by manufacturers of office equipment). Indeed, the possible application of this concept is so wide that "system selling" is used for a company whose philosophy is not to sell a piece of hardware but a total system, whether it is of production equipment, office organization, or something else. Under this concept, the supplier aims to sell a package deal—the product, plus ancillary equipment, advice, staff training, management consultancy, and whatever else may be needed. Thus the buyer proceeds with the utmost ease to receive the full benefits of the product.

One writer (Simon) suggests that the objectives of technical service should be analyzed into three main groups.[32] Service policy and service action should be controlled by these objectives as with other departments. The groups proposed are shown in the table on the following page.

It is a convenient simplification to distinguish presales service, which is generally carried out in pursuit of short-term sales objectives, from postsales service, which is commonly concerned with product performance, and this distinction is used below. Often, however, technical service will be part of the continuing relationship with the customer which links one sale to the next.

Before a sale, a supplier will commonly be willing to supply a limited amount of free advice, usually without charge or obligation. For example, a supplier of lubricants may willingly survey the plant of a company, identify all the points at which lubrication is necessary, recommend those grades of his own make which are appropriate at these points, and prescribe the frequency with which lubrication should take place. In general, the cost of this is modest in relation to the potential business, and a survey is part of the routine sales function. Not all companies may want this service. The larger ones with their own lubricant specialist, for example, may prefer to do this for themselves.

Where the presales service cost is high in relation to the usual size of order, the policy of free surveys and similar benefits can become expensive. The cost of such a survey is treated as a part of normal sales overhead. Very rarely is it possible to charge separately for advice, although occasionally it can be reflected in a marginal price differential. Sometimes care in making an advance appreciation of inquiries may eliminate a proportion which have a low probability of developing into business. Where the survey is extensive, it may be possible after limited preliminary work to discuss progress with the prospect and at this stage form a view of the possibility of business eventuating and perhaps even obtain a commitment that an order will be placed.

Similar problems arise with engineering design. Plant designs may be prepared to meet a particular customer's needs, and the customer may then circulate them as the basis on which bids are to be submitted. No doubt the company which prepared the designs should be well placed to bid successfully. On other

Sales objectives
To broaden the available market.
To maintain an account.
To increase sales of the total product line.
To encourage present purchasers or users to purchase again in the future.
To satisfy the customer that he has made a useful purchase.
To stabilize large fluctuations in sales.
To increase profit through increasing sales.
To remain competitive.
To contribute to the reputation of the company in the market place and in the public eye generally.
To sell a different product from the one on which the service is being given.
To permit evaluation of new products of interest to the customer.

Product performance objectives
To extend the output life of the customer's equipment.
To build up a backlog of operating experience in the manufacturer's own products.
To get the product to perform to specifications.
To obtain feedback on the quality and acceptability of products in terms of design, materials, operations, etc.
To have an arbitrator to settle warranty disputes arising between customer and production.
To be able to investigate customer problems.
To overcome the inability of the customer to do the work himself.
To teach customers how to use products most practically and effectively to achieve lower maintenance and/or production costs.
To preserve the end value of the product in its use.

Nonsales competitive objectives
To provide an opportunity to meet people high in the customer's organization.
To obtain feedback on competitors' equipment.
To gain access to customers' plants to keep abreast of their production needs and policies.
To increase consciousness of the need for certain types of service.

occasions, it may be bidding on designs prepared by a competitor.

There are, however, many industries in which the company is able to provide continuing service by design, individual product development, and research-based technical know-how and can expect to receive a bigger volume of inquiries. Buyers also will often prefer to deal with such a company, even at the expense of a modest premium.

AFTER-SALES SERVICE

After-sales service, whether expressly agreed by contract or implied because of the reputation and image of the company, can usually be identified clearly and costed in relation to each unit of product or each particular contract. In some industries, the service requirement is trivial and can be met by good technical literature and a well-informed representative, apart from the occasional complaint which requires attention from a specialist. In other industries the requirement for service is widespread, because of the lack of the required specialized knowledge among customers. The needs will often tend to be highest among products which are technically complex and new, with fast-growing demand, so that there is widespread ignorance in the customer firms and little expertise to alleviate this. Under such circumstances, technical service can be of tremendous value in the marketing strategy and a link which the customer will be reluctant to break because of the possible loss to him. A continuing relationship is thus forged.

Again, the market may be divided into segments by the need for service. Some parts of the market—perhaps the larger firms or those concerned with technical products themselves—may have no need for service.

Where the volume and type of postsales service required differs from customer to customer, the costs involved can sometimes be charged back to the customer directly or reflected in his individual price. At the minimum, it is necessary to check that each customer or group of customers makes sufficient contribution to cover the costs incurred.

Where, however, the need for technical service is pervasive and service costs on the average only a small proportion of the value of the business flowing from it, then it will not be charged separately but will be "free." It helps to cement relations between the supplier and the customer and will often give the supplier access to decision-makers in the customer firm whom it might otherwise be difficult to contact. Under these circumstances, it can help to cut down the cost of obtaining repeat orders. The customer's staff becomes familiar with this supplier's product and will tend to be influenced by this knowledge when preparing designs and specifications. The supplier will be aware of the customer's developing plans and will be able to anticipate his needs and have new products well forward in development when the need becomes apparent.

What sort of supplementary services should be offered? The range is tremendous.

The provision of maintenance and spares is a widespread requirement. Maintenance provided under some form of express or implied warranty, including the meeting of justifiable complaints, is a cost which a company must be prepared to bear. Often a supplier will go beyond this to maintain customer goodwill. Logically this should be treated as part of the sales costs. Some large companies find it difficult to ensure that maintenance charges cover expenses. To overcome the difficulty, company policy may seek to avoid business which involves maintenance and may try to leave this to intermediate manufacturers or distributors. Spares are normally profitable and sometimes very much so, as demand is obviously insensitive to price. Spares do, however, often involve considerable costs in stock-holding, clerical work, packing, and transport which should be fully recognized.

A supplier of packaging may very well run a service to help customers by designing packages that sell their products rather than by simply supplying what the customers request. He may take the further step of carrying out studies of the final consumer markets to identify opportunities for customers' products so that business in packaging may result. He is likely to be better informed than many of his customers on the consumer reaction to packaging.

A company making electronic products may assist customers to design products into which these components go and may also undertake development of the final market. Their technicians may attend at the designing and development of the prototype, through the preproduction stage and through the first stage of production.

In selling computers, service has proved a vital element, as the following extract indicates:

> In marketing the 1900 Series, I.C.T. are selling not just a machine but a service—a service that includes education, installation, software maintenance, spares, supporting documentation and expert guidance throughout the life of the computer. The customer is never left to go it alone.
>
> For example, over 900 I.C.T. personnel are engaged exclusively on 1900 Series software development. Almost 2,000 man-years of effort have gone into it so far, bringing the cost of software development to over half that of the 1900 Series hardware development. And these figures exclude

some 160 programmers working with the sales force whose advice and assistance is always available to i.c.t. customers. They also exclude 200 programmers in the company's User Programming Service, which can undertake to write programs for customers.

In addition, i.c.t. maintains over 3,000 service engineers throughout the world. Wherever the installation, a skilled i.c.t. engineer is never very far away. And he is capable of site preparation, installation, maintenance and is supported by an efficient spares organization.

Then there is education of the customer's staff in the operation, programming and management of their computer installation. i.c.t. retains 220 full-time instructors, and almost 7,000 customer students passed through i.c.t. Schools last year.[33]

This was written in early 1967, and since then the company (now merged into International Computers Ltd.) has greatly expanded its service function.

In some industries suppliers have even taken on the role of general management consultants to smaller customers.

In each case, the effective test has been the long-term value of service in creating sales and the net cost of the service after allowing for possible economies in other selling costs.

TECHNICAL SERVICE AND THE SALES FORCE

Technical service is an arm of marketing and must be closely integrated for the best results. Where the service requirement is not of too sophisticated a nature, it may well be possible to train the sales engineer or equivalent to carry out the bulk of the work. This is particularly appropriate for presales service. Where, however, technical service is highly complex, it may well be better to limit the technical role of the salesman and support him with specialized technicians. In some instances a variety of specializations may be needed to provide what is required. The relationship between the technical advisor and the negotiating salesman must be very close, and the lines of communication and organization should be designed to facilitate this. It is possible to envisage a situation in which there are nontechnical salesmen selling standard products, and specialists selling more complex products; from this it is a short step to the point where the sales team consists of nontechnical salesmen working with service representatives responsible for maintenance and similar after-sales service.

THE ELEMENTS OF PRODUCT SERVICE

Simon[34] suggests that all technical product service can be broken down into the following ingredients:

Anticipation	Prediction of customers' needs for technical services and provision for these predicted needs.
Accuracy in problem definition	The determination with the customer of the precise problem on which the service organization is to work.
Completeness	The scope, range, or number of technical services provided for customers.
Responsiveness	The speed with which the service organization responds to emergency situations.
Problem-solving efficiency	The time necessary to achieve a technically correct solution of the problem which permits the customer to accomplish what he expected with the aid of the service rendered him.

He recommends that, to evaluate the efficiency and aptness of the technical service, results under these headings should be assessed.

Certainly, the importance of service in industrial markets is often high. The failure to consider it which has sometimes occurred has probably resulted from the earlier and fuller attention given to consumer marketing, in which this aspect is of less importance. Nevertheless, it must be appropriate to customers' needs and its economics must be reviewed to ensure that a reasonable benefit accrues.

13

Planned Advertising

The traditional definition of advertising describes it as communication by an identified sponsor through a paid impersonal medium. As sometimes interpreted, it is by no means clear whether this usage would include direct mail advertising. It is, however, convenient to include direct mail in this chapter, and in general it is customary and reasonable to consider both display advertising in journals and mail advertising together.

While the role of advertising in industrial markets is less striking than it is in consumer markets, and advertising budgets are, on the whole, lower as a percentage of turnover, it is by no means unimportant. It is one link in the chain of effective marketing, and if the advertising link is weak the total marketing effort will suffer.

One way of looking at the role of industrial advertising is to regard its prime purpose as a method of making the sales force more effective and more economical. In this way it reduces selling costs and boosts turnover. To achieve this, advertising has to be woven into the complex pattern of communications methods in general use in industrial markets; this requires close cooperation between the advertising agency and the marketing company to ensure that there is a comprehensive overall design in the approach to marketing communication. Display advertising must tie in with mail shots, exhibitions, seminars, the literature which the company uses, and the presentations of the salesman.

This general task is effected in a number of ways. Frequently, advertising prepares the ground before a call. It briefs the buyer and other executives whom the salesman will meet so that they are aware of the company, its reputation, its products, its product features, its technical service, or any other points which they must know. The salesman then finds he is starting an interview with a man who is already aware, interested, and if the advertising has been good enough, somewhat inclined to deal with him.

Advertising also helps to convey a message in depth to a prospect company. The decision-making network is complex and normally the salesman will not be regularly in touch with more than two executives. The rest of the network will be hard and expensive to reach. An important task of advertising is to contact others on the network and move them to a fuller appreciation that this is the right product to buy and the right company to buy it from.

Where the market for a product is widespread and many companies make a small volume of purchases, the salesman's calls on them will be infrequent—perhaps once or twice a year. The gap between calls must be filled, and this is a role which advertising can play.

Advertising also may have the responsibility of generating leads which can make the work of the sales force more effective. This is particularly valuable when much of the sales force's work is in searching out new prospects because the product is one which is bought infrequently. In some exceptional circumstances, where the sale is by mail, advertising has the entire responsibility for making the sale. It is also used to back up the work of distributors and intermediate manufacturers to motivate them to greater selling effort.

No review of what advertising has to offer is complete without reference to its contribution to projecting the company image. This is a function which extends beyond that of directly assisting the making of sales. It is considered more fully in Chapter 14.

In general it may be said that the marketing executive tries to use advertising when it is the most economical way of undertaking a particular part of the total communication function. It is not easy to assess when this applies, and as a practical matter it is very hard to give more than general suggestions.

Managers sometimes see the problem of advertising expenditure as a question of whether to spend extra money on advertising or to use that money to employ another representative. This is often the wrong way of looking at the problem. The sales force and advertising are part of a unified package of communication and the decision is on how big the total package is to be. There is no point in selling the buyer on a product unless others in the company are prepared to accept his recommendation. Similarly, there is little point in trying to persuade a customer to purchase a particular textile yarn unless the consumer is willing to accept and perhaps even prefer it to others.

ADVERTISING OBJECTIVES

By the time that the advertising is being planned, the marketing man's thinking should have developed through a number of prior stages. He has first settled his overall approach to the market, he has determined the general nature of his communication strategy within his overall marketing plan, and now for the first time he comes down to the specific question of determining the role of advertising. A common difficulty that advertising agencies in this field have to face is that advertisers come to them without having gone through this initial process. The marketing goals which are to be supported by advertising should have been decided; the task of developing goals for advertising which are as precise and quantified as possible follows from this.

The brief to the advertising agency must therefore set out:

The marketing goals.
The nature and size of the target audience.
What is the role of the audience in the decision-making process.
What change in information and attitudes is sought.

There may well be several groups of people who will be targets for the campaign. Each group can involve different objectives, different advertisements, and different media. Thus a company might specify its objectives as follows:

To inform 100 top executives in industry X that the company is a reliable and trustworthy source of supply.
To inform 1,000 design engineers in that industry that a new product of the company is suited to a particular application.
To explain to 1,000 buyers that the price has been reduced and delivery is prompt.

In practice this degree of precision is hard to achieve. Nevertheless, unless the purpose of the advertising is defined in terms which have a reasonable degree of precision, the advertising effort may well be dissipated and of little value.

THE ADVERTISING APPROACH

At this stage, responsibility is shifting onto the shoulders of the advertising specialist who is being briefed, although the process of briefing is in the nature of a dialogue in which an exchange of views promotes clarity and greater understanding on both sides about what is sought and what is feasible. The raw message has to be turned first into a general approach and then into copy. Media have also to be selected. While it is convenient and necessary to look at these steps individually, there is of course a process of feedback by which thinking on one aspect affects thinking on another.

The approach is the general basic idea about the way in which the chosen message may be put over effectively and convincingly. It may be desirable to put the message as a straight exposition of the merits of the company, or it may be by way of testimonials (although this method seems less popular in the United Kingdom than in the United States). Facts about applications may be put over by a case-history approach, telling how other users have successfully used the product, or even by some question and answer approach which involves the reader in the advertisement by requiring him to respond to it, mentally at least. To the buyer, the message about the price change may well be put over straight. Service may require different handling, for example by showing that the company has a technical service representative available within one hour's traveling time of every major company in the country.

Some of these approaches may be more effectively interpreted at an exhibition, by issuing a press release, or by a mail shot rather than by display advertising.

The creation of effective copy is described in specialist texts. This matter is, of course, complicated by the difficulty of testing whether or not the copy has been effective. The copy itself should always be based on what interests the target reader in relation to the product or service offered. Like the salesman, the advertising man talks in terms of customer benefits. This is an obvious guidline—yet it is easy to forget. In technical and industrial advertising, the arguments are almost invariably on a rational level, supported by factual evidence. Different classes of decision-makers have different interests, and each message may require a different medium and separate tailoring to a particular audience. Before settling down to the development of copy, the advertising man will spend a great deal of time on the basic problem of understanding the product and what it does and on thinking through the likely reaction of his different target audiences.

As in most advertising, the first task of the copy is to

attract the right readers. Individuals who may only be flicking through a journal need to be impelled to study a particular advertisement. The target audience is picked out by the headline or illustration of the advertisement. Each reader must react as if, at the back of his mind, a voice were saying, "This is something I should look at." Messner, in his well-known text,[35] says: "A good industrial advertisement has about it an air of *promise* for the reader," and he gives the following advice on the headline:

> To do its job well, a headline should:
> 1 Seek out the kind of readers which you would like to read your advertisement.
> 2 Encourage them to read further in the copy.
> 3 Inspire belief.
> 4 Communicate an understandable message.

From there on, the copy must pick up and intensify interest. If the product has well-defined advantages, this is not a big problem. When, however, the product is much the same as other products on the market, the good copywriter must take more obvious facts and bring them to life in a manner which adds interest, impact, and credibility. Enlivening the advertisement with a touch of emotion and human interest has been known to reinforce it.

This is a real challenge to the copywriter's abilities. His objective may be to *maintain* rather than create goodwill and a positive awareness. Under such circumstances an indirect approach may be used—for example, by highlighting service or dramatic examples of product application. Finally, the general tone of the advertisement and its layout will have an effect, over time, on the way in which the reader may think about the company. Creating good copy is no easy task.

Normally, a company's specific advertisements are part of a larger campaign. Advertisements may well appear in a series in the same journal, and they strengthen each other if there is a family likeness and perhaps a unifying theme to intensify impact. For example, a campaign to show the versatility of a product may feature in successive advertisements a series of dramatic instances in which the product has been used in an unexpected and intriguing way.

Frequency and size of advertisement is a difficult problem, and at this stage the advertising man has little more than rule-of-thumb judgment to guide him. Is it better to have a quarter-page advertisement every month, half a page every two months, or a full page every four months? The valid answer "Whichever does the job better" is not often helpful as a guide to action. A common view is that size is important, and the advertisement should be large enough to make an impact or even to dominate the medium. To some extent it depends on the journal concerned. Some journals are studied with loving care and filed as a source of reference, and even the smaller advertisements are noted by the relevant reader. Others are read more casually, and the probability of being noticed will depend very much on the size and location of the advertisement.

MEDIA SELECTION

Industrial advertising uses many different media. The object is to find a channel which goes to the target audience and is likely to combine the appropriate emphasis and acceptability with economy. Sometimes the choice is at first sight surprising, but the varied problems of industrial marketing require an equally wide range of answers. Television, for example, is not an obvious selection for industrial goods. It has, of course, a place in back-selling campaigns for influencing consumers. Sometimes it has been used for the direct promotion of goods to decision-makers in industrial markets. Rank-Xerox, for example, introduced their copying equipment to the United Kingdom market through this medium, among others. The reason appears to be that there were very many companies who could be expected to be interested in the product, there could be several buying points within each company, and the total number of people who could influence buying decisions was very great indeed. Because the product could be demonstrated on television, the message could be transmitted with a credibility and impact which other media would find hard to match.

The same medium has been used in a somewhat different way for the sale to farmers of fertilizers, seeds, and other requirements. For these, the advertisers selected a television station (in this case Anglia Television), which served an area with a strong agricultural bias, and chose a suitable time for promotion. Here it was a case of contacting a moderately large audience, and television was considered an economical medium.

Industrial advertising is also carried in the "quality" daily and weekly press and journals. Some of this is image projection, but there are frequently advertisements more directly concerned with developing short-term sales. These are generally products of a nontechnical nature which would be of interest to a wide range of industries; in particular they are often items of direct interest to the administrative and commercial staff.

A quick look at this press reveals advertisements for

automatic tea and coffee units, towel services, leasing of motor vehicles, and secretarial, financial, and commercial services of all types. These advertisements aim to appeal to various levels of management in business, government, and elsewhere. Some industrial advertising uses posters as a medium—for example, posters outside agricultural shows promoting goods to farmers. One company used advertisements in London underground trains to promote drain-cleaning services to businessmen.

More important in most industrial advertising, however, is the wide range of trade and technical journals which circulate in Britain, and the main problem of media planning is concerned with deciding which of these to use and to what extent.

Dicussion of trade and technical media has developed its own language. The prime distinction is between "vertical" and "horizontal" media. Vertical media penetrate many different levels in a particular industry; for example, *British Printer* is read by many different executives in the printing industry, whereas *Modern Purchasing* caters for purchasing officers across a wide range of different industries.

Life being what it is, media do not always fit neatly into these classes. When considering journals reaching a specific industry—particularly a large and growing industry such as electronics or chemicals—there are some which penetrate to many different executives in one sector of the industry, others which reach one class of executive across the industry (that is to say, they are vertical or horizontal within the industry). Some media are L-shaped (part vertical and part horizontal) and others overflow from one industry into another.

Another important distinction is between journals which are issued free to a controlled circulation and those which have a paid, but unrestricted, circulation. The former are distributed only to certain categories of eligible executives. The entire income is from advertising. The object is to ensure that the circulation of the journal is directed to a particular professional or industrial audience. In this they differ from the general run of journals sold to any subscriber.

To achieve his objectives of selecting media to reach the right audience with the right quality of impact, the media planner needs to know the profile of the target audience and to choose media whose readership matches this profile. One general problem is the lack of a clear and standardized nomenclature for different executive functions in business. This makes both definition and matching of the audience profile difficult.

Readership data on different journals is, therefore, essential. Prior to 1966 the only information widely available was that provided by the certificate of the Audit Bureau of

Circulation Ltd. For member journals the ABC certificate gives the following audited information:

Paid subscription journals	(a) Sales at cover or annual subscription rate, and (b) sales at reduced rate.
Controlled journals	Number of qualified readers on the mailing list at their request. (A qualified reader is one who is in the professional/industrial group to which the journal is directed. This definition requires the reader to have asked for the journal, by returning a reply-paid card or otherwise, and excludes copies sent out to people who did not request them.)

Currently some 600 of the trade, technical, and professional journals are audited in this way.

This information was augmented in 1966 when the British Industrial Advertisers' Association, the Incorporated Society of British Advertisers, the Institute of Practitioners in Advertising, and the Periodical Proprietors' Association's Trade and Technical Council jointly issued a new Media Data Form, part of which is produced as Fig. 11. This form is a standard basis on which publishers are asked to provide fuller information. At the time of writing, some 350 journals now provide this data. This number includes most of the journals of major importance in industrial advertising.

For paid journals, the form collects information on sales on normal terms, special terms, and about free issue. A separate analysis is adopted for controlled journals. A breakdown of readers by location, industry, and job title is also required. Supplementary information is asked about the history of the journal, its editorial policy, and any special readership research.

The number of publishers carrying out special surveys to provide a fuller breakdown of their readership is increasing. For media planning, what is needed is a study of different categories of executive, identifying the journals which they read. There are few such studies as yet, but the numbers are slowly increasing, mainly as a result of pressure from advertising agencies.

There are other considerations as well as readership figures which must be taken into account when selecting media. One is the quality of the journal: some are more authoritative than others, and this may be reflected in the reader's attitude to the advertisements. Some are studied closely by readers, while

● INDUSTRIAL PROFESSIONAL & TRADE
Media Data Form

Issued jointly by:
British Industrial Advertising Association
Incorporated Society of British Advertisers
Institute of Practitioners in Advertising
PPA Trade & Technical Council

NAME OF PUBLICATION

Filing Code
★

© COPYRIGHT Institute of Practitioners in Advertising 1966

CIRCULATION DETAILS Average number of copies distributed per issue for 6/12 months period ending _____

A. Paid Circulation Journals

17 (a) Are the figures below audited? YES/NO   (b) Is the journal a member of ABC? YES/NO

(c) If not ABC figures, by whom were they audited?

	HOME	OVERSEAS	TOTAL
18 Number of copies sold at normal trade terms or by subscription at not less than 85% of cover price			
19 Number of copies sold			
(a) at less than normal trade terms			
(b) at subscription rates below 85%, but not less than 50% of cover price			
(c) at subscription rates under 50%, but not less than 25% of cover price			
(d) at subscription rates under 25% of cover price.			
20 Number of copies distributed by or on behalf of a Society			
(a) to members as part of normal subscription to the society			
(b) against payment in addition to normal subscription to the society			
(c) to non-members against payment			
21 Total net sales			
22 Average unpaid distribution to qualified readers			
23 GRAND TOTAL			

24 Are you able to provide percentage of subscription renewals? YES/NO

25 Any other relevant facts.

B. Controlled Circulation Journals

26 (a) Is the total against 32 audited? YES/NO   (b) Is the journal a member of ABC? YES/NO

(c) If not ABC figures, by whom were they audited? _____

	HOME	OVERSEAS	TOTAL
27 Regularly, i.e. every issue unpaid to qualified readers			
28 On a rotational basis unpaid to qualified readers			
29 Other unpaid distribution to qualified readers			
30 On subscription (a) at full rate			
(b) at reduced rate			
31 Other sales (a) at cover price			
(b) at less than cover price			
32 TOTAL			

33 Please give details of any circulation not on a regular (every issue) basis, i.e. explain method of distribution of copies in 28 & 29 above.

34 Is your circulation list open to inspection? YES/NO

35 Is journal addressed to individuals or to job titles? YES/NO

36 Any other relevant facts.

Fig. 11. Part of Media Data Form. (By courtesy of the Institute of Practitioners in Advertising.)

others are read in a more relaxed mood. Some journals are normally filed and kept for future reference by the executives who read them, and advertising may have a longer-term value. To assess the journals in this way, the media planner can study their content and reinforce his views by inquiry among readers.

Finally, the facilities which the journal offers may influence the decision. The availability of color, the willingness to accept inserts, and whether or not there are reader reply cards at the end can be relevant. There are occasions when there is no journal which serves the particular audience. In that case the advertiser must create his own medium. This is one reason for the development of direct mail and the house journal.

DIRECT MAIL

This is a valuable medium for the industrial advertiser, and its popularity is high. The term is self-explanatory: it is the sending by mail of promotional material direct to customers' and prospects' staff. It is an extremely flexible medium, since in addition to national campaigns it is possible with careful planning to carry out local campaigns which tie in closely with the salesman's calls or the work of a local distributor.

A key factor in successful direct mail is an up-to-date list of the people who are the targets for promotion. The preparation and continuous updating of the mailing list thus requires regular attention, and in a large organization several staff may be employed on this task. The list is, if at all possible, a list of people's names. Turnover rates in particular jobs may be up to 20 percent per annum. If a mailing list contains tens of thousands of names, this means thousands of alterations annually.

All mail returned undelivered must be carefully handled to ensure that changes are recorded, and feeding back information to keep the list up to date becomes an important job for the salesman. Where direct mail is used frequently, the records must be classified by industry and by function in order that addressees with a particular interest can be identified and appropriate material sent to them. Their time and the advertisers' money is then not wasted on irrelevant mail shots.

Mailing lists for a market which is being entered for a first time can often be purchased from specialized suppliers. However, a company with regular interest in a particular market will normally maintain its own list. This may begin with a purchased list, but this is developed and updated from such sources as directories, association membership lists, exhibit visitors, salesmen's information, and inquiries received. The cost of direct mail is often more expensive than that of an insertion in a journal with a comparable readership. There is not only the initial preparation of the material, but also the printing of the literature and the actual mail cost. Having met this cost, there is still the possibility that the shot, although addressed to the individual technician, purchasing officer, or other executive by name, may still be unread or may never see the light of day because it is intercepted by a secretary or even thrown away unopened. People who receive a large amount of literature in this way sometimes seem to develop some sixth sense for mail advertising material!

Direct mail requires as much care in writing as any other advertising. Effectiveness may be increased by starting any covering letter with "Dear Mr. ———" and addressing the individual by name. With large-scale mailing lists the cost of entering each individual name is high, and the marketing executive must weigh the extra cost against the effect or response rates.

Much direct mail is concerned with developing leads, and the system for recording and acting on these leads must be carefully planned. Direct mail is, of course, also used for keeping customers up to date: sending out literature of all sorts, catalogs, servicing information, and suggestions on applications and uses. The pressure of direct mail is growing and the competition in many an executive's in-tray is intense.

New ideas are therefore at a premium, and the advertiser is continually seeking new forms of presentation which will catch the executive's attention and encourage him to read on. These include pamphlets mailed under "first-day" covers with new postage stamps, three-dimensional devices, and samples. Yet still the search for originality continues. Commonly there will be a series of shots (analogous to series of advertisements in a journal) in order to make the fullest impact at the right time.

The assessment of advertising effectiveness is discussed more fully later in this chapter. Mail advertising which aims to produce inquiries does, however, have the advantage that it is often possible to test response to different variations of a message before embarking on a large-scale campaign. Some regular users of mail advertising have carried out small sample experiments of this nature and assessed relative effectiveness of different copy from inquiries received; they have found that useful comparisons are possible. The "samples" for such experiments must be chosen according to the basic rules of sampling.

There are also certain operating considerations which need attention, such as the need to conform to post office regulations.

SETTING THE ADVERTISING BUDGET

Against this background, the advertiser is forced to decide how much to spend on the budget for media advertising. Methods of making this decision vary from those which are easy to apply but difficult, perhaps impossible, to justify on logical grounds, to those founded on a sound theoretical basis but difficult, and sometimes impossible, to apply in practice because of the problem of making the necessary estimates.

In the first category are a number of rule-of-thumb formulae. These are:

1 Allocate a percentage of past sales.
2 Allocate a percentage of profit.
3 Allocate a percentage of expected sales.

The actual percentage chosen may be derived from past company practice or by examining what competitors are doing. The logical deficiencies of this approach are easy to see. It is more an appropriation than a budget since it is not based on any consideration of the relationship between the amount of expenditure and the expected increase in company revenue which will flow from that expenditure. The best arguments that can be advanced are that it has some relationship with past experience, and if the company has been intelligent in its approach to the market it may have approximated to a reasonable figure. If competitors' figures are looked to for a guide, it ensures that the company does not fall behind in its relative expenditure (although it is not always easy to obtain information about the relative advertising expenditure of competitors, and when it is obtained it is often not on a comparable basis).

Any historic relationship between advertising expenditure and turnover, even if it were correct in the past, is not necessarily the right figure for the future. Changes in the rate of innovation in the industry leading to more new products can lead to a change in the need for advertising. If a company sets out to expand its sales by seeking greater market penetration, entering new markets, or developing new applications, then this will affect the role of advertising.

Faced with this difficulty, some companies seem to have given up any idea of a logical approach to the advertising budget, and the figure is determined by no clear method. Others have attempted to move toward a method which has the merit of logic—the task method.

In this method, the company works back from the amount of advertising needed to the estimate of what the budget should be. That is to say, the logical flow of thought is

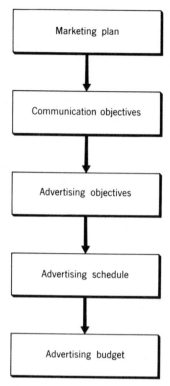

Fig. 12. Setting the advertising budget

as in Fig. 12. In this way, the amount to be spent on advertising flows in a logical manner from the total marketing program. In developing the advertising budget, it is necessary to make difficult assessments about how frequently to insert advertisements or send out mail shots in order to achieve the advertising objectives.

Yet when it comes down to it, this difficulty cannot be avoided. The percentage share methods are ways of closing one's eyes to the problem. It seems far better to face the basic issues and, with an awareness of the limitations of what is being done, nevertheless use all possible skill and judgment in trying to arrive at an answer which is capable of reasonable justification. As advertising expenditure is commonly less than 1 percent of turnover in industrial markets, an honest and intelligent endeavor to apply the task method can result in a figure which may be described as of the right order of magnitude.

When companies are currently using some variation of the percentage method, it is still possible to examine the question "How is the task which advertising has to do next year changing, and how is the budget requirement changing as a result?" This question is often easier to answer approximately and avoids having to face the task of working through a whole year's forecast of advertising requirements and then having to seek sanction from a board which may suspect that the task method is simply a way of trying to expand the budget for advertising. Finally, of course, the budget must be within the company's resources, and an advertising submission that is beyond this is in trouble! Such a situation would indicate that the company's marketing plan is basically defective.

ASSESSING THE EFFECTIVENESS OF ADVERTISING

At the back of all the discussion on advertising there remains one question which is hard to answer: "How effective is the advertising which has been put out?" This question has not been answered with complete satisfaction even in consumer advertising, where appropriations running into millions of dollars can be at stake. What has happened is that research has set out to measure the efficiency of the communication rather than the effect on the volume of sales resulting from the advertising. The reason for this is that, whereas communication results can be reasonably attributed to advertising in consumer markets, sales depend on many other variables as well.

There is much to be said for the view that this is the right thing to measure, except where the goods are sold entirely by advertising, when the results can be directly examined by comparing cost of advertising with volume of sales generated. This, however, is an uncommon case; in most instances advertising is one part of the job. It may be most valuable to maintain a warm goodwill toward a product among purchasing officers, but if in fact the salesman fails to call on those particular officers, then the goodwill may be wasted. Advertising may have carried out its role well in the chain of persuasive communication, but sales may not have been consummated.

Where a principal function of the advertising is to generate sales leads, then replies received may be an appropriate basis for assessment of results. It is necessary to take account of the value of the replies, and the real test should be the sales generated by the leads received.

However, if there is a long gap between the date of the original inquiry and the placing of an order, as there is in many industries, then the assessment is long delayed and less reliable.

In these circumstances the salesman who follows up the inquiry is often asked to report on the quality of the lead. Is the inquirer a genuine prospect? Is business likely to result in the short term? In the long term?

The need for a systematic procedure for following inquiries relatively soon after they are received hardly needs stressing. An efficient system of recording and control is necessary to ensure that this in fact happens.

Ideally, advertising should have specific quantitative objectives which are capable of being measured by market research. For example, it might be decided that in order to generate sufficient volume of demand for a building product the aim should be to make 75 percent of the architects in southern England and London aware of its special properties. Prior to the campaign, a survey shows that only 10 percent of them are aware of this information. After the preliminary campaign (or at some convenient point in it) further market research is carried out to measure progress toward the target.

While this is the ideal, the cost of market research may seem disproportionate to the advertising expenditure. The choice then is either to carry out the market research anyway, for if the company does not have it done (even at a comparatively high price) the marketing plan may be damaged by inefficient or misdirected advertising, or to use informal methods to assess how the advertising is going over. The latter method can often give useful indications when the cost of research seems too high. Information is sometimes obtained from representatives, provided it is made clear to them that it is the customer's view that is wanted, not the representative's own, and that what the company wants to know is whether the advertising message has got through and *not* whether the prospect thought it was a good advertisement. This can be backed up by information received at trade exhibitions, comments in the press, and information from distributors. Even competitors' reactions may be illuminating.

In the United States, research on industrial advertising in a formal way is more common, though far from universal. One of the best-known services is the Starch service (by Daniel Starch and staff) in which a sample of readers of some of the larger-circulation industrial journals are asked whether they have:

(a) "noted" the advertisement, that is remembered having seen it;

(b) "seen—associated"—whether they remembered seeing the advertisement *and* associated it with the advertiser (or brand);

(c) "read most"—that is read more than 50 percent of the advertisement.

In Britain some work is done by publishers sending out copies of a magazine to subscribers and asking them to indicate which of the advertisements they remember seeing. This method is obviously much less satisfactory than the full personal interview approach. Even, however, with the most conscientious of methods the respondent may well have great difficulty in giving an accurate answer to a question like "Did you read more than half this advertisement?"

THE ROLE OF THE ADVERTISING AGENCY

In view of the wide range of possible ways available for communicating to the market in industrial products, the advertising agency which goes into this field must be prepared to take a much wider view of its function and accordingly widen the range of services which it offers the client. It has to plan a related sequence of messages blending both personal and impersonal communication. Thus it must work very closely with the client and be well briefed on his sales and service operations, as well as obtaining the more customary information. It must ensure that the timing of the advertisements is appropriate and must be ready as a normal service to provide related material to assist in face-to-face selling and to brief the sales force on the many marketing communication tools which are in use.

Traditionally, the advertising agency has lived by the commission system. Agencies evolved from the function of agents who sold advertising space for newspapers on a commission basis. Gradually, they found that the best way of selling space was by helping the buyer of the space to decide what to put in it! Nevertheless, agencies still substantially retain the system by which the remuneration comes from the medium-owners as commission, and not from the client who is their true employer and to whom the agencies' loyalty should be directed.

The commission system is subject to much criticism in relation to consumer advertising. It certainly seems inappropriate to industrial markets. In Table 7 the Institute of Practitioners in Advertising illustrates the way in which the pattern of advertising expenditure may be divided between different channels for three separate companies.[36] These budgets illustrate the variety of approach to industrial marketing communications.

A fee defined as a percentage of turnover has little

Table 7 Comparison of advertising budgets*

	SIZE OF BUDGET		
	$24,000	$96,000	$480,000
Literature	35%	16%	17%
Press, space and production	20	37	45
Exhibitions	15	15	10
Direct mail	15	4	5
Agency service fee	10	6	4
Films	—	—	2
Advertising dept. costs	—	10	8
P.R. service fee and costs	—	8	8
Contingency	5	4	1
Total	100	100	100

* Amounts, originally in pounds, have been translated into dollar equivalents.

relevance to this situation, and the commission system in industrial advertising has sometimes been modified by two other methods:

1 Agreeing a service fee for the work to be done.
2 Guaranteeing the agency a certain level of payment. If this is not achieved through commission, then the balance is made up by the advertiser.

MAKING THE MOST OF ADVERTISING

When a campaign is carried out, its benefit can often be increased by exploiting it through all possible channels. Its value should be brought home sharply to the sales force, and material in the campaign can often be adapted for use by the salesman in making a presentation to a customer. Distributors also should be kept fully briefed and supplied with copies of advertisements. Reprints can be used as mail shots. Publishers usually provide reprints on reasonable terms, providing inquiry is made in good time. Publishers and advertisers have a common interest in working together in this way.

14

Print, Promotion, and Public Relations

This chapter brings together a range of communication methods which are of considerable importance in marketing industrial products and have not been covered earlier. Some of them are complex in the range of alternatives which they offer and the purposes they can serve. If the executive is looking at his whole communication problem, he will probably readily identify his need for print, although there is room for imagination and ingenuity in deciding in detail what form it shall take. With promotion and public relations, it is often more difficult to decide what exactly their role shall be and to assess their effectiveness.

THE FORMS OF PRINT

This term is used for all the literature produced by, or specifically for, a company, thus distinguishing it from advertising media owned by third parties, such as the trade and technical press. The concept overlaps with direct mail.

Literature also reaches the customer through channels other than mail: it is a tool of the salesman in making a presentation, it is distributed at exhibitions, and it will also be passed on by distributors and agents. The term "direct advertising" is sometimes used to cover this entire field.

Literature is essential in most industrial marketing situations, yet it has not been much discussed by writers on marketing, perhaps because until recently most of them have been more concerned with consumer markets. Frequently a marketing man who has clearly understood what he is trying to achieve will have little difficulty in deciding what literature is necessary. "When you have your task defined, print needs fall into place," said one specialist in this field.

The process of analysis by which this point is reached must be painstaking, for it requires considerable attention to detail. Lack of the right literature at the right time can mean a sale missed and, since good literature does much of its work when the salesman is not around, no one ever knows until it is too late and the order is lost. The literature must thus be suited to its purposes and well designed. Its quality must be influenced by the standing of the company which issues it and the status of the proposed recipient.

The range of possibilities under this heading is infinite. With display advertising, the advertiser is constrained by the need to fit the requirements of the medium, but with print he is creating his own medium and the only constraints are those of effectiveness and cost. This, of course, makes classification difficult. The following breakdown is generally accepted as being most convenient,[37] but much of the material has more than one function.

PERSUASIVE

Material under this heading serves the prime purpose of directly creating favorable attitudes toward the company and what it has to offer. It includes such items as personalized letters, printed and illustrated letters, leaflets, folders, booklets, and business reply cards.

INFORMATIVE

This includes reference material such as catalogs, price lists, spare-parts lists and wall charts, technical and other aids to using and maintaining the product, and a wide range of other material including external house journals, letters, and posters.

REMINDERS

Calendars, blotters, notebooks, and diaries are intended to serve the primary purpose of keeping the supplier's name and other details in mind.

UTILITARIAN

This includes labels, letterheads, envelopes and business cards, and similar material.

Where there are a very large number of people slightly involved in the buying decision, it is often desirable to have a small and informative leaflet which can be given away liberally. Such a leaflet will be inexpensive and not too technical, but it can still be well designed. It is an easy way of putting in the picture many people whose individual influence may be small but whose collective impact can matter. It ensures that discussion at all levels in the prospect company is reasonably well informed and reduces the possibility that adverse eddies of opinion may develop. It seeks to leave a favorable impression of the supplier, his products, his service, and his general reliability.

A leaflet of this type is by no means sufficient for the decision-makers more closely concerned with the product purchase decision. Fuller literature is necessary, and commonly there is a need for two classes of document. The man who is concerned with commercial policy requires literature which puts over the story of the company which is supplying the product and shows how the decision will bring commercial gains. This document will stress advantages such as cost saving, extra sales, and government invested grants which will accrue and will provide factual evidence and accounting or statistical calculation. It may also bring out the reliability of the supplier, if this may not be well appreciated by the customer.

The technical man will benefit from a different class of literature, explaining how the product works, product characteristics, and applications, helping him to satisfy himself that it is for his purpose. These documents have a workmanlike air. Drawings and diagrams could be of the "blueprint" type, probing the inner workings of the product and giving details of laboratory and field tests. It should aim to help the technician decide on the product and select a model which will suit his purpose. This class includes individual data sheets.

It may be necessary to produce different literature for different industries, and in some instances suppliers have found it economical and efficient to produce a brochure solely for executives of one major company which represents substantial potential business, showing how a raw material or component can be used in the prospect's own product.

The job of this class of literature is to aid the salesman and to be a silent salesman when he is not around. The target decision-maker can browse over it at his leisure, he can talk about it with colleagues, and the literature can penetrate through to people whom the salesman has never met. Often when the buyer or the works manager has made a favorable decision, he then has to recommend that decision to a committee or superior for approval. The literature gives him the tools to back his case. It strengthens the salesman's approach and helps reduce the time required to achieve a sale.

"Reference material" is a convenient expression for that literature which the buyer and others in his organization keep for consultation when a need for a purchase is identified within the company. The executive's files and shelves are an extension of his own memory, and up-to-date material in a form which is easy to locate adds memorability to the products.

Commonly used items include the catalog (or its equivalent), price lists, spares lists, and data sheets. These are designed to be efficient tools.

For many products, the catalog is extremely important, and companies are taking great care to make them simple and speedy to use. This involves improving the clarity of type and headings, good indexing at the front, and other facilities such as thumb indexing and color-coding page edges. Some companies are experimenting with unorthodox methods of locating entries, for example by recording details on edge-punched cards for quick and easy tracing.

Technical and instructional handbooks must be provided when the nature of the product requires it. These may describe installation, operation and repair, and maintenance. They may need to be durable enough to stand constant use, perhaps in the works under arduous conditions. In some departments, the collection of shelves of technical literature seems to become a sort of status symbol with some executives. To these may be added training material for customers' production, maintenance, and sales staff.

The size of any document which is to be filed and kept for a period of time or included in a folder to be sent to a client or senior executive must conform to the practice of the industry concerned. A recent development is that in some industries specialist agencies now offer to provide buying firms with a filing system containing the literature of suppliers and to keep this up to date on payment of a rental. The supplier of the literature is also charged a fee for inclusion in these records.

The house journal is often used with advantage. The range of possibilities is very wide, depending upon the purpose which the journal is designed to achieve and the audience which it is to serve. Leaving aside the internal house journal of staff news—which is irrelevant for this purpose—one finds prestige-type journals (of which the reviews of the major banks are an example) which have no immediate selling purpose but maintain the standing of the organization concerned. Others are addressed to maintenance men and have a content of lighter material plus a core of useful advice. Journals may be addressed to technologists, and the content is suitably matched to the readership. Again, the aim is to provide a useful and respected publication with only indirect promotion of the company, and that primarily through items with interest value. The major part of the material may be about scientific and technological developments. The costs of such journals show great variation.

The value of calendars and diaries is difficult to assess. No one seems really to know exactly what benefit they achieve, or even if they are retained by the original addressees or passed on to junior members of the staff. In theory, they keep the supplier's name in front of the recipient, but a man who receives three or four diaries only uses one! Including reference material of particular interest to him which is not conveniently accessible elsewhere may encourage the addressee to retain a diary. Calendars present a similar problem.

ASPECTS OF PROMOTION

The word "promotion" is widely used and seems to have a variety of meanings. The term is used here to cover any method of putting over a message which goes beyond the use of media and personal representation and backs them up with a short-term attention-drawing "boost."

The most common method under this heading is the exhibition, which can be a major trade exhibition or a special exhibition organized by the supplier himself or on his behalf. Personal observation is one of the ways in which people obtain information, and the exhibition provides a suitable opportunity to see products and sometimes to see them in action. This is a great advantage in some markets.

The trade exhibition is, however, often a source of much heart-searching. It can be the biggest item in the industrial communication budget (apart from personal representation).

Some companies are carrying out research to decide what the value of attendance at the exhibition is, but the results do not yet seem to help settle the issue. Sometimes it appears that the majority of new contacts at the exhibition represent unimportant executives in present customer firms or casually interested inquirers representing little, if anything, in the way of business. Other inquirers may already be known to the company's sales force. Some companies report receiving a useful volume of business at the exhibition but are uncertain whether or not most of this would in any case have been picked up when the salesman next called. More attention is being directed at determining the type and number of visitors to the exhibition and noting the booths which they visited. Companies putting on exhibits keep as full a check as is possible of callers at their booth.

A major influence in deciding whether or not to attend is concern about what competitors may be doing. The fear is that if the company does not attend and the competitor does, then this gives the competitor a chance to cultivate the company's present customers and perhaps gain the orders which are now due or at least establish a bridgehead for the future. The result is that attendance seems sometimes to be contagious—one year all the companies making a certain product attend, the next none of them!

Certainly, companies appear keen to find out whether competitors propose to be at particular exhibitions. Overseas exhibitions are not quite the same, and a well-attended exhibition overseas is often a good way of breaking into a foreign market.

Once a decision has been made to attend an exhibition, then it is necessary to extract every ounce of benefit from the heavy cost involved. The stand itself must attract, and much thought and money is given to this. Customers and potential customers must be invited and often entertained as well, although exhibitors try to keep entertainment costs in proportion. The public relations staff must see that the press is kept well informed and well catered for by information, photographs, and so on. The stand must be well staffed, properly supplied with literature, and care taken to ensure that serious inquirers are given all possible assistance and that proper follow-up by the sales staff takes place afterward.

Some companies avoid the national trade exhibitions and stage their own exhibitions, perhaps on coincident dates to catch the same audience. Their products do not then have to compete with those of competitors. It is, however, necessary to generate an audience for the show, since it cannot rely upon the audience which is automatically generated by the trade show. This means that customers must be circulated by mail and the exhibition must also be advertised in trade journals. In some way, prospects not on the company's mailing list but who might attend the national show must be reached.

Another alternative for the smaller-size product is a traveling exhibition—perhaps in a specially built caravan or in a room rented in each locality, or a distributor's showroom. This permits a wider range of customer's staff to attend and will also attract people from smaller companies and institutions who may not travel to a national exhibition.

Rather similar is a procedure by which executives of prospect companies are invited to attend "open days" at suppliers' works. This is particularly suitable when the product is such that the chance to see it operating may make all the difference in securing business. These occasions can be given a very high status, and directors or other very senior executives may well be interested in coming. Such an audience is given VIP treatment and may be brought by special plane or other special transport to heighten the intensity of the occasion. To have a captive audience at this level is often of great value for capital equipment. Even though the cost per guest appears high, it can pay off. All the details need careful planning, and again the contact must be followed up in order that other levels of influence in the customer's company also receive the necessary attention. Selection of the right audience to attend is vital or the outlay can be wasted.

Sometimes it is possible to go one step farther and stage a visit to a customer's works to see a product actually in use. Naturally, the customer will be concerned at guarding what he considers to be his trade secrets from people who may be competitors, and this can sometimes be a complete bar to this approach. Some companies have found that with suitable precautions this type of promotion has been possible and successful. Ingenuity can find other variations on this theme. One company held an "at home" on the product—the product in this instance being a ship! Such occasions as these are of interest to the trade and perhaps also to the general business press.

P.R. IN MARKETING

At this point it is convenient to recognize that the border is being crossed into the field of public relations. The subject of public relations in its entirety goes well beyond the scope of this book, and those who wish to explore it in detail should go to more specialized texts.[38] It has, however, much of value to offer in industrial marketing, and the marketing executive is interested in its effective use.

The best definition is perhaps that by the Institute of Public Relations, which describes public relations as "the deliberate, planned and sustained effort to establish and maintain mutual understanding between an organization and its public." The practice of public relations is commonly seen as a way of putting across information about the company and its point of view to the world at large in an effective way. "The world at large" includes customers, shareholders, employees, government, and the electorate. The definition identifies public relations in terms of its objective and not in terms of a particular method. It includes the projection of the corporate image of the company, and thus numbers corporate advertising, press relations, films, exhibitions, and seminars among its techniques.

In fact the chief role of the public relations executive today is to act as guardian of the image of the company. The fact is that every company has an image—that is to say, a way in which the public sees it; indeed, it probably has several images which vary among its several publics. Whether these images truly reflect reality is another matter entirely, and it is this which is the concern of public relations. The image is of importance in marketing as the background against which sales are made and in its effect on the authority and credence which are given to the company's sales force, literature, and other promotions.

There is also a more specific contribution to be made in transmitting particular messages to particular audiences—drawing the attention of its customers to what the company has to offer through its products and services.

The hallmark of the public relations approach is indirect communication. Press relations is a case in point. One of the prime functions of many public relations men is ensuring that editors are kept informed of newsworthy matters affecting their clients. The decision to publish or not to publish belongs to the editor. The final responsibility is his. The public relations advisor must, therefore, be well acquainted with the different publications and be able to advise what their editors will consider the right material for their particular readers.

The appropriate trade and technical press will often be very glad to receive worthwhile information on many aspects of the company's business. The task is both to identify what is relevant and to bring it to the attention of the editor concerned by press release or another appropriate way. New products are, almost by definition, newsworthy, but so may be major contracts, the completion of large orders (particularly exports), advances in research, works and other visits, and a whole range of other happenings. The experienced P.R. man will often see a news angle which escapes the nonspecialist and be able to identify what is likely to interest a particular journal.

Even for a small company, public relations will at times extend beyond the trade and technical press to the business and other national press and even to television. Press work is not confined to the press release, although that is probably the most common. It includes the contribution of special articles, including even articles signed by top executives up to the managing director himself (although not always written entirely by the signatory).

Public relations does not end there. A company can make itself recognized as a leader in a particular field if a senior executive writes a book which can be accepted as authoritative, thus establishing its name in that field. Executives can also speak on their subject to conferences, professional bodies, or universities and thus widen general knowledge of the area in which the company operates. An executive who is to do this can often benefit by training in public speaking.

Seminars are now becoming a popular way to gain understanding of a company's contribution to technological advance. These appeal to technicians, designers, R&D executives, and others with a professional and scientific approach to their work. The seminar, usually of one but sometimes two days, consists of lectures, discussions, and other material of professional interest to the audience. It must provide value in terms of ideas and is not a selling situation. Speakers can be drawn from a variety of backgrounds: universities, scientific bodies, government, and even perhaps from competitors' staff, as well as from one's own company. The object is to draw attention to a field of interest which the company is developing and to put over the fact that the company is a progressive contributor to advance in this field. The implication is that the audience should listen to its technical representatives when they call, should read its literature, and keep a sharp eye on its new products. But the seminar itself must be honest and may well be put on by a neutral body—a university, research institution, or professional organization. The basic objective is to open the audience's eyes to what is going on and to the company which is doing it.

The key thought in this chapter is that all these tools of communication are, so far as marketing is concerned, given point and coherence by approaching them from the analysis of the customer and the information which he needs to make clear to him the merits of the supplier company and what it has to offer. This must then be followed through to make sure not only that he buys the product, but that he does in fact receive these benefits. Given clarity about this concept, and the necessary understanding of the customer—including perhaps his manufacturing techniques, his staff organization, his market, his R&D organization, and many other details of the company —the executive will then develop clear objectives (what is to be said to whom?) and devise planned ways of putting over the necessary messages. Even the apparently simple process of entertaining the customer's managing director to lunch requires more thought than is often given to it. Applying these principles may well result in a deep rethinking of the entire process of marketing communication.

15

Price Determination

Determining the price of a product implies that the executive has some freedom of choice in making this decision. At the very beginning, it is worth examining the question "What discretion does the executive have in choosing the price for a product and what are the factors which set limits to the price which he can select?" An alternative is to ask, "What are the conditions which give him this discretion and how can the area of discretion be enlarged?"

There are some market situations in which no discretion exists. These are circumstances rather like those described in elementary economics textbooks under the term "perfect competition." The product is exactly the same irrespective of the source from which it is bought, and no individual supplier or purchaser is so important that his actions can influence the market price. In this situation, the price is "given" as far as the business executive is concerned; it is outside his control and he has no choice but to accept it. This situation is brought out most clearly in the major organized commodity markets on which zinc, rubber, copper, etc., are bought and sold. Price does, however, become the prime criterion for many products which are standardized, and in respect of which buyers have low requirements for technical service, either because the product is a simple one or because the buying firm has the necessary competence. This situation is more frequent toward the "saturation" stage of the product life-cycle. There may then be little basis on which the purchaser can distinguish between the offerings of different suppliers other than that of price.

Price discretion on the other hand arises from the fact that there *is* some other basis on which the buyer can discriminate. He may discriminate because of differences in the nature of the physical product: its design is better, it matches his specification better, and so on. He may discriminate because of better technical service and advice, or because a supplier has a better reputation for fulfilling delivery promises. Discrimination also occurs because of promotional reasons: one company is better known or more respected than another in a particular field, or the representative has maintained better contact with the buyers.

Additional price discretion arises from the fact that a manufacturer of a differentiated product may have a choice between selling a relatively large volume at a low price or a smaller volume at a higher price. Both price and unit cost are related to the valume to be produced and sold. At any particular time, the more it is hoped to sell, the greater will be the pressure to reduce price, and as volume produced increases, the unit cost will often fall. Output, demand, and cost are three interacting factors affecting price. Demand sets the upper limit and cost the lower limit, at least in the long run. Pricing is thus an area of great complexity, in which all these variables have to be brought into calculation, and the calculation itself involves evaluating the uncertain future. How will customers react to a price change? What will competitors do and how will this react on demand? These questions require answers with as high a degree of confidence as possible.

Before becoming involved in the detailed arithmetic of pricing, it is necessary to decide the company's total marketing strategy for the product and the role of pricing in that strategy. If this is not done, the short-term decisions on pricing may not fit the company's long-term strategy. Rarely is the object of pricing simply to maximize short-term profits.

Examples of policy objectives in pricing are as follows (some of these will be discussed in more detail later in this and the following chapter):

1 To penetrate and preempt the market for a product by charging a low price.
2 To cream the market and to obtain early profits and liquidity by charging a high price.
3 To assist in phasing out an obsolescent product by making it unattractively expensive.
4 To discourage competitors from entering the market.
5 To avoid customer and political criticism.
6 To support a company image.
7 To encourage market expansion by a low price/high volume policy.

8 To avoid unduly provocative competitive action which could lead to prices falling to a level inconsistent with long-term profitability.

Such guidelines as these must be consistent with the way in which the company plans to move toward long-run profitability and give a necessary background to specific price decisions. Senior executives may have such ideas as these at the backs of their minds, but if they fail to specify them there may well be consequent confusion and misjudgment at a lower level.

THE ARITHMETIC OF SHORT-TERM PRICING

It will be assumed that the problem is to set one basic price for the product which is to be the general level. The problems of differentials between different customers and different market segments is deferred. List prices may sometimes differ from the true basic price where it is the custom of the trade concerned to allow discounts to customers.

The arithmetic of pricing uses data derived from the company's past history, from marketing research, and from personal judgment. In general, the aim is to determine the price which will give maximum short-term contribution, and this price is then modified by additional considerations to the one which is deemed most appropriate to the fulfillment of the longer-term objectives of the firm.

In some form or other, the calculations bring together the following variables:

1 The prices which different customers are prepared to pay for the product.
2 The terms on which competitors are likely to sell, taking account of their reaction to the price which will be determined in the present calculations (this obviously reacts on Item 1 above).
3 The costs of producing and marketing the product.

Each of these elements will first be discussed separately and then the possible procedures by which these can be harmonized in a price will be considered.

PRICE AND THE BUYER

What the customer is prepared to pay is discussed in any introduction to economics, and the following summarizes what is commonly found in any elementary textbook.

The concept of the demand curve is basic. In general, it is asserted that as the price of a product declines, so the amount of a product which customers will buy tends to increase. This statement requires the qualification "other things being equal," for clearly the volume of demand will depend on other things than price. There are even some examples of consumer goods for which the demand will (over a limited range) increase as price rises, because the buyer assesses the quality of the product by its price. (This phenomenon is not completely unknown in industrial marketing.)

In consumer goods, the demand for a product will increase with a price reduction as a result of extra business from two main sources (and conversely as it rises):

1 Customers who are at present buying the product will increase their purchases (perhaps by reducing their purchases of another product).
2 Customers who now do not buy the product at all may consider it sufficiently attractive at the new price to justify buying it.

These remarks apply to what is commonly called "primary" demand, that is, total market demand for the product as a whole, irrespective of supplier. The demand for the individual brand or company's product ("selective" demand) is further increased by business attracted from competitors, unless competitors follow suit and cut prices. The distinction between primary and selective demand is by no means straightforward, as there are often differences in the products supplied by competing companies.

In industrial markets, primary demand may expand as price falls for a number of reasons. Firstly, if the price cut is substantial, the intermediate manufacturer may pass the benefit on to the final consumer, who may therefore increase his purchases. This, however, is rarely an important influence. Any individual component or raw material is likely to be only a small part of the total cost of the product into which it enters: the price change thus has a very diluted effect on the price which the consumer pays for the end-product. This is a reason why demand in many industrial-goods markets can be relatively inelastic to price change.

A more substantial reason for sensitivity of demand to a price cut is that the product may now prove to be relatively cheaper or dearer than a competing product in particular applications. A rise in the price of copper, for example, may open the way for its replacement (wholly or partly), for certain purposes, by aluminum. There may be a time-lag before demand reacts to such a price change. Customers may have to redesign products and retrain staff. They may, therefore, wait and see if the price advantage is likely to be lasting before deciding to make the arrangements which permit them to change to the product which has been reduced in price.

With capital equipment, a price change may affect the rate of return which can be expected on the investment involved. The gradual fall in the price of computers has been an important factor in their widening use.

All this is, of course, examining the reaction of demand to price change in isolation. Other forces influencing demand are discussed in Chapter 6 on forecasting.

PRICE ELASTICITY

The marketing executive is concerned to try to assess how much demand is likely to vary with a particular price change. The demand curve which indicates how much of a product will be bought at particular prices is very attractive as a concept, but in practice the shape of this curve is unknown, although some interesting attempts to define it have been carried out by a few market researchers.

It is, however, frequently possible to make some useful conjectures in broad terms about the sensitivity of demand to price changes. Some factors tend to make a product's demand more sensitive to price and others to make it less sensitive. Sensitivity in relation to price change is commonly called the "elasticity" of demand. A product for which a 1 percent fall in price would lead to an increase in the quantity demanded by more than 1 percent is referred to as having an elastic demand. If the related change in demand is less than 1 percent, then the demand is inelastic.

Demand tends to be more elastic when the product has a wide range of uses and a wide range of possible substitutes. As the price falls, so the area of demand is widened as in one market after another the product takes over from competing products. Sometimes technocommercial studies of different markets or market segments will indicate approximately at what price level the product can be expected to take over from the competition, and this can then be used to provide rough estimates of elasticity.

As has already been mentioned, reaction to a price alteration may take some time to show itself, because the substitution of one product by another in the buying firms takes time. Previous equipment may have to be written off, existing contracts terminated, and experimental work and assessment carried out on the product to make sure that it becomes attractive from the price point of view. Once the product has been adopted, it may require a considerable and prolonged reversal of the price change for the market to be lost. Sensitivity to price in many industrial products does not mean that in the short term primary demand can increase with a price fall and then revert to the former situation when the price trends are reversed. It may mean a longer-term process of adaptation of productive processes.

COMPETITION

On the whole, most companies are cautious about deciding to change prices. This is partly because of the sheer mechanics of printing and amending price-lists, partly because of the fear that if the company seems to be uncertain in its pricing, then representatives will often find themselves faced with demands for price cuts. It is thus desirable that in making a decision on price, the long-term implications should be considered, including the nature and magnitude of competitors' reactions.

The concept of competition is a very wide one. Fig. 13 shows three circles. In the center is competition from other products which are virtually identical. A firm which manufactures paint finds itself in competition with all the other manufacturers of paint, the oil company competes with all the other oil suppliers, and different makers of wire rope are in search of the same customers. As the circle widens, competition is with different products offering to satisfy the same need in related ways—paint against other protective coatings, oil against natural gas, wire rope against chain. Wider still, the competition may offer a product which is fundamentally different but provides the same ultimate benefit. Paint competes with products not requiring protection, energy with products which conserve energy or increase the efficiency of its utilization (such as insulating materials), and wire rope for lifting purposes finds itself in competition with fork-lift trucks and systems

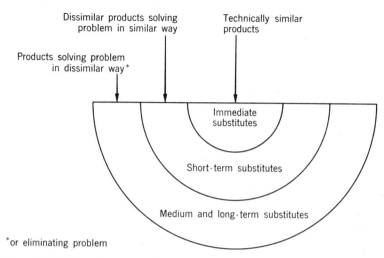

Fig. 13. Circles of competition

which obviate or reduce the need for lifting within the plant. In the illustration, it is generally true that the further the competition is away from the central point of homogeneity, the more long-term is the nature of the competition and the more important are the longer-run aspects of the strategy. Competitors include potential competition, such as the possibility that customers may themselves manufacture the product.

In economic theory, competitive situations are divided into a number of classes:

PERFECT COMPETITION

This has already been briefly referred to and is the situation at the center of the circle where the product is homogeneous, plus the additional requirement that there are so many buyers and sellers that no one of them can exert an influence on price.

IMPERFECT COMPETITION

This is the usual situation and covers all those situations in which either there is product differentiation or a relatively small number of competing buyers or sellers, or both.

1 *Oligopoly* is one of the most common situations of real life. There is a small number of sellers of the product, and each seller is directly affected by a price change by one of the others and is likely to react to it. If one firm lowers its price, it will gain business from the other firms, who may react by cutting their

prices also. This factor—possible retaliation—has to be considered in deciding price action.

2 *Monopoly* is defined in the textbooks as control by one firm of the supply of a product. Such a firm has considerable power over the price of its product, subject to the limitations imposed by the demand. These powers are limited by the possibilities of rival firms entering the business, customers deciding to make the product themselves, or by competition from one of the outer rings shown on the diagram. It is not necessary to control 100 percent of supply to have strong influence in the market; for the purpose of the British monopoly legislation, control over one-third of the supply of a product counts as a monopoly.

At one time, agreements on prices and related matters were very common among companies in an oligopolistic situation. These agreements have to a very large extent become illegal under the Restrictive Trade Practices Acts.

Competition in oligopolistic conditions has been known to have the effect of forcing prices down below long-term costs, so that overheads are not covered in the short term. This is because the direct effect of a price cut on the sales of a competitor may force him to retaliate and a price war may follow. This can happen particularly in a capital-intensive industry, where overheads and fixed costs are high but variable costs are low. If excess capacity arises, companies may be tempted to improve output by cutting prices to a level where fixed costs are not covered. This situation is less probable if one company has sufficient standing in the industry to emerge as the leader in price setting. The price leader is likely to be the largest company but could be a smaller company whose decisions are followed because of general respect for the judgment of its executives. If costs rise, no other company is likely to raise its price until the price leader has done so. If costs fall, the price leader may well lead the way down, although in some cases smaller firms may find it advantageous to make minor concessions before the general price drop. Similarly, if there is a drop in demand, the smaller firm may be the first to offer special discounts or price concessions.

However, companies are not *forced* to follow the price leader. Leadership, judging from experience in the United States and the United Kingdom, depends upon a number of factors: the relative size of the "leader," the logic of its decisions, and whether it seems to be overaggressive in its actions. Katona[39] points to the importance of habitual behavior, and in pricing it is likely that leaders who do not conform to the industries' ideas of habitual behavior may not be followed.

THE MEANINGS OF COST

The word "cost" has a deceiving air of simplicity. The range of meanings which may be attached to it is very wide, and one of the most difficult problems is to define which concept of cost is relevant in a specific situation. The term *opportunity cost* is basic and fundamental. It is not a difficult concept to understand (although it can be quite tricky to apply), and every executive should be at home with the term.

Because the plant, staff, and other resources of a company are limited, it follows that if they are used in one way, they cannot be used in another. Machine time and labor used for making one product cannot be used for making another; a representative calling on one customer cannot at the same time be calling on another. Thus the essence of the cost of doing one thing is that the opportunity to do something else is sacrificed. The normal books of account of a company show the outlays of that company and spread them between products and periods of time; they do not show how much profit would have been made if a different "mix" of products had been made or if the salesman had called on different customers. The accounts cannot measure opportunity cost.

Moreover, the accounts include certain charges which are not opportunity cost. Depreciation, for example, in no sense measures the opportunities for an alternative usage of that machine. Depreciation is simply an allocation of past expenditure over a number of years, and the actual amounts charged in any one year may be determined more by accounting procedures than by any other consideration. A product which is made on a particular item of equipment represents one way of obtaining value from that equipment. Other alternatives are:

(*a*) to sell off the equipment; or
(*b*) to use it for another product.

The opportunity cost is measured by the next best net return among those alternatives which are rejected. The word "net" may need some further explanation in this context. It means only that whichever course of action is adopted, there will be some income which will be received and some costs which will be incurred, and it is the difference between the two (the net return) which is relevant. For alternative (a) above, the opportunity cost is measured by the sales revenue *less* selling costs; for (b) it is the revenue from the product *less* the direct costs of producing and selling the product.

The concept implies that the manager should examine the alternatives open to him, and that past costs are not relevant to future decisions. At the date of the decision he must evaluate the different possibilities of the future. This guides him to the use of his resources in a way which produces the best return.

A related concept is that of *avoidable cost*. This is the answer to the question "What cash outlays can I avoid if I do not produce this product (or make this call)?"

To make the point clearer, assume that the costs of an imaginary product, as conventionally estimated, consist of the following:

1 Direct materials and labor.
2 Depreciation of the plant.
3 Administrative, selling, and other overheads.

If production is terminated, the cost of direct materials and direct labor can be eliminated and is therefore avoidable (if it cannot be eliminated then it is not avoidable). Depreciation is not an avoidable cost; the plant is already bought and depreciation is simply the spreading of that cost over a period of years. Likewise, for a small change of total output, overhead costs are unlikely to be affected, and these therefore are not avoidable. If a major *long-term* change is contemplated, then certain of the costs mentioned are avoidable. While present equipment lasts, its cost, except for maintenance cost, is not avoidable—it is a *sunk* cost. When the time comes for the equipment to be replaced, a new situation arises. At this time the cost of the proposed new equipment *is* avoidable.

Similarly, if the cost of the call on a particular customer is under examination, the concept of avoidable cost can be applied. To omit one customer saves the traveling and out-of-pocket expenses involved and the commission on any sales, but the representative's basic salary and superannuation are not avoided. If, however, the appointment of a further salesman to call on a new group of customers is contemplated, then all the costs associated with that salesman are at that stage avoidable and can be evaluated against the return expected. Again, the accounting system does not directly provide this sort of information, but it has to be calculated to a reasonable degree of accuracy for a particular set of decisions.

A distinction which is often relevant is that between

traceable and *nontraceable* cost. Some costs are clearly identified with particular departments, products, or operations while others are not so identified. Thus administrative overheads, such as the general manager's salary, cannot be related to the output of specific products or to the costs of servicing particular markets. For many costing purposes this is treated by a system of apportionment, but clearly there is no such thing as a true basis by which this cost can be related to particular products. For example, such costs are commonly allocated to particular products in proportion to direct costs or to turnover. These will have no particular relation to the way the general manager's time is spent.

The distinction between traceable and nontraceable cost would, in most companies, be roughly equivalent to the distinction between direct and indirect (or overhead) cost. Indirect or overhead costs are often allocated on a basis which has little relevance to many managerial decisions.

Finally, the distinction between *fixed* and *variable* costs deserves attention. This is a common distinction in costing and for many purposes, if handled with discretion, it is a valuable one. The basis is that there are certain costs, generally taken to be bought-in materials and parts and direct labor costs, which vary with the volume of output. Other costs represent a fixed outlay which, once production has started, remains virtually unchanged whatever the volume of output may be (at least within the normal range of output of the plant concerned).

This theory requires some refinement. First, like almost all generalizations, it contains substantial elements of simplification. Variable costs are not wholly variable in the short run: some skilled workers will not be laid off if the volume of business declines temporarily. Nevertheless, variable costs are usually a serious attempt to approximate reasonably realistically to short-run avoidable costs. Secondly, the fixed costs contain a large range of costs with different meanings. They contain the tooling-up which is directly attributable to that particular job. They contain administrative expenses frequently allocated in accordance with some arbitrary rule.

Some costs which are primarily overheads contain semivariable elements, so that as total company output expands there is some increase in cost but not in proportion to the increase in output. By simple statistical techniques, the semivariable costs can be treated as though there were two parts, one part behaving as a fixed cost and the other as if it were variable. This enables the problem to be resolved.

More complex approaches allow for all sorts of relationships between costs and output. The main difficulty is often not the statistical problem, but the problem of obtaining the necessary information analyzed in the right way and of sufficient accuracy.

THE FULL-COST MODEL

In practice, one of the best-known, oldest, and perhaps most widely used methods of determining price is what is known as the "full-cost approach." In this approach direct costs are calculated, and percentage additions are made to this figure for overheads of various sorts and for profit. The percentages for overheads commonly represent the actual or expected average for the company. The calculations are something like the following fictitious example:

Direct cost	Materials	$60 per ton of output
	Labor	36
	Total	96
Factory overhead*		24
Factory cost		120
Administrative and selling overhead†		96
Total cost		216
Profit‡		22
Price		$238

* Taken as 25 percent on direct cost.
† Taken as 80 percent on factory cost.
‡ Taken as 10 percent on total cost.

This type of approach to pricing is very common yet is the subject of severe criticism among economists and others.

The first criticism is that the final price depends entirely on the direct cost content; customers' willingness to pay and the state of competition are ignored. What has happened is that in the example the direct cost has been taken and increased by 147 percent to arrive at the selling price. Whether the product is a new product with high risk but for which buyers may be expected to be willing to pay a high price, or a product in decline where the market is falling away, this procedure, applied literally, is to offer this product at $238, take it or leave it. Yet the new product, with specialized qualities, may well earn $264 or $288 or even more. The aging product may not sell at $238 but might sell well at $192, a price which well covers all direct costs and gives a useful contribution to overheads.

Most overheads are more or less fixed over a certain range of output, and if the ailing product provides a contribution, then there is that much less overhead to be recovered from other products and that much more available for profit. The word "contribution" may be defined as the excess of price over avoidable costs. In the short term, avoidable costs may be taken as variable costs plus perhaps variable overheads where these are significant.

The second criticism is that since the essence of an overhead cost is that it cannot be related to particular items, the device of allocating it in relation to the direct cost is completely arbitrary. The same argument applies to any arbitrary rule of this sort, for example allocating overheads according to volume of sales.

Finally, the criticism is made that however the overheads are allocated, their cost per unit must depend on the number of units sold, which in its turn depends on the price. Therefore, until the price is known, no forecast of sales can be made and no unit cost in a meaningful sense is achieved. The "cost plus" formula which implies that unit costs do not vary with the amount of throughput thus has a built-in fallacy.

Those who make this criticism argue that overheads should be recovered where they can, that management should seek to obtain a substantial contribution from those products where the market will support an appropriate price and accept a low contribution where the market will only pay a more modest one. The rule here then is to maximize the contribution, and this is a very important point of view which will be discussed later.

The arguments in favor of full-cost pricing should, however, be given their due. First, the full-cost approach does keep before the executive the need to recover overheads and profits, an objective which has to be achieved overall if the company is to succeed. Second, it is watered down in practice: once the formula figure has been calculated, it may be possible to amend the formula price with a better understanding of the implication of such a variation. Such variations can be made either before the product is marketed or after some market reaction is received. In other words, this can be a trial price and can be adjusted by feedback from the market.

Secondly, if experience within the industry has shown that on the average it is possible to achieve the target (including the various percentage additions), then this is some attempt at an opportunity cost.[40] This point has not been strongly argued but has something to commend it and might well apply to a standardized product. Thirdly, where there is a large number of products to be priced, and no one has any clear means to forecast market reaction to the price, this is a quick and inexpensive method of determining at least a first approximation.

Finally, the concept of a just price is still a very strong

one, and there appears to be a feeling that a "full cost" price will appeal to the government, the buyer, and the company's competitors as a reasonable and fair means of fixing a price. These arguments perhaps indicate why this method has been so widely used. In today's conditions, management which seeks to succeed in competitive business should analyze more deeply.

THE "MARGINAL COST = MARGINAL REVENUE" MODEL

This model is taken from elementary economic theory. In its simplest form it considers the position of a business executive in the one-product firm on the hypothesis that he seeks to maximize his profit. It is derived from a comparison of the *change* in costs of production as his output rises with a comparison of the change in the amount which he can charge his customers and yet sell his total output. It is usually assumed in elementary economics that the unit cost of production falls as output increases until it reaches a point of minimum cost and then begins to rise again. On a graph this produces the famous U-shaped cost curve of traditional economic theory. It is also assumed that as output increases, so the price has to be reduced to persuade customers to buy all the output (except under conditions of perfect competition, where the price is assumed to be constant). These assumptions are progressively relaxed in more advanced texts.

Three concepts are defined in respect of cost—total cost, average cost, and marginal cost—and similarly for revenue. The theory then demonstrates that under circumstances of price competition, profits in the short run will be maximum when marginal cost and marginal revenue are equal. The definitions of these terms are as follows:

	Cost	Revenue
Total	At any volume of output this is the sum of all costs incurred producing that output.	This is the total revenue from the sale of the output. (If price is constant it equals the price multiplied by the number of items sold.)
Average	Equals total cost divided by output. It is often assumed first to fall and eventually to rise again with	Average revenue is similarly derived and declines with increasing output (except in the special case of a firm in

| | increasing output. | perfect competition, when it is constant). |
| Marginal | Marginal cost is the amount of increase (or decrease) in total cost with a small change in output. | Marginal revenue is the amount of the increase or decrease in total revenue for a small change in sales. As output increases, so the price charged commonly has to be reduced to sell it, and the marginal revenue for a small change in output is affected by this price cut. |

The theory is difficult to apply as a whole. The circumstances of perfect competition which the theory fits best are rare and are not of chief interest in pricing practice as there is then no pricing discretion. The theory breaks down in the case of the oligopolistic situation because in that situation there can be no clearly defined demand curve; everything depends on the way in which the few competitors react to a price change. Finally, of course, it is extremely difficult even to guess the shape of the demand curve.

Table 8, which follows, gives an arithmetic example of these concepts for a situation in which the company's product has no close competitor and it is therefore reasonable to accept the hypothesis of a downward-sloping demand curve. The table is illustrated in Fig. 14. It will be seen that profits increase until quantity of output is about 6,300 tons and price about $600. This is the point at which marginal cost and marginal revenue are equal. Subsequently the profits decline because the marginal (extra) cost of producing each unit of output is more than the marginal (extra) revenue which it generates.

While the doctrine as a whole is rarely capable of use, for small changes in output the test "Will marginal revenue exceed the marginal cost?" is a useful one to apply. In such cases it is worth noting carefully that it is the *change* in *total* cost which is the measure of marginal cost, and it is sometimes hard to assess how a certain decision may affect total costs of the company. However, for small changes these can often be identified with sufficient accuracy to assist in decision-making, even after allowance for some margin of error is made. This is further discussed under "Marginal-cost pricing" in Chapter 16.

Some of the following ideas are linked to this marginal analysis approach, which is valuable for the extra insight which it gives into the basis of pricing.

Table 8 Revenue, cost and profit*

QUANTITY (× 1000)	PRICE ($)	TOTAL REVENUE (× $1000)	MARGINAL REVENUE ($)	TOTAL COST ($)	AVERAGE COST (× $1000)	MARGINAL COST ($)	PROFIT (× $1000)
0	—	0		1,200	—		−1,200
1	912	912	912	1,776	1,776	576	− 326
2	852	1,704	792	2,160	1,080	384	− 456
3	792	2,376	672	2,448	816	288	− 72
4	732	2,928	552	2,688	672	240	+ 240
5	672	3,360	432	2,904	581	216	+ 456
6	612	3,672	312	3,120	521	216	+ 552
7	552	3,864	192	3,360	480	240	+ 504
8	492	3,936	72	3,696	461	336	+ 240
9	432	3,888	−48	4,152	461	456	− 264
10	372	3,720	−168	4,800	480	648	−1,080

* Figures, originally given in pounds, have been changed to dollar equivalents.

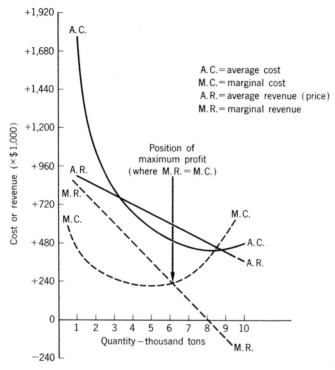

Fig. 14. The "marginal cost = marginal revenue" model

THE BREAK-EVEN MODEL

A more practical approach to price determination comes about from the sensitive use of the classical break-even diagram. It has long been a useful tool in this field.

Fig. 15 is a typical example. The product concerned has fixed costs amounting to $120,000 per annum, including such items as factory overheads, tooling-up, plant depreciation, and other allocated overheads. Variable costs at the rate of $36 per ton produced are shown in the upper section of the diagram. Semivariables are not shown separately, and it is assumed that they have been separated into variable and fixed elements as already described. Sometimes a more detailed analysis of costs is used, but this does not affect the basic issues.

This approach differs from that above in that it assumes that variable costs per unit are the same whatever the level of output, and thus average costs will decrease throughout. Within

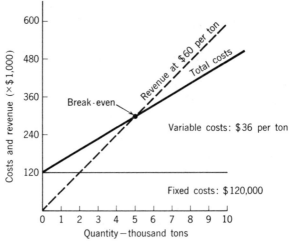

Fig. 15. Traditional break-even analysis

a range, limited by present capacity, this is often a reasonable approximation.

Some adaptation is necessary if it is desired to relax this assumption. Suppose that after a certain volume of production is achieved it is necessary to add more equipment, then the fixed cost will take a step up to a higher level, reflecting the cost of the addition. If employees have to work overtime to attain a certain volume of production, the variable costs per unit of output will increase and total costs will rise more sharply. Minor modifications in the diagram will allow for these variations.

If, for example, a net price of $60 per ton is proposed for the product, it is possible to identify the sales volume required to break even. Unlike the "full cost" approach, the interrelationship between variations in fixed and variable costs, volume, and price can be examined.

The break-even point can, of course, be calculated without reference to the diagram by a simple formula. First the contribution per unit of output is calculated. The contribution is the difference between the price and the variable costs. In this example it equals $60 *less* $36, i.e., $24 per ton. The break-even point is then obtained by dividing the fixed costs by the unit contribution; in the example, $120,000 ÷ $24 shows that break-even is reached at 5,000 tons, as shown in Fig. 15.

The break-even point depends on the size of the unit contribution in relation to fixed costs, and current thinking stresses the importance of the contribution as the key determinant of short-term pricing decisions (subject to the overriding importance of pricing objectives in the long term). Once the decision is made to manufacture the product, fixed costs cease to be a relevant factor. The objective becomes to maximize the contribution. If this maximum covers all fixed costs and yields a profit in excess of allocated overheads, all well and good. If it fails to do so, then the original decision to enter the business was mistaken, but at least the decision-maker has done all he can to minimize the ill effects of that wrong decision.

IMPROVED BREAK-EVEN ANALYSIS

A sharper focus on contribution is obtained by modifying the traditional form of the break-even diagram so that variable costs are at the bottom and fixed costs at the top, as in Fig. 16. Costs have been divided as follows:

1 VARIABLE COSTS
Variable cost is in fact an approximation to the short-term avoidable cost. It indicates the extra cost of producing one more unit of output (until the point is reached where it is necessary to step up fixed costs).

2 SPECIFIC PROGRAMED COSTS
These are fixed costs attributable to the product under review which flow directly from management policy decisions

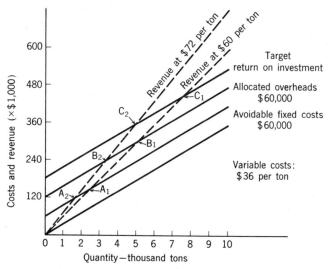

Fig. 16. Modified break-even analysis

to manufacture the product on a particular scale. These costs are avoided if there is a policy change and the product is discontinued, and may sometimes be varied by management decision. They include such costs as promotion, plant, and continuing R&D costs specific to the product. Unlike variable costs they do not vary directly with output. They are in fact avoidable fixed costs.

3 APPORTIONED FIXED COSTS

There are general overhead costs which are not generated in any identifiable way by particular products and whose allocation is arbitrary. They are the basic costs of being in business.

Target return on investment is also included in the diagram; that is what the company aims to achieve and if possible to exceed.

The same figures are used as for Fig. 15: variable costs are $36 per ton, fixed costs $120,000 (of which $60,000 are specific programed costs and $60,000 apportioned overheads). Target return on investment is $60,000.

Consider first the line indicating revenue at a price of $60 per ton. This naturally runs above the variable-cost level of $36 per ton throughout, and the vertical distance between these two lines is the contribution to all fixed costs and profit.

Prior to the point A_1 the product revenue covers variable costs and provides some contribution to its own fixed costs. Not until revenue reaches A_1 does it contribute to general overheads. B_1 is less significant; it is the point at which revenue meets the arbitrarily allocated overheads. While general overheads must be covered if the company is to survive, the real extent to which a product contributes to general overheads depends on what can be realized in the market. At C_1, target return on investment is achieved.

A separate line shows the revenue obtained from different volumes of sale at a second price, $72 per ton. Three points (A_2, B_2, C_2) are shown where sales revenue at this price would cover specific programed costs, general overheads, and target return on investments.

These points are compared in Table 9.

The key question which at this stage remains unanswered is "What is the customer willing to pay?" or more precisely, "What are different customers prepared to pay in relation to different applications?" plus the question "How will competitors react?" All the market information which is available is called on to formulate a view on these, but while it serves to reduce uncertainty it never produces complete certainty.

Table 9 Sales to achieve certain targets

	AT $60 PER TON	AT $72 PER TON
	($\times$ $1000) TONS	
A To cover specific programed costs	2.5	1.7
B To cover allocated overheads	5.0	3.3
C To cover target return on investment	7.5	5.0

It is, however, now possible to frame questions on these lines: "At a price of $60 per ton, what is the amount we can expect to sell?" "What is the *least* we are likely to sell?" and "What is the *most* we are likely to sell?" and similarly for $72 (or any other price which the marketing manager considers worth examining).

These questions cannot be answered with complete certainty. Marketing and sales executives, with their knowledge of the prices of competitive products, their relative merits in different applications, and the existing ties between various buyers and sellers, can usually produce meaningful approximations. These can be explored on the diagram, or by elementary arithmetic, so that the planner knows the worst, the average, and the best results which each price may produce. He then makes his decision with awareness of its implications both in terms of maximizing contribution and reducing risk.

CONTRIBUTION/VOLUME RATIO

Focus on contribution leads to consideration of the concept of contribution/volume (C/V) ratio, also sometimes referred to as price/volume (P/V) ratio in some texts.[41] The C/V ratio indicates what proportion of each $1 of revenue is available as contribution, as illustrated in Table 10; it is obtained by dividing contribution per unit by price.

The data is illustrated in Fig. 17. Sales revenue is on

Table 10 Contribution ratio

	AT $60 PER TON	AT $72 PER TON
Price	$60	$72
less variable costs	36	36
Contribution	$24	$36
Contribution ratio	0.40	0.50

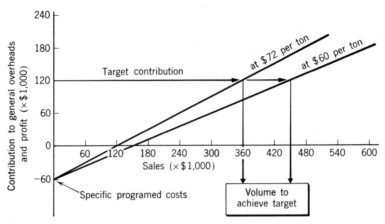

Fig. 17. Contribution/volume analysis

the horizontal axis (note that this is revenue and not volume in tons) and contribution to general overheads and profit on the vertical axis. Specific programed costs are measured negatively—below the line—as a first charge against the product's contribution before anything goes into the general pool. The two lines plotted on the graph show for the two different prices the contribution generated by different sizes of revenue.

Not only does this approach focus on contribution, but it permits its relationship to specific programed costs to be considered, with consequent clearer thinking about them. It is also possible to set a target contribution level and identify easily what volume of sales is required at each price to achieve it. Setting this target is a management decision based on considerations of what is feasible in the market and what is desirable for the company.

The probability of reaching this level can be considered, as was done in the previous section. It is also possible to examine pricing policy for a range of related products by arriving at the average C/V ratio for the range and then carrying out the above analysis.

This approach highlights more clearly than others the interrelationship between price, contribution, volume, and the programed costs and how they affect the probability of achieving target contribution levels.

Finally, it must be emphasized that the stressing of the concept of contribution in this chapter does not diminish the marketing department's responsibility to develop annual and long-term plans which provide adequate return to cover all costs and generate profit.

16

Special Aspects of Pricing

The previous chapter was concerned with the basic price, set in a framework of pricing objectives. General models of price determination were outlined.

This approach now requires widening to build more subtlety into the analysis of pricing decisions. All the models were essentially static, yet it is an axiom of marketing that change occurs and that every effort must be made to anticipate and adapt to it. In addition, the company's problem is one of fixing a structure of prices for related products, which are often either partly competitive or partly complementary, and perhaps to set different prices for different markets.

PRICING AND THE PRODUCT LIFE-CYCLE

The clearest and most effective account of the developments which take place over time is in the concept of the product life-cycle, which has been discussed in Chapter 7. Price performs a different role at different stages of the cycle, and the quality of pricing decisions can be improved by awareness of the life-cycle considerations.

When a new product is first launched, the marketing executive of an innovating company has a difficult pricing decision to make. Just how difficult it is will depend upon just how new the product is. If it is not greatly different from existing products, then the price of those products can provide a very valuable guide as to the price which is likely to be acceptable for the new product.

If the product is a more radical departure, then the problem becomes more difficult. Whatever task is to be performed by the new product is already being carried out by some other product, but in a way which is less satisfactory. Nevertheless, the costs and benefits of existing products can be compared with those of the new product. This cost comparison, together with a comparison of the benefits involved, should help to delineate a zone within which will be found the price which customers will be willing to pay.

Different market segments will, of course, differ in their reaction to price, and some assessment of these differences is required. The question "What are the advantages of this product in different industries, for different customers and for different applications?" is often not too difficult to answer in general terms and provides a basis for judging the sensitivity of demand to price.

For the initial marketing of a product, there is usually a choice between two price policies:

1 A *skimming* (*or creaming*) *policy* which introduces a product to the market at a relatively high price, the price then being lowered progressively over the life of the product.
2 A *penetration policy*, the product being introduced at a relatively low price, which it is intended to maintain unchanged throughout much of its life.

For most industrial products, the first policy is the one commonly selected. It has a number of advantages which are very attractive in industrial marketing.

Generally, even after the most careful research, there is considerable uncertainty about the amount which customers will pay. The customers find it hard to assess what the product is worth to them, and test marketing as practiced in consumer markets is hardly ever feasible.

The rate of market expansion may not depend primarily on price. Prospective customers require time to evaluate the product, train the operatives, and perhaps install ancillary equipment. Thus initial demand is often small, whatever the price within wide limits. Under these circumstances, a low price offers no advantages in promoting market expansion. A higher price helps to meet the heavy initial first costs and generates the maximum short-term flow of cash. Thus the innovating company can exploit the period of monopoly which it has before competition enters the field. Initial targets are carefully selected segments where the product offers most benefits.

The skimming price can be gradually adjusted as market reactions to it are better understood. It largely avoids the danger of having to increase prices, and it is more effective for salesmen to meet buyers in circumstances of reducing, rather than of increasing, price. Moreover, the process of gradually reducing prices reflects the decline in unit costs which takes place in many products as experience and scale of production increase and probable competitive production builds up.

Penetration pricing has two major objectives: to expand the market for the new product rapidly and to deter competition. The ability to expand the market implies that it is appropriate where price elasticity is high and market expansion depends primarily on the price of the product and less upon other factors. Capacity must be available to meet this early expansion, and the case for penetration pricing is higher if the economics of the production process favor large plants and high-volume output.

The low price may act as a deterrent to competitors, although if the market is likely to be substantial and existing products made obsolete, competitors will almost certainly enter the market irrespective of price. The early penetration may, however, lead to a situation where the innovator can retain an important share of the market, either from brand loyalty and reputation or from the more efficient cultivation of the market and the close contact with decision-makers which can arise from the earlier penetration. If the product is one which competitors can easily and quickly produce, this rapid grasp of the market may well be an asset to be sought if a reasonable proportion of what is gained can be held. Conversely, if the product is protected for a while, a slowly reducing price permits each market segment to be exploited.

On the whole, penetration pricing is uncommon in industrial marketing, although there are a few occasions on which it has been used effectively.

In fact, it is not always an advantage to keep competition out. If the initial promotional work in expanding the market is heavy and expensive, then it may be a positive advantage for two or more firms to share the burden. Otherwise one firm may carry the cost of market development and others reap much of the benefit. For some items, customers may be reluctant to purchase the product unless there is more than one source of supply.

As the life-cycle progresses, market growth is normally assisted by product improvement and adaptation, as well as by price reduction. The relative importance of each of these depends upon the pricing policy originally adopted.

At the same time as products tend to be improved, there is sometimes also a tendency toward standardization. That is to say, as customers develop understanding, so there is more pressure to obtain common specifications of the products from different suppliers. Price then becomes a more important factor in the buying decision, and it becomes increasingly difficult to resist price concessions. It is sometimes possible in circumstances of price leadership to maintain prices, but a company which persists in trying to hold price in the face of decline may expect to suffer loss of market share.

The choice then is either to move on to the next new product, or to exploit such tolerance as exists in the market. If elasticity of demand is high, the conscious lowering of price will expand sales and may improve the return on the product. If, however, elasticity is low or there are overriding longer-term considerations, then a company may prefer to price somewhat above the competitive level and aim to justify this by relying on additional service or reputation.

MARKET SEGMENTATION PRICING

So far, discussion has assumed that at any one time one price is set for all possible customers. The demand curve can, however, be considered as representing a number of different buyers, some of whom are willing to pay more for the product than are others (see Fig. 18). It may therefore be possible and profitable to charge several prices: a high price to those with the keenest demand, a medium price to those in the middle, and so on down the scale. This policy may be crudely described as charging what the traffic will bear.

This is possible under certain circumstances only. Clearly, there must be no legal objections to this discrimination. In addition, buyers must not be expected to object or react so strongly that the suppliers concerned suffer loss of sales and profit.

Implementing this policy may have some problems. Circumstances must be such that if one customer is supplied with the product at the low price, he cannot resell to the high-price market segment. If, for example, customers in country X are charged a higher price than customers in country Y, then the difference should not be sufficient to justify customers in Y reselling to X. The margin between the two prices is limited by the amount of costs (such as transport) involved in transferring the product from Y to X. Services cannot be transferred, and some products can be differentiated so that the product sold to one customer is less suitable for the purposes of the other. Competition may limit the opportunities for market segmenta-

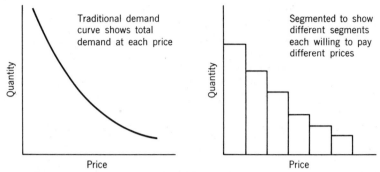

Fig. 18. Segmenting the demand curve

tion. A high-price market segment can be very attractive to existing or potential competitors.

Transport is an extreme example of price differentiation. The "product" cannot be transferred and frequently direct costs are low and overhead costs high. Thus the objective is to follow the rule of maximizing the contribution from each segment of the market separately.

This is illustrated by the international air-cargo rating system, described in *Marketing Management in Air Transport*,[42] which is essentially as follows:

(*a*) A basic rate between each pair of points per pound or per kilogram which will apply to any cargo. The tendency is for these rates to be less per mile over longer distances, because much of the cost of carrying cargo is in the handling at either end, which is constant irrespective of the distance.

(*b*) A multitude of "commodity rates" aimed at attracting particular flows of traffic which cannot bear the basic rate. . . .

(*c*) Rebates for both (*a*) and (*b*) when the consignment reaches a certain size (e.g. 45 kgs.) because some terminal costs—documentation, accounting, etc.—are the same for all consignments. . . .

(*d*) Minimum charges—usually set quite high—because of the heavy incidence of terminal handling and documentation costs. . . .

(*e*) A "volumetric" surcharge to ensure that very light but bulky cargoes pay for the space they take up in the aircraft.

(*f*) A "value" surcharge, so that exceptionally high-value cargo, such as gold, pays what it really can bear!

Where a few large customers dominate a market for a product, they will normally expect lower prices. Costs of supplying these customers will usually be lower, because bulk business provides economies in administration, selling, and delivery, and perhaps also in production. However, their buying power may be such that they may obtain price advantages in excess of the cost saving involved. Under these conditions, the wider margins of profit obtainable on smaller customers' business may be very important in the total economics of the product.

The arithmetic of pricing segmented markets thus has three main rules:

1 To charge each segment according to the sensitivity of demand to price in that segment. If demand is inelastic, the price will tend to be high (because the demand will be no greater if price is reduced); conversely, if it is elastic, the price will tend to be lower because this will expand the market. In assessing demand behavior it is necessary to remember that demand for one supplier's product will depend on how existing and potential competitors will behave.

2 To ensure that the price to each segment makes a contribution over direct costs of the product, plus any special costs associated with that segment (e.g., special packaging costs, costs of representation, and so on).

3 To ensure that differentials are not sufficiently great to permit buyers in low-price segments to resell profitably to high-price segments (unless there are special reasons why this should be permitted).

These rules are, of course, subject to the overriding policy considerations already discussed.

PRODUCT-LINE PRICING

The preceding section discusses price differentials related to the type of customer. This section deals with price differences between products of the same general character. In terms of demand, differences in the product line relate to products which are all expressions of the same essential concept but differ from each other in respect of such tertiary factors as size, strength, versatility, presence or absence of supplementary features. To some extent they may be competitive, in that if the customer is buying, say, steel plate and has to choose between alternative specifications, if he chooses one grade then by the same decision he refuses another.

In a wider sense such products often support each other, for if a customer does not find a specification which matches his requirement with a sufficient degree of precision, then he may well not purchase from this supplier at all; he may buy from a rival supplier of steel plate or use another type of material.

Costs of a product line are to a degree interrelated. While each product has traceable direct costs, many overheads of administration, selling, research, and development are not logically attributable to specific products but to many products jointly. Sometimes these joint costs exceed the direct costs.

Prices for the product line can be of the simple "full cost" type described earlier. Each product has its direct cost estimated and customary additions are made for overheads and profit. The result is that prices are proportional to direct costs except in so far as overheads differ as a result of differences in, for example, depreciation charges. A somewhat similar device is to make prices proportional to "marginal costs," which in practice commonly means short-term variable cost.

The view taken in Chapter 15, however, was that the allocation of overheads cannot be other than arbitrary. The customer will not pay more for a product than he needs to pay, and some products cannot obtain from the market sufficient to cover the "average" overheads for the producing company; others can receive more than this. On this principle it would be reasonable to charge what the product is worth to the buyer and to regard those products which show insufficient contribution as candidates for withdrawal. This may, however, have to be modified to ensure equitable price relationships between related products.

Product-line pricing is, however, complicated by certain issues of complementarity and competitiveness between individual products. In some cases, the sale of one product may lead to sales of others: for example, sales of a copying machine may lead to sales of the copying medium. It may then be desirable to price the copying machine attractively and recover overheads and profit on the copying medium. Reasonable estimates should, however, be made to ensure that the overall return is satisfactory. It is necessary to make sure that the customer cannot obtain the copying medium elsewhere. Where the relationship between the sale of one product and the sale of another is less clear, it is probably wise to approach the idea that one product should subsidize the other with the utmost caution.

In consumer marketing, a range of products of different

sizes are sold at the same price. This is true of some minor items like hosiery. The cost differences are small and a constant price makes selling easier. There are probably few close analogies to this in industrial marketing.

MARGINAL-COST PRICING

In some texts "marginal costing" is used as an inclusive term for the entire concept of contribution pricing. Here it will be used in a more restricted sense to describe those circumstances in which limited quantities of the product are sold in one special segment of the market on terms which cover little more than the additional costs associated with them. The objective is to utilize capacity which would otherwise be idle. For example, export orders are sometimes accepted on these terms. The phenomenon is most common in capital-intensive industries.

Marginal-cost pricing has its place in pricing strategy as an example of the market segmentation approach already mentioned. Marginal costs are often equated with short-term variable costs, but this definition may in many practical circumstances be too narrow. For example, the marginal costs of exporting must include any special costs of clerical work, packing, insurance, freight, and selling which would be avoided if the business concerned was not accepted. Sometimes, if the additional business is considerable, costs which are normally treated as fixed may vary, and these must be covered.

The danger with marginal-cost pricing is that if the volume increases, the company may find itself requiring extra capacity to meet it, and the returns may not be sufficient to justify the capital costs involved. It can then happen, unless management is alert, that new investment is undertaken, the cost of which cannot be recovered from the expected revenue. Marginal-cost pricing is a short-run approach to selling in minor market segments when existing capacity remains unexploited after more attractive markets are satisfied.

SUBMITTING BIDS OR PROPOSALS

The preparation of bids or proposals raises difficult problems. In some types of industry much of the business comes as a result of proposals made to customers' specifications.

Prior to the bidding stage, the shrewd supplier will have

educated the specifying decision-maker in the advantages of his products so that the specification is framed in a manner consistent with his company's capabilities. He will also concentrate his attention on that part of the market where he is most likely to be successful. Preparing bids or proposals can cost money, and sometimes a preliminary review of the situation will show that there is little or no chance of success. Under these circumstances, the expense of the proposal is best saved. On other occasions, where bids have been invited for standardized products and the specification has been somewhat different from usual standards, some suppliers have offered one of their standard products, superior to the specification. Their terms for this superior product have often been better than those of competitors who kept strictly to specification and whose bids were therefore based on the relatively high costs of a short special run.

Making bids or proposals is, in fact, a special form of segmented market; each customer is a separate segment and the competition varies from case to case. The bidder has to assess the probability of achieving successful results at different prices.

One writer[43] has shown how probability theory can be applied with advantage to this problem. Records were kept of the results of bids over a period of years. The relationship between the successful bidder's prices and the company's own cost estimates was calculated, and this permitted the company to form a view about the probability of success of a bid at a particular figure.

Even making bids requires awareness of long-term objectives. Sometimes a particular bid may provide access to new customers, new know-how, and new opportunities. If the potential market size justifies it, initial bids or proposals may be on terms which offer little contribution to overheads. The potential long-term benefit must, however, be assessed and be worthwhile in relation to the risk involved.

17

Channels of Distribution

Most British manufacturers sell direct to their industrial customers in the home market without the involvement of intermediaries. There are, however, some exceptions where distributors or agents are employed.

An intermediary is a link in a chain of distribution from the manufacturer-supplier to the manufacturer-customer who does not himself perform any manufacturing operation on the product. Sometimes, however, the intermediary may provide certain services such as installation, maintenance, and repair. The relationship which a manufacturing company has with an intermediate manufacturer can sometimes be rather similar.

In the industrial field, the intermediary is used where the manufacturer considers that direct representation is uneconomic. It is a "make or buy" situation in which the sacrifice of marketing effectiveness and control for the original manufacturer is outweighed by the saving in cost. The decision to use an intermediary thus involves a long-term view of the effect on sales and costs, including such internal costs as transport, representation, storage, and other costs of holding stock. This long-term view must include attention to such issues as the problems of providing service, introducing new products, and effect on the company's image. Sometimes the intermediary is able to provide specialized knowledge of local markets which the manufacturer could not easily duplicate.

The intermediary is generally most important in markets where individual orders are small and sales volume low. While the intermediary can provide certain services, he is usually not able to provide those requiring considerable specialized knowledge, as for example design or applications engineering. Sometimes it is also difficult to provide credit and trade-in facilities. To the manufacturer the use of the intermediary implies some loss of control and perhaps effectiveness. These factors together explain the limited use of intermediaries in domestic industrial markets, where some 80 percent of the business is commonly with 20 percent of the customers and where many products are technically complex. They also suggest that much of this business will be in circumstances in which the buyer is the dominant decision-maker in the customer firm and where the salesman with empathy is the key to success. Some of the difficulties which are envisaged can be minimized and the benefits maximized by good cooperation between the manufacturer and the intermediary.

THE ROLE OF THE INTERMEDIARY

The agent does not buy and sell in his own right but on behalf of the principal. He carries lines for several manufacturers, but normally these are not in competition with each other. He is, in fact, a close substitute for the company's own salesman. He may hold stock on consignment, and his prime justification is the ability to carry out the selling process at low cost because he is offering a wider range of products to the same group of customers. The agent's income is from the commission on the sales he makes.

The distributor is independent, buying and selling on his own behalf and making his profit from the mark-up. He is, however, financially responsible for his own stock, although this responsibility is in practice sometimes softened by the manufacturer, who will offer longer credit terms, willingness to take back obsolete stock, and some protection against the impact of price changes. In fact, the distinction between the agent and the distributor in practical terms can become blurred. Discussion below focuses on the work of the distributor, but much of what is said applies with modification to the agent. One distinction, sometimes of importance, is that resale price maintenance legislation forbids manufacturers to prescribe the price at which the distributor sells.

The traditional functions of a distributor are discussed below. The importance of each varies according to the economics of the various situations and the established business habits and commercial relationships.

ECONOMIES OF TRANSPORT
A classic role is that of breaking bulk. Where items are

bought by many customers in small quantities, it is cheaper to transport the goods to convenient centers and from these distribute in small lots. The existence of agricultural and builders' merchants is related to this cause.

Stocks can be held by three different interests: the manufacturer, the intermediary, or the customer. Stock-holding by the customer of reserve supplies of spares and small items in irregular demand is less economical than stock-holding by an intermediary who deals with a number of customers and can average out their demand variations. As he is nearer the customers, his stock can be drawn upon by them more speedily than by obtaining the goods from the manufacturer. The existence of this stock can be a two-edged sword, as the manufacturer can lose touch with what is happening to user demand until he receives an order from the distributor which, if ill-considered, could exaggerate the change in final demand. The relationship with the distributor involves some consideration of how this problem can be dealt with.

ECONOMIES OF REPRESENTATION AND
COMMUNICATION

Because of the small size of the business between one individual supplier and each individual customer, the cost of a salesman calling direct from the manufacturer on each customer can be disproportionate to the business generated. Both distributor and agent normally carry a number of manufacturers' products, and this can keep average costs down by spreading the cost over all these lines. In both cases they may also be able to take advantage of local knowledge and existing customer loyalties to sell more effectively.

CONSIDERATIONS OF CHOICE, DISPLAY, AND
CUSTOMER CONVENIENCE

There are some lines in which the intermediary offers the convenience of choice so that the purchaser can compare products offered by different manufacturers more economically and conveniently than if he had to deal with and evaluate separately the offerings of each directly. He may also appreciate the advantage of seeing the goods displayed locally.

The original manufacturer has, however, some special problems in dealing with the distributor. First, there can be a conflict of interest. The distributor and manufacturer are each interested in his own business and his own profits, and these interests will not automatically coincide. The distributor's interest in making profitable sales implies that he will sell one manufacturer's product as willingly as he will sell the competitor's model of the same product. Loss of control by the original manufacturer follows, and introduces complexities in planning his marketing. He is therefore faced with the need to obtain results by developing arrangements which, while providing profitable business for his own company, will recognize the distributor's legitimate interest in developing his own profits, to the benefit of both parties. The object is to create an alliance between a team of distributors and the manufacturing company which is fruitful for all the parties concerned.

SUPPLIER/DISTRIBUTOR RELATIONSHIPS

The first decision then is whether or not to use distributors, and the answer will in many cases be obvious— preempted by economics and customer habits. In other cases the decision will be less clear-cut and there may be a case for leaving certain parts of the market to the distributor and handling the rest direct, in accordance with the principles already discussed. The split of the market may be decided on the basis of the following variables:

1 REGION
Areas of low demand may be handed to the distributor. For smaller manufacturers in the United Kingdom this might include Northern Ireland and parts of Scotland.

2 CUSTOMERS
This may be further modified, perhaps by reserving to the distributor customers whose business is below a certain annual volume and to the manufacturer those above. This involves certain problems, as individual customers' turnover increases or diminishes. Certain national accounts may commonly be reserved to the manufacturer.

3 TYPES OF PRODUCT
Simpler products will go through distributors, with the more complex technical products being handled by the manufacturer's salesman, perhaps with some commission to the distributor where he plays a part in generating a sale.

4 SIZE OF ORDER
Orders below a certain size are reserved to the distributor, those above it to the manufacturer.

Defining the distributor's market is not straightforward.

Naturally, it is desired to be as simple as possible, but it is not always possible to be both simple and acceptable to both parties.

The manufacturer may adopt a policy of selling to all distributors, subject to the usual considerations of credit-worthiness; this is common in distributing many minor products to the building industry. Alternatively, he may operate a policy which involves a preferential arrangement with some distributors. In return for the preference shown, the distributor may be expected to cooperate in the overall marketing plans of the manufacturer. Preferential arrangements can vary from complete exclusivity, under which the distributor has sole rights for a particular part of the market, to distributors who are limited in number but do not have completely exclusive rights. It may be a scheme under which some distributors are "approved" to work in close cooperation with the manufacturer, who gives them particular backing, while still being prepared to supply other distributors.

In choosing which of these principles to adopt, the manufacturer will have to be fully aware of what is involved in marketing the product concerned. If the product is to be sold through all suitable outlets, it is assumed that the potential user of a product in wide demand will be motivated to ask for the product and that the supplier's brand will be acceptable, perhaps even preferred or insisted upon.

The important marketing function of the distributor is that of stocking the product. The process of back-selling operates to produce customer inquiry, and this needs the support of widespread distribution and availability. Sometimes it is possible to obtain some display of the product or promotional material on the distributor's premises, and this will remind the customer of the brand concerned.

Thus the supplier's salesman will seek to ensure that all distributors are stocking the product and that the stock is maintained at reasonable levels. Advertising, public relations, and promotion will seek to keep the name of this product not only before the customer but before the staff of the distributor, so that they are well informed about the product and firm in their selling of it. The object is to concentrate the selling efforts on the product of the manufacturer concerned. The representative when he calls on the distributor will try to ensure that everything that can be done is done to move the product out. Such factors as clarity of packing so that the storeman can quickly identify a type and size of product and good literature for the use of the staff and customers of the store are imperative.

If some preferential arrangement is adopted, then the supplier/distributor relationship becomes closer. In choosing a distributor who is to represent him, the manufacturer will check the quality of product knowledge among the sales and technical staff concerned and will, if it can be arranged, provide formal training about his product. He will cooperate to provide literature benefiting both parties and provide a wide range of advice to make sure that the business of the distributors is growing and profitable. He may provide finance or management consultancy service. The manufacturer's own sales staff may at times undertake selling to distributor's customers on behalf of the distributor. This would be appropriate on a short-term basis, when a new market is being opened or a new product introduced.

The closest relationship is the one of exclusivity in which the manufacturer has handed over certain business within a particular area to one distributor with the assurance that no other distributor in the same area will be appointed to handle these products. This, of course, puts the distributor in a favored position if the product is a good one which can expect to meet a ready market reaction. The manufacturer should choose such a distributor with particular care and ensure that his staff has, or can reasonably soon obtain, sufficient expertise (technical, selling, and managerial) to make the product a success, and also that the quality of the management is such that the product market can be exploited fully and efficiently.

The distributor may well cooperate with the manufacturer on stock planning to ensure that stocks of sufficient size will be carried. In addition, the manufacturer will offer, and expect the distributor's personnel to attend, training programs to ensure that the standard of competence and knowledge of his products is maintained and developed. Some manufacturers will go to great lengths to help distributors, making available all manner of management services on subsidized terms or free of charge. Where they have not considered existing distributors efficient, or where there has not been a distributor network in existence, a company may recruit promising applicants, train them, back them with finance, and thus produce good-quality distributors.

Exclusive distribution generally requires that a distributor will meet his obligations and will cooperate willingly in developing the market. Cooperative advertising and other cooperative ventures to enlarge the market may be developed, each party paying part of the cost. Before appointing the dealer, checks may very well be carried out among customers to ascertain what qualities they look for when deciding to deal with a distributor. How much importance do they attach to quick delivery, good advice, and other factors?

The distributor may be asked to accept an obligation

not to offer directly competing products. Sometimes this may be an unreasonable requirement, when competitors' brands are well known, sought after, and conveniently purchased and sold in conjunction with other products. In these circumstances, perhaps the distributor may handle these products but will cooperate in pushing those which are the subject of the distributorship. He will also be asked to provide stock and other market intelligence at appropriate intervals.

The idea that the representatives who work with the distributor should be a separate section of the sales force has much to commend it. The problems of the distributor are sufficiently different to require specialized attention and knowledge, and this is one way in which these can be provided.

One interesting use of distributors in Britain is the Authorized Industrial Distributor in the electronic equipment field. The number of small users for electronic products is many and varied—laboratories, industrial users, educational establishments, and others.

Manufacturers "authorize" distributors for particular areas of the country. Within this area orders received are dealt with on the following basis:

Small orders—handled by the distributor.
Intermediate orders—handled either by the manufacturer or the distributor.
Large orders—handled by the manufacturer.

It should be noted that under this arrangement "small orders" received by the manufacturer will be transferred to the distributor, and vice versa for the large orders.

In the intermediate zone, orders may be handled by either party, but if one of them is unable to give prompt attention to an order, for example because the goods are out of stock, it will be transferred to the other. The size range covered by the terms "small," "intermediate," or "large" will, of course, be specified in the agreement between the distributor and the manufacturer. In general, manufacturers agree to the distributor stocking competitors' products, as the well-balanced product line is the attraction to the buyer.

The relationship between the manufacturer and the distributor is summed up in the following extract from an article by the general sales manager of a company manufacturing electronic components.[44]

The Authorized Industrial Distributor exists to meet the immediate requirements of original equipment manufacturers with the prompt availability of small to medium quantities of a wide selection of components. It must be borne in mind that much of a Distributor's success depends on the product line-up which is carried. For profitable operation, the Distributor must feature only the products of leading manufacturers who, by their acknowledged quality and sound marketing techniques, are assured of nation-wide acceptance. It is inadvisable for any manufacturer, therefore, to use a Distributor which has not proved itself in the Distributor field, and which is not already well known as a Distributor of quality components. To do so may be catastrophic from the point of view of the manufacturer.

For the Distributor to be of maximum value to both his customers and the component manufacturer, he must maintain stocks of a range of top-quality components, the quantities of which are scientifically calculated to provide the optimum available service linked with a turnover rate which ensures continued replenishment and avoids "shelf life" complications. Top-line Distributors in the United Kingdom operate modern inventory management and close liaison with the manufacturer on delivery lead time changes which could avoid the fatal situation of being out of stock.

18

Organizing the Marketing Function

This book is built upon a very wide view of what marketing is. The purpose of the company is seen as the achievement of sales on terms which promote its financial and other objectives. The act of sale is the tip of an arrow, and all the functions of a company must be organized behind it to give direction and effectiveness.

This view is well expressed in the widely-known definition of the marketing concept: "A corporate state of mind that insists on the integration and co-ordination of all marketing functions which in turn are melded with all other corporate functions for the basic objective of producing maximum long-range profits."[45]

Marketing is therefore not the sole concern of the marketing department. The aim is to achieve company-wide focus on the market. The marketing department has a direct responsibility for the collection and interpretation of marketing information, for drawing from this information its implications in terms of management decision and action, and finally the task of communicating, negotiating, and perhaps also distributing to the customers the products and services which result from this process.

THE MARKETING MANAGER

The marketing manager (using that term to designate the top executive of the marketing department, whether he is in fact called manager or director) thus has not only a departmental responsibility, but also the duty of developing the marketing attitude throughout the whole company. This task is most heavy when the department is newly established. There is much misunderstanding about the nature of marketing, and some existing departmental heads may see the new department as derogating from their authority. In fact the contrary is the case, for through the marketing plan the marketing department provides a framework which should improve the commercial effectiveness of all sections of the company.

Formal authority is not itself a sufficient basis for developing a different company attitude, and the new marketing manager who expects a ready acceptance of his views is often disappointed. Even those executives originally responsible for making the appointment have sometimes been found not to have appreciated fully the implications of their decision, and one of the early needs is to obtain understanding and acceptance by top management of the full implications of the marketing approach. Even with subordinates, new attitudes cannot be developed solely by issuing orders. An important quality of the man selected for this post when it is first created is the ability to command sufficient personal acceptance to clear this hurdle.

The new marketing manager must have the skills of management in its fullest sense; he cannot hope to carry weight in discussions with the finance officer, for example, unless he is well informed about the basic financial and accounting concepts of managerial significance. He must be versed in the principles of management and skilled in their application. His own department must be run crisply and efficiently. He will find that a leadership role among his colleagues in the company is not his inalienable right but must be won by his abilities in practice and by the cogency and skill with which his own ideas are presented.

THE BASIS OF ORGANIZATION

Organizing a company or department is a process of dividing it into a number of sections and relating those sections in the way that best promotes the achievement of its objectives. A section is "a group of workers under one control,"[46] and in classical organization theory a company is composed of a hierarchy of sections. The chief executive at the apex has under him a number of sections, each headed by a senior manager. Each of them has a further layer of sections subordinate to him, and so on down through the company.

In this scheme each individual is aware of his personal responsibility and where he is placed in relation to the rest of the team. These details are set out in his job description.

The head of a section has work delegated to him by his superior and will himself delegate to subordinates. He remains responsible to his own superior for the work of his section, including the work which he has delegated.

This classical approach is a convenient way of expressing relationships, and it is certainly difficult to describe a company as a whole without its aid.

Nevertheless, the basic ideas behind the classical approach are often subject to criticism. It treats the people who are being organized as passive instruments and not as human beings and does not give attention to the informal groups which develop and the need to involve subordinates' interest and emotions behind the objectives of the department and organization. It is claimed that many organizational structures give rise to frustration and prevent job satisfaction, and that they do not develop the sense of common purpose and shared values which are essential if people are to work cooperatively together.

While it is impossible to explore the different theories or organization here, in marketing the cooperation of the individual staff member should be regarded as important. Because the problems of the marketplace tend to be ever-changing, the search for new ideas is continuous and it is doubtful if these are best obtained by autocratic methods. While controls are necessary, they should be handled in a manner which promotes cooperation between different sections of the organization.

Designing an organization is a problem of trying to satisfy a number of different and sometimes conflicting criteria. The most important for the present purpose are:

SPAN CONTROL

No manager should have more subordinates than he can satisfactorily control. This is not a set number but depends on a variety of considerations, including the amount of interaction between the subordinates.

ECONOMIES OF SCALE

When similar activities are brought together, the cost of carrying them out efficiently is often reduced.

UNITY OF OBJECTIVE

Activities serving a common objective can be grouped together to increase effectiveness.

Problems of coordination (and therefore of communication) should be minimized.

RESPONSIBILITY FOR KEY DECISIONS
Decisions which are not easily reversible in the short term should be made at a high level.

Under the chief executive a company has main departments broadly classifiable into production, finance, research and development, engineering, and marketing.

The marketing department will have full or very substantial responsibility for those activities which involve interaction with the customer and the market in the short and medium term, and its influence should guide the company toward "melding" all its activities in the long term.

From this, one would commonly expect to see the following main headings in the responsibilities of the marketing department:

Marketing planning.
Marketing research and forecasting.
Selling and service operations.
Advertising and publicity.
Physical distribution.

The exact content of these items is not scheduled here, because of the inevitable variation. Each is discussed in its appropriate chapter. Moreover, when the detailed content is examined it becomes more difficult to say where precisely marketing responsibility begins and ends. The criterion of quick coordination and communication is one which should be given much weight in relation to those matters which particularly affect competitive advantage at the time the sale is closed. If an early delivery date is the key, then production scheduling authority may well be with the marketing department; if minor price variation is the nub, then sufficient authority must be with marketing, and so on. The ideal would be so to decentralize these decisions that the salesman could make them, but there is difficulty in achieving this because of the wider implications which such decisions may have.

DEPARTMENTAL ORGANIZATION

Within the department the problem of organizational design is concerned with the reconciliation of three pressures:

1 The pressure to organize by function, because this gives functional economies of scale.
2 The pressure to organize by products, because of the natural technical and economic requirements of the productive process with which marketing must coordinate.
3 The pressure to organize by customer or market segments in order to best meet differing needs.

In the simplest of cases there is no problem.

Where there is one major product or a group of naturally related products sold to many customers, the natural organization is the very simple functional basis illustrated in Fig. 19.

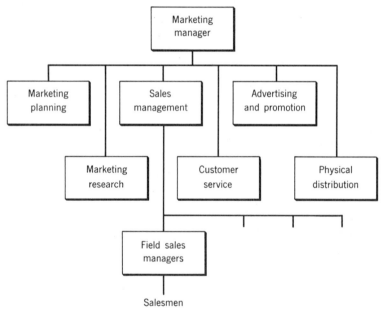

Fig. 19. Marketing department: functional organization

Here each of the main functions is separately responsible to the marketing manager, and all work on any one function is grouped together. Sometimes two or more functions may be combined, for example service with sales management.

Where there are two or three major product lines, each line sometimes has its own marketing organization, headed by a deputy marketing manager with a full range of functional departments to support him. This arrangement does not make it easy to use specialist staff economically. More usual is for the functional organization to be retained for planning, research, advertising and publicity, and perhaps physical distribution, but with specialized sales forces. The sales forces may be specialized either by product or market segment, as discussed in Chapter 11.

The planning section is an important part of the marketing department. It is responsible for developing the overall marketing plan, including special projects such as the launch of new products. It has to work closely with marketing research, which provides the information on which the plan is based.

In many companies, the sales section has more staff than the rest of the department together, and the sales manager is a powerful and influential figure. His post is an important one, but his influence can lead to a department concentrating on the short-term sales volume and losing sight of the goal of long-term profitability. Today's problems are pressing; they arrive as letters, memoranda, and telephone calls demanding immediate answer. Long-term problems seem to lack the same imperative demand for action. Unless the responsibility for looking ahead is clearly specified, it can fail to receive the attention it deserves.

The marketing research department may well have functions wider than its name implies. In some companies it operates to assist not only as a provider of information but as a diagnostic aid in the analysis of marketing problems and the identification of the information needed.

Often it will provide a regular service of economic and commercial information. Part of its work will be as a recorder of information culled from its regular study of the commercial, technical, and general press and from other established sources. It will also be responsible for desk research, for the briefing of outside research agencies, and for the execution of its own field surveys when necessary. It must interpret to management the implications of research findings in a form which identifies the needed marketing action. It may also be the most suitable section for evaluating the efficiency of the marketing operation. For example, the quantitative and objective approach of marketing research is of value in planning sales territories, setting quotas, advising on proposals or bids, and other aspects of marketing action.

The advertising department will normally place its media advertising through an agency but may itself be responsible for some or all of the company's literature and mail shots. Practice varies. Where the company decides to accept responsibility for literature, it must employ an experienced writer, either full-time or perhaps part-time if someone suitable can be found on this basis. A production department will also be needed; some of the work may be contracted out, but bigger departments usually prefer to do much of it themselves. Public relations and press relations may be associated with advertising or directly responsible to a higher level. If it is within the advertising section, the P.R. man may need a flexible relationship with authority to consult senior executives, even the managing director, when matters of sufficient consequence arise.

Physical distribution is a specialized area, varying from industry to industry; in some companies it is highly complex, with goods being transported by pipeline, express freight train, and road vehicles, and in others it may consist of a simple van delivery service. The matter is not explored in this text. It is nevertheless worth noting the extent to which physical distribution and handling is increasingly being studied as a self-contained system, and there may well be more consideration to distribution logistics in the future, including in this term the whole of the issues arising from storing and handling from the receipt of the raw material to the delivery of the finished product.

Technical service is frequently responsible to the sales manager but may be a separate section within the marketing department when the emphasis is on postsale service such as repair and maintenance.

In order to deal with the problem of reconciling function, products, and customers' problems in the organizational structure, the post of product manager has been created in some industrial marketing departments. A similar post under the title of "brand manager" has been common in mass-selling consumer goods for a number of years.

The product manager is given responsibility for overseeing a group of products. His task is to develop integrated plans for these products, to recommend them to the marketing manager for approval, and after approval to use his influence to see that these plans are successfully implemented. His job is to persuade and he is not normally given line authority, although his role in planning gives weight to his representations. He keeps check on the profitability of his products and ensures that plans are attuned to the market in all aspects from production to delivery.

Clearly this is not an easy job to fit into the traditional types of organization. The product manager must, for example, liaise with the sales force to see that they have all necessary aids, call on the right customers, spend an appropriate amount of time on his products, and stress the right points in their presentations. In doing this he could conflict with the authority of the sales manager over his sales staff or develop into a sort of supernumerary salesman concentrating on a few major accounts.

Yet the idea of having one focus for information, planning, and supervision of marketing action is an attractive one. It corrects the difficulty which can arise, particularly when one sales force is selling somewhat different lines to the same customers, of there being no one in the company who has a complete view of what is happening to a particular product class, and who is able to form an opinion as to why it is happening and what action is necessary.

Some companies have taken the further step of giving the product manager line authority and responsibility for the product from production to selling. Another alternative is to appoint market managers to oversee action aimed at particular markets.

One particular function over which there can be dispute is the location of the product planning section in the company as a whole. In consumer marketing, it is commonly in the marketing department. This gives the marketing department decisive influence over what is to be produced and the detail of the product.

Clearly it is important that the views of marketing shall have full impact. In consumer markets most product changes flow from an evolutionary adaptation to customer and market pressures, with fundamental research only a factor in a small proportion of the changes, except perhaps in pharmaceuticals. The emphasis is more in development than research. Moreover, promotional costs are also a much greater factor in consumer marketing, and the question "Can we promote and sell it successfully?" often far outweighs in difficulty the question "Can we develop and make it?" In industrial marketing, the proportions can be different. Product changes are more concerned with the primary and secondary levels of product concept. Yet, given that the company has determined explicitly or implicitly a particular corporate strategy, the question "What products will potential customers need in a few years' time?" must determine the general direction of research and development, and the question "What product detail is appropriate for today's customers?" is the specification of current products. These questions are ones which the marketing department must answer.

The problem then is whether the answers given by the marketing department can most effectively be integrated with the company as a whole by placing product planning within that department, or by setting it up separately, directly responsible at top level within the company. Its major proposals might be reported to an interdepartmental committee, and much of its detail controlled by project groups as proposed in Chapter 8.

The solution will depend upon a number of considerations. Features which would encourage the location of product planning in the marketing department include:

1 High cost and risk in marketing the finished product.
2 Rapid change in the market.
3 Importance of tertiary features of the product.
4 Assurance that R&D will have a high probability of devising the types of product normally required.
5 Ample opportunity to expand in present markets.
6 Low probability of marketable ideas being generated by other departments, for example R&D, as a by-product of other work.

Where the opposite emphasis is present, it is more difficult to resist the arguments for a central product planning department independent of other major departments. Finally, much would depend upon the individual marketing director concerned. His need for objectivity is very important, and the area of new products is one in which objectivity can be difficult to achieve. Even if product planning is separate, the marketing planning section will have special responsibility for giving attention to this subject.

Supplementing these basic sections, some companies have found it desirable to have other sections for special purposes. Market development is an example. This is a separate section to negotiate with substantial customers when marketing new products or entering new markets. Market development has more authority to agree prices or enter into long-term commitments than has the regular sales force.

ESTABLISHING A MARKETING DEPARTMENT

When a company is establishing a marketing approach and a marketing department for the first time, it is faced with the problem of changing from the present structure to a new one with minimum disruption of existing staff relationships. The sales manager has ranked at the level of other departmental heads and will not relish the prospect of a marketing manager above him.

The change from existing organization may then take place in several steps phased over a period, the company having clearly in mind the ultimate structure which it seeks to create.

If the sales manager is a suitable individual for appointment to marketing manager, the process of adjustment is easier.

It can be a logical step in his career; he knows the company and its customers and may be willing to learn the new skills and develop new attitudes to take his place as a key man in the company's top management. His claim deserves careful consideration.

If he is not so inclined, the alternative is to bring in a man from outside, who may be a good marketing man but may have to learn about the company, its products, and its customers. One solution which has been adopted is to appoint a marketing manager at the same level as the existing sales manager. His job is then to focus on the planning, profitability, and long-term aspects of the marketing role, until such time as it may be expedient to take the further step in sharply defining the marketing organization. Marketing research will inevitably come into prominence in the company as the planning procedure develops.

19

The Skills of
the Manager

The pervasive role of marketing in the business firm today imposes a severe test on the manager of this function. It is not sufficient that the marketing manager be competent in his understanding of the market; he must be proficient in all the skills of management. The whole area of management thinking today is changing continuously. New ideas come forward to replace the old. Some are hailed as panaceas yet prove to be short-lived in their impact on management thinking. Others stay and make an important contribution to better management.

The idea that management is a profession demanding knowledge, skill, and a disciplined expertise in addition to personal qualities has been slow to take root in Britain. This is now changing, but some executives who have trained to acquire these attributes have been hesitant about deploying them before colleagues and superiors who may lack them. It looks as though in the next few years the situation may at last be achieved, so that to be a trained manager, rather than a sciolist, will become a source of pride. To achieve this, an individual must be prepared to discipline himself so that he maintains and develops his knowledge of current thinking about management and effectively applies this knowledge.

Management may be defined as the deployment of resources under his control by an individual for the achievement of the overall purpose of the organization. Every person who has some control over staff, over money, or over material assets is, in this sense, a manager.

One of the most useful steps is for a manager to look

at the management of his own time to consider whether he is using this to the best advantage. If his own time is not well used, he will never be able to spare the necessary thought to the improved running of the department under him.

It is often salutary for a manager to keep a detailed log of the way in which he spends a typical week. At the end of the week, he should summarize his time into four categories:

1 Interruptions.
2 Wasted time.
3 Minor matters.
4 Major matters.

Section 4 is the key category of the work, concerned with matters which really justify his attention. Section 3 relates to matters which he should aim to delegate, Sections 1 and 2 to those which he should try to eliminate. It will never be practicable to achieve the ideal—even a manager cannot control circumstances to that extent—but it is nevertheless usually possible to make an improvement, often a big one. Once he has decided how much time he can gather together for his key matters, he should try to reserve parts of his week on a systematic basis, so that he can work uninterruptedly for a reasonable period of time on those tasks which distinguish the successful from the commonplace. He has great responsibility for putting over ideas to his own board and to other organizations.

An ability to speak in public and to prepare a clear and well-presented report are assets which he should develop in himself and in the subordinates on whom he depends. It is worth noting the particular need of the marketing research department to prepare reports of clarity and conciseness. Large parts of these are frequently included in, or appended to, the reports sent by the marketing department to the board.

THE FUNCTION OF MANAGEMENT OBJECTIVES

Clarity about objectives has been stressed as an essential element in any process of conscious striving toward efficient management, and this idea has been codified and given shape by the development of the concept of "management by objectives." This aims to provide a framework for planning by which objectives of individual executives in a company are clearly organized behind the ultimate purpose of the company and each executive is motivated to achieve his immediate objectives and thus to promote the purpose of the company.

Objectives start at the top of the company with the determination of its corporate strategy, so that the board knows what it is aiming for and the standards it seeks to achieve. These broad objectives do not directly help the salesman to decide which customers to call upon, or the advertising manager to decide what literature is to be produced. They must be translated into subobjectives which indicate to senior managers what action is expected from them. In turn, these are translated into sub-subobjectives for the next line of management, and so on down the scale until each member of the entire staff has objectives consistent with his role in the company.

It is not, however, sufficient to set these up at each level unless the individual who is supposed to aim for these objectives as targets feels a personal commitment to them. If objectives are handed down from above, then the individual recipient is likely to receive them suspiciously and to feel that any failure to reach objectives is due to some inherent defect in the objectives rather than deficiency on his part.

Much current thinking, therefore, stresses the advantages of the subordinate devising his own objectives after having been given complete information from his superior. This means that, having determined his objectives, he is committed and motivated to fulfill them because they are his own.

The problem of this arrangement is in the opposite direction: the subordinate may set objectives which are too easy to fulfill and thus safeguard him against criticism but do not provide adequate targets. In practice, some compromise process of consultation may occur in companies which apply this procedure. Some individual managers put the emphasis on leaving the subordinate to arrive at a figure with little guidance from above, while others consult the subordinate but largely fix the objectives themselves. Whichever way the emphasis is, it seems to help, at least at first, to have a specialist appointed within the company to attend these consultations as an aid to the process of setting objectives and perhaps also as a catalyst.

The great value is that in many companies this process makes clear to the individuals concerned what is the primary purpose of their efforts for the company and what is the measure of their success. This may sound as though it is an unnecessary refinement of management practice, but experience has proved the contrary. Many executives are by no means clear about what they should be doing, and achievement is often measured by the wrong yardstick.

Like many management techniques, management by

objectives has its roots in the practices which good managers have to some extent adopted in the past. Developed and made explicit, it has removed much of the fuzziness which prevailed under past practices, and companies which apply it consider that it has materially improved efficiency.

DEALING WITH PEOPLE

Much of the manager's job is delegating to other people the performance of certain tasks and checking to make sure that these are carried out to the required standard. This is partly a problem of setting measurable objectives and installing a control system which measures results against objectives, so that discrepancy can be picked out and investigated, and remedial action taken. It is also a matter of obtaining satisfactory personal relations within the organization so that subordinates will accept and feel committed to challenging objectives.

Working with subordinates in this way demands from the manager considerable sensitivity to people. Every individual has his own attitudes, beliefs, and motivations which are expressed in what he says and the way in which he behaves. The manager has to recognize his own, so that they do not impede his relationship with other staff, and appreciate those of others, even though they are not directly expressed but must be deduced from the more subtle overtones of what people say and how they behave.

This human skill is part of the continuing relationship between the manager and his subordinates in particular, and other staff members generally. The man who has been a salesman should have some advantage in developing this skill, since it is rather like the skill which he uses in negotiating. It is, however, easy to overlook the fact that it has to be part of the manager's instinctive and natural behavior in his regular dealings with staff and not a "gimmick" to create a good impression on special occasions.

THE LANGUAGE OF BUSINESS

The language of finance and accounts is the ultimate language of business. Figures of cost, revenue and profit, or contribution are the criteria by which key decisions are tested to see if they make the best use of the resources of the business. Much of the information which the marketing manager uses comes to him in this language, and his results must eventually be summarized in this way. The man who is not reasonably at ease with financial data and concepts is unlikely to make that impact on top management which is required to achieve the corporate attitude to marketing.

This does not mean that the marketing manager must understand every detail of bookkeeping. He must, however, be familiar with the main ideas of accounting and finance so that he can work with the finance department, understand their arguments, and discuss them from a position of insight rather than ignorance.

Financial accounts, properly understood, give much information about the company they describe. The 1967 Companies Act has required more companies to publish more information, and this will therefore be a route to assessing not only one's own company, but competitors, customers, distributors, and companies which might be worth taking over. Fuller understanding comes from following trends over a period of years. The explanatory notes accompanying the accounts require careful attention.

The balance sheet reveals major aspects of the financial position of the company. Traditionally, it has been laid out in two columns, headed respectively liabilities and assets. Liabilities were then divided between claims to be settled in the short term—current liabilities (notably creditors)—longer-terms claims by debenture holders, and capital and reserves attributable to shareholders. Assets were similarly divided between current (cash, debtors, and stock) and fixed (property, plant, and equipment). To the uninitiated, this format caused unnecessary difficulty. Happily, this practice is being replaced by a simpler one for many purposes.

Increasingly, accountants adopt a single-column layout for the balance sheet. This shows first net current assets—the company's working capital representing the excess of current assets over current liabilities. To this is added fixed assets to show the total assets available to meet long-term claims. Among long-term claims, the claims of debenture holders and other outside lenders have priority, and the balance of reserve accounts, undistributed profit, and share capital are all the ultimate property of the shareholders.

The ordinary shareholders are legally the "residual legatees" of the company's assets. What they own can be assessed by deducting from the total assets of the company sums due to prior claimants such as creditors, the Inland Revenue, debenture holders, and preferred shareholders. This is one way to assess the value of ordinary shares. On the stock exchange it can be, and often is, outweighed by additional considerations such as dividend policy, profit potential, consistency of past profits, merger possibilities, and special factors. Much depends on the purpose for which the valuation is made.

The values of assets for the purpose of the balance sheet are not necessarily the values which would in fact be realized if the company were wound up or taken over as a going concern. Values for building and equipment are affected by certain conventions about the way in which they are depreciated. The tradition of accountancy is to be cautious and write off assets quickly, and thus understate their value in the balance sheet.

Land and buildings which have appreciated in value over many years because of the decline in value of money and the demand for good sites may stand in a company's books at the prices at which they were originally purchased many years ago. This problem may be less serious now than it used to be prior to the introduction of capital gains tax. This legislation encouraged companies to revalue property to provide a better measure of its value. If this has been done, it is usually stated in the notes. As a going concern, a company may well have intangibles of value to a take-over bidder—an efficient sales force, customer goodwill, and so on. These are not in the balance sheet. The valuation of stock also raises problems of principle.

TESTS OF PERFORMANCE

In conjunction with the profit and loss account, the balance sheet shows the rate of return which the company is earning both on the total capital employed and on the shareholders' equity. These are key tests of company performance.

It is also possible to assess whether changes in financial results from one year to the next arise from variations in the profit earned as percentage of sales or from changes in the rate at which the net assets of the company are turned over. Sometimes comparison between firms in comparable circumstances can indicate where improvement in results is likely to be found. The analyst can also extract other valuable ratios.

In the short term the liquidity of the company ranks high in importance. The word "liquidity" has a more subtle meaning than "cash" because it includes all the ways in which the company can obtain cash quickly (e.g., from debtors or by selling quoted securities). Small businesses particularly have run into difficulty, not because they were unprofitable, but because they were unable to meet their creditors in the short term, having spent too much of their immediately available funds on the purchase of fixed and other assets which could not be turned into cash at short notice. This situation is brought to a dramatic climax if a credit squeeze makes finance particularly difficult to obtain. The finance department should stand guard over the cash of the company, but considerations of liquidity will often react upon the policies which can be pursued by the marketing department. Excessive liquidity, on the other hand, may mean that management is not using assets as well as it might.

In reading a balance sheet, there are two ratios which are commonly used as tests of liquidity—the current ratio and the quick asset (or acid test) ratio. These are defined below:

$$\text{Current ratio} = \frac{\text{current assets}}{\text{current liabilities}}$$

$$\text{Quick asset ratio} = \frac{\text{near-cash and cash items}}{\text{current liabilities}}$$

A low current ratio indicates shortage of working capital. A high ratio may indicate too much capital tied up in stock or held in cash. What is "high" or "low" depends on the industry concerned. The quick asset ratio should be regarded suspiciously if it is less than 1. A number of other important ratios can also be extracted by examining the balance sheet, profit and loss account, and turnover figures taken together.

Finally, the analysis of the flow of funds through the business, which can be derived by comparing successive financial statements, greatly increases understanding of a company's operations.

BUDGETING

The budget is one of the key tools through which the manager exercises control over the organization under him. Derived from a company's overall plans which flow from the sales forecast for which the marketing department is responsible, the budget sets out the amount of business expected and the expenditure involved in obtaining that business. The budget, in fact, is a tool to control expenditure in advance of its occurring and penetrates to all aspects of the company. It also has an important role in motivating staff.

In preparing a budget for any department or individual, it is illogical to include any item not under the control of the individual concerned. The purpose is to measure his results against the performance which can reasonably be expected from him.

The budget, however, extends beyond cost and also covers profit, contribution, and flow of funds. It is of value to have such analyses for major groups of customers and for product lines, so that these can be kept under review.

In some circumstances it is not appropriate to use fixed budgets. For example, certain sales expenses depend upon the volume of results achieved by the salesman, and thus a fixed figure is of little value as a control device. A system of flexible budgeting which allows for controlled variation in cost can then be used.

Control by detailed budget of costs is an approach requiring centralized consideration of individual cost forecasts. Alternatively, control may be exercised by establishing a section of the company as a profit center. This means that all costs and all revenue are brought together for that department and success measured by the net profit arising.

This procedure is occasionally used for the marketing department. The department buys products from the production department. After selling the goods to customers, it can calculate its "profit" by deducting from revenue the sum due for goods plus its own operating costs. One problem is that it is difficult to settle on the transfer price at which the marketing department "buys" from production.

Related to budgeting is, of course, the usual process of costing and standard costs.

THE CAPITAL INVESTMENT DECISION

This major decision arises when a company is contemplating the expenditure of a large sum of money in the near future in return for an expected profit which will be delayed by some years, as when an additional plant is being installed, when the company is taking over another, or when a new product is being launched. The decision whether or not to make this investment depends on the evaluation of three factors, which have to be forecast by the company. These factors are:

1 The amount of return it is expected that the investment will generate.
2 The years during which this money will come in and the expected return in each year.
3 The risk involved.

The financial assessment of future return is now generally related to the flow of cash out of and into the company and not primarily to the traditional form of profit calculation.

When looking at cash flow, the distinction between items normally treated as capital and those normally treated as revenue is irrelevant. The inflow and outflow of cash in any one year as a result of the project are brought together to provide a net figure, plus or minus, of cash flow in that year.

It follows that "depreciation" does not appear as an item in the calculation. Depreciation is not a movement of cash in or out; the movement of cash in respect of the asset concerned takes place at the time of payment and is brought into the calculation then. A payment of $48,000 in buying a plant is treated within the calculation for a project in the identical manner as is $48,000 spent in building up a customer network.

The treatment of taxation and government grants is on an analogous basis. Tax is cash out at the time of payment, and grants are cash in when received.

Cash movements generated by the project are the basic element, because cash which is "out" cannot be used to produce revenue for any other purpose. While it is out, it is sunk in the project. When it returns from the revenue generated by the project, it is available to be used beneficially elsewhere.

The logical conclusion is that the timing of the cash flow is important. It is not simply the total amount of cash received, but the interrelationship of cash and time. When there is a period of years before the investment is recouped, it must return with profit compounded over those years.

The discounted cash flow (DCF) calculation is a relatively simple method of arriving at the figure of the real percentage rate of annual return received from a project. It takes account of the points made above. There are now many useful texts explaining this technique.[47]

However, having calculated the rate of return, the manager must decide whether the level is sufficient to justify the project. This depends on a number of factors, including the other alternatives open to the company (could the cash involved earn more elsewhere?), the long-term cost to the company of obtaining capital, and the risk in the project. The greater the risk, the higher is the return required to compensate for the greater danger of losing the money involved.

The DCF approach is of wide application, and used with discretion it can provide valuable guidance on most projects where direct profits are required. As risk partly depends upon time—the longer the time-lag before the return is achieved, the more chance that something can go astray—DCF can therefore be backed up by an estimate of the "pay-back" period. This is a very simple concept. It answers the question "If our company invests $120,000 this year in this specific project, how many years will it be before we recover this sum (ignoring interest)?" In general, the shorter the period which it takes to recover the initial outlay, the less risk is likely to be involved.

THE AGE OF THE COMPUTER

The last twenty years or so have seen the dawn of the age of the computer. With each year that passes, management feels the impact of this development ever more strongly.

At first the computer was the tool of the giant firm, but its use has now spread out far beyond this limited group, and it is clear that it will eventually become an everyday tool to be used in the firm in the same matter-of-fact way as is the typewriter, the telephone system, and the traditional calculating machine.

The cost of acquiring a computer and its associated equipment was at one time one of the biggest barriers. Now not only have costs come down, but the principle of time-sharing is making it possible for even a quite small company to be linked to a central computer. The costs involved are the hire of the terminal required to link a company with the computer and payment for the use of computer time. Little space is required.

Cost has not been the only barrier. Communicating with the computer has been almost as serious a difficulty. Even when a computer system has been installed, the need to employ an expert programer and to have programs written for the tasks which were done by the computer have inhibited its use. Gradually, the fearsome job of programing has been reduced in complexity. The development of "autocodes" and more advanced languages is making it possible to write instructions for the computer with much greater ease. Autocodes are not difficult to learn and make programing for the nonspecialist practicable.

For most computers, there are now libraries of programs from which it is possible to obtain ready-written tested programs for most of the commonly occurring problems of the manager, statistician, and market researcher.

The computer offers management the potential for the storage of data in a way in which it can be rapidly retrieved and the ability to process figures and other logically planned data to carry out analyses of great complexity in a very short time and to print out results. However, to use the computer to anything like its full potential, the organization, ideas, and thinking patterns of the company and its management often require to be substantially changed. This is a long process and can impose very severe strains on the people affected.

In the first instance, most companies on introducing a computer used it as a "super clerk" which it was expected would undertake the work which had hitherto required a large office staff. Among specialists there is an ill-concealed feeling that this work is somewhat beneath the computer's dignity.

Nevertheless, it frequently gave an initial economic justification for installing the equipment, while management grew to understand it better. Gradually, more comprehensive systems of data handling are being introduced, such as that by which, from the original receipt of the customer's order, a chain of events controlled by the computer is set off within the company. In principle, this chain could include the issuing of all necessary documents from acknowledgment of order to the sending out of the invoices and might involve optimum scheduling of production, requisitioning of supplies, controlling stock, and the preparation of statistical analyses of sales and contribution, both for the company as a whole and for individual products and sales territories.

The integrated data-processing system thus becomes a major management aid in a deeper sense. It promises the manager more and quicker data but leaves him to decide what data he wants and how he will act on it. The manager must decide what steps to take to avoid being engulfed by a possible tidal wave of paper.

This justifies more attention to the concept of management by exception. This is not a new concept, but it has been of less importance in the past when the amount of data which could be produced in time to be useful and on economical terms was less. The essence is that, once the plan and related budget is prepared, the vital information for the manager is the *difference* between what he intended to happen and what actually did happen. Moreover, the manager is not interested in small differences but only in those which justify attention with a view to possible action. If the sales force consists of fifty representatives, and forty-seven are reasonably on target, then the manager need only concern himself with studying those three who are significantly out.

The manager then has to ask himself: "What limits of tolerance should I allow?" so that the computer can be programed to identify those exceptions which are outside the limits. This means considerable thought to decide what the limits are, and whether they should be set on each month's figures, on quarterly figures, or on moving annual totals. Once these tolerances have been set, the computer can monitor the results and leave the manager free to address his attention to the crucial areas, as identified by the computer in accordance with his instructions. He may like to see all the figures (and not just the exceptions) at less frequent intervals.

Sometimes management can move on to the third stage and hand over to the computer part of the decision-making. This implies that it is possible to identify the action appropriate to a given set of circumstances sufficiently clearly to permit the inner logic of the decision-making to be programed for the guidance of the computer. This has been done in such areas as stock control, where the computer can make a short-term forecast of sales, calculate stock requirements, and reorder.

The growth of the computer as a decision-maker is an area of great potential importance for the future. It requires the manager to search out ever more deeply the logic of his actions and to reduce the role of intuition. He must examine possible contingencies before they arise and develop decision rules to meet them.

The marketing department of a company gains first by the greater control which the computer offers, and second by the way in which it relieves (or can relieve) the staff of the detail. Where, however, the company is selling in a market where the number of customers is very few, the advantage of rapid data-processing is not great.

The computer when first introduced was often most closely associated with the finance department, because that department takes responsibility for much of the clerical staff employed by the company, being concerned with payroll and customer accounts and for the provision of much internal financial and statistical information for management decision. Moreover, in most industrial marketing companies the marketing department in its full sense had only recently arrived. Consequently, marketing has not often worked as closely with the computer as it might have done. When the marketing department did wish to use the computer, it was faced with the problem of having a program written and then finding time to run it on the computer. These stages could absorb so much time that the benefit from the computer's speed was lost.

The marketing manager might well consider whether he should, as a matter of course, seek the regular allocation of a proportion of computer time for the purposes of his department. Even if he has no specific prior task, it will result in his department developing familiarity with the use of the computer, and the knowledge that the time is available can result in a more experimental approach to the utilization of information. He may well find that there are many neglected aspects of the market and marketing operations which will show unexpected gains from analysis. Market research results cannot only be analyzed, but statistical relationships within the data can be explored more fully. In forecasting, several different methods of arriving at forecasts can be examined and their sensitivity to changes in assumptions studied. Experiments in mail shots and comparative studies of contribution by customer, product, and salesman are all worth examining if the facilities are available. Now that programing is easier, at least one member of the department should be familiar with the language of the computer.

TOWARD QUANTIFIED MARKETING

As management becomes more sophisticated, so it becomes more important that managers become numerate. This is not to assert that the manager needs to be a front-rank statistician or mathematician. There is, however, very often a totally unjustified fear among managers of even the simplest of mathematical formulae. As a result, statistical data are not given the attention they deserve.

Many of the matters with which the marketing manager is concerned cannot easily be quantified. The reaction of customers and competitors to a price change is a matter of judgment. This is sometimes advanced as a reason for not attempting calculation in this field and for not trying to make explicit the reasoning processes by which the price is decided. It might, however, be true to say that it is worth examining various assumptions about buyer behavior and studying their implications before making a decision. Various techniques are under development by which these matters can be explored. There seems little doubt that management is moving toward the stricter use of models of a quantitative type.

ON BEING A MANAGER

The manager of today must be forever learning and relearning. Ideas which first arrive in one area of management are frequently transferred to or react on other areas. Critical-path analysis is used in marketing for launching products and for other complex purposes. Value analysis is of relevance to the marketing man, because it affects his own products and the customer's buying decision. The technical salesman should seek a place on the customer's value analysis team.

In present circumstances, the manager must be a deeper, more conceptual, thinker. That is to say, he must be able to see the elements in a situation, the way they interrelate so that one part affects the other, and so to identify the key elements in the situation. This requires more than repeating successful solutions of the past; it involves the ability to reason from fundamental principles to the new solutions for tomorrow. This more light-footed theoretical thinking must be allied to practical skills so that the solutions work.

Marketing is the way in which the management of a company seeks to identify long-term opportunities and to mold the company in order that it is so organized and endowed with assets and skills that it can benefit from these opportunities as they emerge. In the shorter term, the company has a range of decisions to make to ensure that it meets the needs of its chosen customers in its chosen market on a mutually satisfactory basis and uses all the marketing tools to bring this about. To achieve this, marketing must be backed with efficient management throughout the enterprise.

Finally, marketing seen in this way is not solely a philosophy for the company. It is a basic approach which individuals can and do use to plan their own career developments and personal achievements.

NOTES AND REFERENCES

1. Based on a definition in E. R. Corey, *Industrial Marketing*, Prentice-Hall, 1962.
2. For further discussion, see R. M. Cyert and J. G. March, *A Behavioural Theory of the Firm*, Prentice-Hall, 1963, and J. G. March and H. A. Simon, *Organizations*, Wiley, 1958.
3. For further discussion, see F. E. Webster, Jr., "Modeling the Industrial Buying Process," *Journal of Marketing Research*, 1965, and P. J. Robinson and C. W. Faris, *Industrial Buying and Creative Marketing*, Allyn & Bacon, 1967.
4. K. Lawyer, in an unpublished paper, "Product Characteristics as a Factor in Marketing" (Case Western Reserve University, 1967), identifies the concept of product complexity.
5. H. I. Ansoff, *Corporate Strategy*, McGraw-Hill, 1965, pp. 5–6. Copyright material, used by permission of the McGraw-Hill Book Co.
6. A. Shonfield, *Modern Capitalism*, Oxford U.P., for the Royal Institute of International Affairs, 1965, p. 378.
7. Ansoff, p. 44, speaks of a "proximate" period of three to ten years up to the planning horizon and a long-term period thereafter.
8. Ibid., p. 104.
9. C. H. Kline, "The Strategy of Product Policy," *Harvard Business Review*, July–Aug. 1955.

10. P. Ward, "The dynamics of business planning," *Marketing Forum*, Nov.–Dec. 1967.
11. E. P. Learned, F. Christensen, K. R. Andrews and W. D. Guth, *Business Policy: Texts and Cases*, Richard D. Irwin Inc., Homewood, Ill., 1965. Reproduced with permission.
12. B. White (Arthur D. Little Ltd.), "Market Planning," unpublished paper to a seminar on Industrial Marketing, Polytechnic School of Management Studies, 1968.
13. F. T. Pearce, *The Parameters of Marketing Research*, Industrial Marketing Research Association, 1965, p. 5.
14. On sampling, see R. D. Crisp, *Marketing Research*, McGraw-Hill, 1957; for further reading, see N. Stacey and R. Wilson, *Industrial Marketing Research*, Hutchinson, 1963.
15. Pearce, p. 50.
16. D. Chapman, "The Psychology of the Interview Situation," paper to an Industrial Marketing Research Association basic course, 1967.
17. Useful works are M. H. Spencer, C. G. Clark and P. W. Hoguet, *Business and Economic Forecasting*, Irwin, 1957, and W. F. Butler and R. A. Kavesh, *How Business Economists Forecast*, Prentice-Hall, 1966.
18. J. V. Gregg, C. H. Hossell and J. T. Richardson, *Mathematical Trend Curves: An Aid to Forecasting*, Oliver & Boyd, 1964.
19. G. A. Busch, "Prudent Manager Forecasting," *Harvard Business Review*, May–June 1961.
20. S. A. Tucker, *Pricing for Higher Profit*, McGraw-Hill, 1966.
21. For example, S. Dixon, *The Case for Marginal Costing*, Gentrial Product Ideas," *Journal of Industrial Marketing ants*, 1966.
22. R. V. Arnfield and D. Roxburgh, "Generating New Industrial Product Ideas," *Journal of Industrial Marketing Research Association*, vol. 3, no. 4, Nov. 1967.
23. C. Shannon and W. Weaver, *Mathematical Theory of Communication*, University of Illinois Press, 1949, p. 95.
24. Ibid., p. 96.
25. R. H. Colley, *Defining Advertising Goals for Measuring Advertising Results*, Association of National Advertisers Inc., 1961, p. 38.
26. E. W. Duck, "The Integration of R. & D. and Commercial Functions," in A. Keynes (ed.), *Economics of Research and Development*, Polytechnic School of Management Studies, 1967, p. 124.
27. "Search for the Perfect Package," *Dun's Review* (Dun & Bradstreet Publishing Corporation), Nov. 1963.
28. E. Gunther, "Evaluating Corporate Image Measurements: A Review of Techniques," *Proceedings of the Fifth Annual*

Conference of the Advertising Research Foundation Inc., USA, 1959.
29. T. Levitt, *Industrial Purchasing Behavior,* Division of Research, Graduate School of Business Administration, Harvard University, 1965.
30. D. N. Chorafas, *Sales Engineering: The Marketing of Technological Products,* Cassell, 1967, p. 6.
31. J. O'Shaughnessy, *Work Study Applied to a Sales Force,* British Institute of Management, 1966.
32. L. S. Simon, "Measuring the Marketing Impact of Technical Services," *Journal of Marketing Research,* Feb. 1965.
33. International Computers and Tabulators, *Submission for the Marketing Award 1967,* I.C.T., 1967.
34. Simon, op. cit.
35. F. R. Messner, *Industrial Advertising,* McGraw-Hill, 1963, p. 108. Copyright material, used by permission of the McGraw-Hill Book Co.
36. Institute of Practitioners in Advertising, *Industrial Marketing and the Advertising Agency,* IPA, 1966.
37. Direct Mail Advertising Association, "Forms of Direct Advertising" (leaflet).
38. For example, P. I. Slee-Smith, *Industrial Public Relations,* Business Publications, 1967.
39. See G. Katona, *Psychological Analysis of Economic Behavior,* McGraw-Hill, 1951, for a fuller discussion of the role of habitual behavior.
40. W. T. Baxter and A. R. Oxenfeldt, "Approaches to Pricing: Economist *vs.* Accountant," *Business Horizons,* vol. 4, winter 1961, quoted in S. F. Otteson *et al., Marketing: The Firm's Viewpoint,* Macmillan, 1964.
41. Tucker, op. cit.
42. J. L. Grumbridge, *Marketing Management in Air Transport,* Allen & Unwin, 1966, pp. 61–62.
43. L. A. Williams, *Industrial Marketing Management and Controls,* Longmans, 1967, p. 44.
44. H. C. Walford (of International Rectifier), "The Manufacturer/Distributor Relationship," in "Distributor Survey," supplement to *Electronic Components,* March 1967.
45. A. P. Felton, "Making the Marketing Concept Work," *Harvard Business Review,* July–Aug. 1959.
46. J. O'Shaughnessy, *Business Organization,* Allen & Unwin, 1966.
47. G. Wright, *Discounted Cash Flow,* McGraw-Hill, 1968.

INDEX

Geographical concentration of industry, 17

House journals, 194–95

Incentive schemes for salesmen, 142–44; competitions, 142
Incorporated Society of British Advertisers, 180
Indirect customers, use of term, 13
Industrial buying: motives for decision, 121–24
Industrial Marketing Research Association, 53
Industrial markets, 11–26; analysis of goods and services, 11–12; characteristics, 14–17; customers and users, 12–14; informal influences, 25–26; making buying decisions, 20–24; market segmentation, 18–19
Information collection, 62–69; by telephone, 62; personal interviews, 67–69; postal surveys, 62–67
Institute of Practitioners in Advertising, 180, 188
Institute of Public Relations, 197
Institutions, use of term, 13
Instructional handbooks, 192–93
Intermediate manufacturers, 26, 60; use of term, 13
International trade, changes in pattern, 28
Interviewing for information collection, 68–69; cost, 68; validity of replies, 69
Inventory of company resources, 35

Linear trends, 76–78
Literature, see Print
Lockheed Aircraft Corporation, 85
Long-term forecasts, 71–86; basic elements, 74
Long-term period, 30

Maintenance, provision of, 169–70
Management objectives, function of, 252–54
Management skills, 251–64; and quantified marketing, 263; budgeting, 257–58; capital investment, 258–60; cash flow and DCF approach, 259–60; computers, 260–63; dealing with people, 254; familiarity with accounting and finance, 254–56; function of management objectives, 252–54; management by exception, 261; preparation of reports, 252; public speaking, 252; understanding financial statements, 255–56; use of time, 251–52
Marginal costs: and marginal revenue, 214–16; pricing, 230
Marketing and corporate strategy, 27–39
Marketing departments, 244, 246–50, 257, 261–62; advertising section, 246–47; establishment of, 249–50; main responsibilities, 244; marketing research, 246; physical distribution, 247; planning sections, 246, 248–49; product and brand managers, 247–48; production, 246–47; public and press relations, 197–99; sales managers, 246, 249; sales section, 246
Marketing function, organization of, 241–50
Marketing in perspective, 1–10; and business planning, 9–10; anticipation of change, 8–9; customer orientation, 2–3; problem solving, 3–4; service, 4–5; synthesis with environment, 5–8
Marketing managers, 241–42, 245, 247, 249; and management skills, 251–64
Marketing plans, preparation of, 41–52; components of plan, 42–43; development, 44–45; development of strategies, 46–47; elements of plan, 47–49; layout of plan, 49–52; objectives, 42–43; period of plan, 44; product life-cycle concept, 47
Marketing research, 53–69; briefing, 54–56; choice of respondents, 59–61; collection of information, 62–69; desk research, 58–59; planning of survey, 56–68; sampling, 60–69; structural survey and forecast of